QUIRIGUA REPORTS

UNIVERSITY MUSEUM MONOGRAPH 49

QUIRIGUA REPORTS

Robert J. Sharer
General Editor

Edward M. Schortman
Patricia A. Urban
Volume Editors

VOLUME II

Papers 6-15

Published by
THE UNIVERSITY MUSEUM
University of Pennsylvania
Philadelphia
1983

Design, editing, production
　Publications Division, The University Museum

Typesetting
　The Publications Office, University of Pennsylvania

Printing
　The Sheridan Press
　Hanover, Pennsylvania

Library of Congress Cataloging in Publication Data

(Revised for vol. 2. Papers 6-15)
Main entry under title:

Quirigua reports.

　(University Museum monograph; no. 37)
　Includes bibliographies.
　Contents: v. 1. Papers 1-5, site map—v. 2. Papers 6-15.
　1. Quiriguá Site (Guatemala)—Collected works. I. Sharer, Robert
J.
[F1435.1.Q8Q57]　972.81　79-18188
ISBN 1-931707-48-0 (pbk)

Copyright © 1983
THE UNIVERSITY MUSEUM
University of Pennsylvania
Philadelphia
All rights reserved
Printed in the United States of America

GENERAL EDITOR'S FOREWORD

The present volume marks the second publication in the *Quirigua Report* series. It includes the remaining summary reports of the field seasons conducted by the Quirigua Project in 1977 through 1979 (the 1975 and 1976 season summaries were published in Volume I), and completes the publication of what may be termed "special subject" papers dealing with aspects of this research. The latter include contributions concerning magnetometer surveys (Beven), obsidian analysis (Sheets), control of lichen growth on the monuments (Hale), the 1976 earthquake (Sharer and Beven), the newly discovered Monument 26 (Jones), a comparison of Copan and Quirigua sculptural styles (Miller), and Monuments 23 and 24 (Jones). These special subject papers were selected for inclusion here because their importance dictated publication now rather than awaiting completion of the final reports in this series.

The final reports of the Quirigua Project (*Quirigua Reports* III through VII) are now in preparation—several are nearing completion—authored by various members of the project staff. The next three volumes in the series will present the data and interpretations resulting from the major research programs of the project (investigations of the Site Core, the Site Periphery, and the Lower Motagua Valley). Plans call for these to be followed by a volume describing the artifacts recovered from these investigations, and a final volume devoted to syntheses and conclusions drawn from all phases of this research.

Robert J. Sharer
General Editor: Quirigua Reports

The University Museum
University of Pennsylvania
Philadelphia

ACKNOWLEDGEMENTS

We would like to express our gratitude and appreciation to the many individuals who have been of great assistance to us in the preparation of this volume. In particular, we would like to thank Dr. Erle Leichty and Dr. Maria Ellis, both of the Babylonian Section, University Museum, for their generous help during the initial stages of production. Kathleen Ryan of the Museum Applied Science Center for Archaeology provided vital assistance throughout the preparation process, including setting type for many of the final corrections to the text.

The last stages of proof-reading were ably accomplished by Eleanor King, Department of Anthropology, University of Pennsylvania, and Dr. Wendy Ashmore, Livingston College, Rutgers University, both of whom generously offered time away from their other responsibilities to insure that these and other essential tasks were completed. The numerous jobs usually encountered in the final stages of preparation were overseen by Dr. Robert Sharer, who was ably assisted by Keven Duff, an undergraduate student at the University of Pennsylvania.

The drawings of the Quirigua monuments included in this volume were expertly rendered by Dr. William Coe (Paper 15) and Dr. Carl Beetz (Paper 13); both have thereby furnished definitive records of previously undocumented Maya sculptures. The line drawings (Figures 1 and 2) for Paper 10 were skillfully produced by Raymond Rorke. Permissions to reproduce previously published materials were kindly granted by the Peabody Museum, Harvard University, and the Carnegie Institution of Washington (Paper 8, Figures 9 and 10, respectively).

The final steps in the publication process were under the expert guidance of Barbara Murray, Publications Coordinator for the University Museum. We are especially grateful to her and her staff, especially Raymond Rorke for guiding this publication to a successful conclusion.

Finally, we wish to express our thanks to Dr. Robert Sharer for all of his help during the preparation of this volume. Not only was his advice and encouragement of great assistance to us in the completion of our own tasks, but he provided the necessary continuity in editorial supervision during the last stages of preparation after we had left Philadelphia. Without Dr. Sharer's untiring efforts this volume would not have been possible.

Edward M. Schortman
Patricia A. Urban
Volume Editors

Kenyon College
September 1982

TABLE OF CONTENTS

PAPER No. 6   1
THE QUIRIGUA PROJECT: 1977 SEASON
By Christopher Jones, Wendy Ashmore and Robert J. Sharer

PAPER No. 7   39
THE QUIRIGUA PROJECT: 1978 SEASON
By Robert J. Sharer, Wendy Ashmore, Edward M. Schortman, Patricia A. Urban,
John L. Seidel and David W. Sedat

PAPER No. 8   55
THE QUIRIGUA PROJECT: 1979 SEASON
By Wendy Ashmore, Edward M. Schortman and Robert J. Sharer
Appendix by Bruce Bevan

PAPER No. 9   79
A MAGNETIC SURVEY AT QUIRIGUA
By Bruce Bevan

PAPER No. 10   87
GUATEMALAN OBSIDIAN: A PRELIMINARY STUDY OF SOURCES
AND QUIRIGUA ARTIFACTS
By Payson D. Sheets

PAPER No. 11   102
CONTROL OF BIOLOGICAL GROWTHS OF THE MAYAN
ARCHAEOLOGICAL RUINS OF QUIRIGUA, GUATEMALA
By Mason E. Hale, Jr.

PAPER No. 12   110
QUIRIGUA AND THE EARTHQUAKE OF FEBRUARY 4, 1976
By Bruce Bevan and Robert J. Sharer

PAPER No. 13   118
MONUMENT 26, QUIRIGUA, GUATEMALA
By Christopher Jones

PAPER No. 14   129
STYLISTIC IMPLICATIONS OF MONUMENT CARVING AT QUIRIGUA
AND COPAN
By Arthur G. Miller

PAPER No. 15   137
NEW DRAWINGS OF MONUMENTS 23 and 24, QUIRIGUA, GUATEMALA
By Christopher Jones

PAPER NO. 6

THE QUIRIGUA PROJECT
1977 SEASON

by
Christopher Jones, Wendy Ashmore and Robert J. Sharer

INTRODUCTION

As in past seasons, the 1977 research at Quirigua extended over a period of nearly four months, beginning in January and ending in May. After two weeks of preliminary arrangements in Guatemala City and set-up time at the site, excavations began on 24 January, continuing for 12 weeks, until 16 April. Backfilling and trench-covering operations continued for another month, ending in early May. Formal closing of research operations took place on 27 April, when responsibility for all materials and facilities at Quirigua was turned over to the Instituto de Antropologia e Historia (IDAEH).

The directorial staff of the Quirigua Project was unchanged from 1976: Robert Sharer was Field Director; Christopher Jones directed the site-core excavations; Mary Bullard managed the laboratory; David Sedat served as Administrative Director; Wendy Ashmore supervised the periphery program; and Enrique Monterroso directed restoration and acted as work-crew foreman. Graduate student field assistants were Arlen and Diane Chase, Edward Schortman, Patricia Urban and John Weeks. Kevin Grey served as Project Architect. Mason Hale continued to direct the effort to control the growth of microflora as part of the Monument Program, while John Glavis again volunteered to assist in the inscription-recording aspect of that Program. Marcelino Gonzalez continued in his capacity as assessor for IDAEH. The bulk of the heavy labor was performed by a crew of local excavators that reached a maximum strength of 80 during the course of the season; a smaller crew of masons and laborers was assigned to the Restoration Program.

As in 1976, financial support for all phases of the research effort was provided by the University Museum (Francis Boyer Museum Fund), the National Geographic Society and the National Science Foundation (BNS 7624189). In addition, generous support was received in Guatemala from the Tikal Association and the Ministry of Defense. In the United States, the Project was once again assisted financially by Mr. Landon T. Clay.

The following report summarizes the results of the 1977 research at Quirigua. Under an evolving policy of IDAEH, the funds from the Guatemalan government used to support restoration were no longer expended exclusively during the dry season period used for the research program. Rather, funding and execution of the Restoration Program was carried out over a full 12-month period. Since the task of restoration is the domain of the Instituto, and since the research team is present during only a small part of restoration activities, summaries of this work will not be included here.

1

QUIRIGUA REPORTS

OBJECTIVES FOR THE 1977 RESEARCH SEASON

In 1977, the Quirigua Project conducted four integrated research programs. An expanded Site-Core Program continued both to document the architectural form and sequence of construction and to test functional hypotheses within the 30 hectares of Quirigua Park. Site-core excavations were carried out within the Acropolis, Structures 1A-3 and 1A-10 and the Great Plaza. The second major effort, the Site-Periphery Program, concentrated upon excavations in 9 loci within the 95 km² region surrounding epicentral Quirigua. Principal objectives of this research included assessments of temporal position and sequence, along with the testing of spatial and functional models. The Monument Preservation and Recording Program continued with the now-routine treatments to halt destruction of the sculpture by microfloral growths. The recording effort, designed to document inscriptions not well recorded by previous scholars, was limited in 1977 to the recording of Monuments 19, 20 and 21 (Stelae S,T and U). Finally, in the laboratory, analysis focused upon temporal and functional evaluation of pottery recovered from both the site-core and periphery programs.

RESULTS OF RESEARCH, 1977

THE SITE-CORE PROGRAM

The 1977 Site-Core Program continued to pursue the objectives of the previous two years with the intention of finishing the deeper trenches and backfilling those that were completed. The season was divided into several semi-independent but interrelated investigations (see Fig. 1): Robert Sharer and Diane Chase supervised and recorded excavations in the Great Plaza; David Sedat and Diane Chase completed the excavation of Str. 1A-10; David Sedat continued his 1975 trench as a tunnel into the Acropolis on axis with Mon. 16 (P); Arlen Chase cleared the rooms of Strs. 1B-6 and 1B-18 and excavated deep under both of these structures on the east side of the Acropolis; Christopher Jones supervised the deepening of the 1975 and 1976 trenches in the Acropolis in an attempt to document the earliest period and subsequent growth of this complex; Kevin Gray and John Weeks completed a record of all exposed architectural forms, including plans, elevations and details, in all six previously excavated Acropolis buildings. Weeks also made counts of masonry sizes, shapes and materials on all exposed platform and building walls, and Gray drew isometric views of the Acropolis at various stages of its development. Finally, Jones supervised a new axial tunnel into Str. 1A-3 at the north end of the Great Plaza, as part of an attempt to locate the tomb of Quirigua's greatest ruler, Cauac Sky, Kelley's (1962) "Two-legged Sky."

ACROPOLIS

The 1977 season did much to clarify the growth of the Acropolis. The complex stratigraphic record revealed during the previous seasons was expanded into unexcavated areas of the Acropolis and existing trenches were deepened at several points (see Fig. 2). To describe the results of this work we have divided the stratigraphic sequence into four provisional construction stages (Table 1).

Construction Stage 4

The earliest defined Acropolis Construction Stage is documented by the excavation of two structures (1B-1-2nd and 1B-6-2nd) and the probing of a third (1B-3-3rd). By typology and stratigraphy these structures seem earlier than Str. 1B-2 and the newly-discovered Acropolis ballcourt (Str. 1B-Sub.4) of Construction Stage (CS) 3.

Str. 1B-1-2nd. The L-shaped building (Fig. 1:t) discovered in 1975 under the frontal stairway of Str. 1B-1 was re-examined in 1976 and 1977 and found to have been built in at least two phases. The earlier phase is stratigraphically prior to Str. 1B-2. It consists of a large single-roomed building on a platform ca. 1 m high, facing north onto the lowest known floor of the Acropolis Plaza. The building walls were constructed of large flat river cobbles, a masonry technique not previously seen at Quirigua. The second phase of the structure is later than Str. 1B-2 of CS 3 and earlier than the rear buttresses of 1B-2 which were built along with the great western platform of CS 2.

The renovation consisted of the addition of a room on the east end of the building, creating the L-shape seen in 1976. The walls of the addition were built with beautifully-cut rhyolite blocks, relatively small in size,

THE 1977 SEASON

with flat front faces and squared corners; these approach the technique of CS 2 and suggest that the renovation was begun late in CS 3. A rhyolite-block bench was built within the room against the back wall. A sandstone-block relining of the interior walls in the west end of the interior might have been completed later. The renovation included an upper-zone molding built upon the original cobble back wall; the walls, however, appear too thin and the room too wide for a stone vaulted roof in either phase.

TABLE I

CONSTRUCTION STAGES OF THE ACROPOLIS AT QUIRIGUA: A PRELIMINARY SCHEME

Acropolis Area

Construction Stage	East	South	West	North
1		New stairs of Str. 1B-1 (a)		Stairs covering Str. 1B-Sub.2
	Str. 1B-6	Str. 1B-1 (b)		Str. 1B-5
9.19.0.0.0. (A.D. 810)				
	Str. 1B-18		Str. 1B-3 (c)	
2			Str. 1B-4	Str. 1B-Sub.3
				Str. 1B-Sub.2
			Str. 1B-3-2nd	
			Str. 1B-Sub.1	
			Western Platform	
9.15.6.14.6? (A.D. 737)				
	Renovation of Str. 1B-6-2nd	Renovation of Str. 1B-1-2nd		Str. 1B-5-2nd
3				
		Str. 1B-2	Str. 1B-Sub. 4 (Ballcourt)	Str. 1B-Sub.3-2nd
				Str. 1B-Sub.2-2nd
9.14.13.4.17? (A.D. 724)				
4	Str. 1B-6-2nd	Str. 1B-1-2nd (d)	Str. 1B-3-3rd	

Associated Radiocarbon Dates (MASCA Corrected):
(a) A.D. 850 ± 50 yr
(b) A.D. 880-860 ± 180 yr
(c) A.D. 890 ± 170 yr
(d) A.D. 590 ± 50 yr

Structure 1B-6-2nd. Early structures were discovered under the east side of the Acropolis in excavations directed by Arlen Chase. Str. 1B-6-2nd (Fig. 2:p) is a terraced platform facing west into the lowest Acropolis Court level. Its construction fill is pure silt, except under the stairway. The structure was found to have two phases, like those of Str. 1B-1-2nd: an earlier one with cobble terrace walls, and a later revision of cut rhyolite and sandstone blocks. The earlier phase was apparently built to cover a burial, Special Deposit 14 (Fig. 2:s), which was placed in a schist-slab crypt at the bottom of a 1.3 m pit dug into the sterile river silt. The pit was refilled with silt and capped with more schist slabs before silt structure-fill was placed over the spot. The burial contained one adult, probably male, lying face-up with head to the north. A jade bead was found in the throat or mouth area. Three of the upper right front teeth were inlaid with small jade discs and several upper and lower teeth were notched. Three small monochrome vessels were placed at the right side of the head. Within the fill of the burial pit was found Special Deposit 13 (Fig. 2:r), a cache of two red, flaring-wall, flat-bottom vessels, similar in pottery type and vessel arrangement to those from the early ballcourt (SD 8; see below). In this case, however, the vessels were empty.

Associated with Str. 1B-6-2nd is Special Deposit 12 (Fig. 2:q), a scatter of ten small ceramic cups and a censer, broken in place on top of the silt fill 4 m above the burial, and covered with the fill of the platform top. The pottery seems typologically later than that of the burial and cache.

The cobble terrace wall of the structure suggests that Str. 1B-6-2nd (and therefore the burial) is comparable in time to the original Str. 1B-1-2nd, and consequently earlier than Str. 1B-2 and the ballcourt, although the similarities of the burial vessels and ballcourt cache vessels argue that they are of the same general ceramic period.

Str. 1B-3-3rd. When explored further, the red-painted bench discovered in 1976 under the stairway of Str. 1B-3 was found to be interpretable as the interior bench of an east-facing building, antecedent to Strs. 1B-3-1st and -2nd, and therefore it has been labeled Str. 1B-3-3rd. This interpretation is based on the discovery of the back wall of the room and of steps leading up into the room doorway. The well-preserved red paint and plaster on the bench also suggest a room interior. However, the danger of trench collapse precluded a search for either doorjamb, so it is not certain that the construction is actually a building. The fill of the building substructure is of two materials: the interior fill is pure river silt, and this is surrounded by cobbles and schist slabs. This fill combination makes the structure similar to Str. 1B-6-2nd (belonging to CS 4) located across the court.

Based on the above evidence, therefore, we have determined that the earliest known construction phase at Quirigua contains structures on the east, south and west sides of the prototype Acropolis Court. The stairs of the eastern and southern structures begin on the original river silt. The walls are made of large cobbles, and the fill has two parts, an interior fill of silt, and a layer of cobbles between the silt and the walls. The interment of an important but not excessively wealthy individual, probably male, occasioned the construction of the eastern terraced platform structure.

Construction Stage 3

Str. 1B-Sub.4. The east-west trench (Figs. 1 and 2) became the main focus of the 1977 Acropolis excavations, on both the eastern and western sides. A tunnel was started in this trench under the high western mass of the Acropolis, and an early construction first revealed in 1976 was recognized as a ballcourt, now called Str. 1B-Sub.4 (Fig 2:k). The tunnel followed the down-sloping eastern bench top, crossed the playing alley, and touched the edge of the opposite (western) bench. The top of the western side of the court was found under the far western edge of the Acropolis construction fill. The court differed from the later Quirigua ballcourt (Stromsvik 1952) in having wider benches and in being oriented north-south instead of east-west (Table 2). In both of these points, this early court bears more resemblance to the courts at Copan than to the later court at Quirigua (Str 1B-7; Fig. 1:a). The walls of the early Quirigua court were built of medium-sized blocks of rhyolite. Against the outside western wall of the court, under a floor of a low platform, was found an intact cache (Special Deposit 8; Fig. 2:v and Fig 6a) consisting of two red-slipped, flaring-wall vessels, placed lip-to-lip, and containing jade gravel, pieces of sea shells, fragments of polished iron pyrite and one-third of a round, flat jade ornament which is carved with a front-view human face.

We suspect that Mons. 17 and 18 (Q and R), the pair of small, round rhyolite "altars" found by Morley at the front corners of Str. 1B-6 in the Acropolis, had originally been markers for the buried ballcourt. They resemble the round markers of the Copan II ballcourt (Stromsvik 1952:Fig. 21) in size and shape as well as in their quatrefoil borders. The north and south limits of the court were not seen, as they are buried under meters of fill; thus the potential original settings for the stones were not discovered.

In the axial trench of Str. 1B-4 (Fig 1:o) was found an

THE 1977 SEASON

east-facing wall decorated along its upper zone with two small projecting moldings and stone knotted bundles placed roughly every meter(see Fig. 6b). This decorated wall might be part of the ballcourt, since its rhyolite masonry is like that of the ballcourt seen in the Acropolis axial trench. However, the wall is two meters west of a projected line of the ballcourt's eastern face, and its top is more than 0.3 m higher than the upper floor of the ballcourt platform; thus, if it is part of the ballcourt complex, it forms a separate element, such as an inset corner, or even part of the end-zone. The decorated wall was followed north by tunneling, in hopes of defining its northeastern corner. Since the wall became more and more deteriorated, the search was abandoned after four meters. It was learned, however, that the western platform did not bury the wall's north end when the ballcourt was first covered.

TABLE 2

COMPARATIVE MEASUREMENTS OF QUIRIGUA AND COPAN BALLCOURTS

	Copan I*	Copan II*	Copan III*	Quirigua Str. 1B-Sub.4	Quirigua Str. 1B-7*
Bench Length	26.80**	26.80	28.45	?	24.1
Alley Width	ca. 7	ca. 7	7.0/7.2	6.09	5.7/5.8
Bench Width	ca. 7	ca. 7	6.8/7.0	7.15/7.53	4.9/5.6
Bench Height	ca. 0.80	ca. 0.80	0.80	0.75/0.80	0.55/0.60
Orientation	-	9° W of true N	4° W of true N	17° W of true N	10° N of true E
Markers:					
End	-	0.71	0.98/1.15	0.67/0.72	-
Center	-	0.73	0.98/1.15	1.02?(Mon. 12)	-
Marker Shapes	-	Round	Square	Round	-

* from Stromsvik (1952)

** all measurements in meters

(Note the similarity on Bench Width, Bench Height and North-South Orientation of Quirigua Str. 1B-Sub.4 to the three Copan ballcourts, in contrast to Quirigua Str. 1B-7.)

Str. 1B-Sub.2-2nd and 1B-Sub.3-2nd. Twin north-facing buildings were discovered under Strs. 1B-Sub.2 and -Sub.3 (Fig. 1:k, l), the north-facing buildings discovered in 1976 north of Str. 1B-4 and west of Str. 1B-5. These buildings (Strs. 1B-Sub.2-2nd and -Sub.3-2nd) probably related to the ballcourt, since the longitudinal axis of the ball-playing alley was in line with the central axis between the buildings. However, the twin buildings were apparently not covered along with the ballcourt, so that this old axis was continued in the alignments of Strs. 1B-Sub.2 and -Sub.3, and the later Mons. 15 and 23 (O and Ó;Fig. 1:c).

The list of structures built or still visible in CS 3 includes Str. 1B-2 and the renovated Str. 1B-1-2nd on the south; Str. 1B-Sub.4 (the ballcourt) and Str. 1B-3-3rd on the west; the renovated Str. 1B-6-2nd and Str. 1B-18-

2nd on the east; probably Str. 1B-5-2nd on the north (Fig. 7a); and Strs. 1B-Sub.2-2nd and 1B-Sub.3-2nd facing out to the north. All these structures except for the ballcourt are repeated again in later structures with the same orientation, even though the axis lines of the new buildings are shifted anywhere from one to nine meters. Thus the early Acropolis had the same basic pattern as the later one, with buildings looking down onto the large central court from all sides, and with two single-room buildings facing north toward the Great Plaza.

Construction Stage 2

Str. 1B-Sub.1. The ballcourt was buried by the fill of the great western Acropolis platform, which supported the *Kinich-Ahau*-decorated Str. 1B-Sub.1, a freestanding wall (Figs. 1:p, 2:d) discovered in 1975 (Coe and Sharer 1979; Sharer et al. 1979). For a while it was thought that perhaps the new platform was a replacement ballcourt covering the first, with the large mosaic figures overlooking the new playing alley. However, this theory was not supported by further excavation, which revealed that the western terrace face of the platform was not the typical side-wall of a ballcourt. The playing alley of the early ballcourt was covered with about a meter and a half of fill but apparently the old western side of the court (like the northern end mentioned above) was allowed to protrude above the new floor level. We were not able to learn the reasons for this incongruous retention of old construction.

Str. 1B-3-2nd. Excavations under Str. 1B-3 struck the front doorjambs of an earlier version of the building, Str. 1B-3-2nd, apparently quite similar in orientation and design to the later one. Str. 1B-3-2nd was built directly upon the western platform top beside Str. 1B-Sub.1, the decorated wall, but we could not discover whether or not it preceded the wall in time. Behind the structure two extensions of the platform were built utilizing the same high, steep terrace facing as on the original, not to sustain a building it seems, but merely to provide additional platform surface overlooking the plain and the river. It is interesting that in the sequence of three superimposed versions of Str. 1B-3 (including the postulated 1B-3-3rd), each interior was painted a bright red, the color of the west. Red paint was not found in any other structure interior on the Acropolis, thus suggesting a ritual use of color in these buildings.

Structure 1B-Sub.2. The axial trench into Str. 1B-Sub.2 (Fig. 1:k), which is northwest of Str. 1B-4, was deepened and extended to meet a new tunnel begun at the base of the great stairway behind Mon. 16 (Fig. 1:b). This trench revealed an addition to the front platform of Str. 1B-Sub.2 before the final stairway had buried the structure.

Structure 1B-Sub.3. The 1977 excavations revealed that Str. 1B-Sub.3 (Fig. 1:l) was a single-room structure with a single doorway facing north, forming a pair with Str. 1B-Sub.2 but slightly smaller. A trench at the west end of the single room exposed a completely preserved stone half-vault, demonstrating that the stone corbelled vault rose only 1.3 m above the wall tops and left a 1.7 m gap between vault bodies that could have been spanned only by wooden beams. A deep axial probe into the filled-up room reached the floor, which was covered to a depth of about 10 cm with burnt earth and charcoal, masses of obsidian chips and flakes, fragments of whole and partial fine-ware bowls and cups, a burnt human tooth and fragments of burnt human bone. The bone and fine pottery suggest a redeposited burial or cremation, but the hundreds of thousands of tiny chips and flakes connote a redeposited obsidian workshop (see *Quirigua Paper No. 10*, this volume for a discussion of the obsidian).

At the northeast corner of Str. 1B-Sub.3 a deep trench revealed that Str. 1B-5-2nd (Fig. 1:m), the buried one-room structure under Str. 1B-5, preceded Str. 1B-Sub.3 but followed -Sub.3-2nd in time. A high wall, built in CS 2, connected the adjacent constructions, apparently as part of the access-restrictive architecture of the Acropolis (cf. Sharer et al. 1979). Another trench showed that Str. 1B-Sub.3 is younger than the great west platform. Thus it was constructed in CS 2, while Str. 1B-5-2nd is earlier and probably was built in CS 3. The masonry of Strs. 1B-Sub.2 and -Sub.3 is typical of walls and buildings of late CS 2, made of sandstone and rhyolite with occasional marble blocks, larger than the blocks of the western platform at the beginning of the stage, and not as well squared or smoothed on the outer surfaces.

Strs. 1B-3 and 1B-4. During CS 2, Str. 1B-4 (Fig. 1:o) was built, Str. 1B-3-2nd was torn down and replaced by Str. 1B-3, and many large platforms (Fig. 2:a, b, c) were built on all sides of the western platform, slowly obliterating it and its decorated free-standing wall. A C^{14} sample sealed by Str. 1B-3 was dated to AD 890 ± 170, too large a margin for our purposes. Two successive raisings of the Acropolis Court floor occurred during this time. Broad new stairways extended around all but the south side of the court by the end of the stage.

THE 1977 SEASON

Strs. 1B-6 and 1B-18. The structures of the east side of the court were built late in this stage or early in the next: Str. 1B-18 (Figs. 1:x, 2:t), a long, low building with mixed masonry and adobe walls; and later Str. 1B-6 (Fig. 1:v), a higher, more square building with marble block masonry. A trench supervised by A. Chase on the axis of Str. 1B-6 extended deep into its fill in search of the tomb predicted by Marshall Becker (1972), but was abandoned in favor of the nearby axis of Str. 1B-6-2nd, in which was found the burial described earlier.

Remarks. Dating of Construction Stages 4, 3 and 2 is conjectural at present, since hieroglyphically datable monuments are not found in the Acropolis. However, as Hewett (1916:159) and Morley (1937-38:IV, 82) have pointed out, there does seem to be a shift in the use of stone material in site-core monuments. The first group consists of the small rhyolite Mons. 12 and 13 (L and M, dated as 9.12.0.0.0-9.14.0.0.0, and 9.15.0.0.0; Morley 1937-38; Satterthwaite 1979) and possibly 14, 17 and 18 (N, Q and R). The second series includes the large sandstone stelae and zoomorphs in Group B and the Great Plaza, dated 9.15.15.0.0 to 9.18.15.0.0. If, as seems likely, the shift from small rhyolite to large sandstone monuments coincided with the change from low buildings of rhyolite construction to elevated platforms of predominantly sandstone block construction, then CS 4 and CS 3 of the Acropolis would precede 9.15.15.0.0 (AD 745, GMT correlation). It has been suggested by Proskouriakoff (1973) and others (e.g., Hatch 1975; Shaw 1976; Marcus 1976) that the repeated date 9.14.13.4.17 is the inauguration date of Cauac Sky from Copan's ruling family, and that the date 9.15.6.14.6 marks the emergence of Quirigua's political independence from Copan under his leadership. Our correlation between masonry and monument changes suggests that the ballcourt and related structures of the Acropolis (CS 3) belong to the early part of Cauac Sky's reign, that the earlier cobble structures and burial (CS 4) preceded his accession, and that the great western platform (CS 2; see below) was built by him after the ties with Copan were severed.

Several facts support this hypothesis. A sample of carbon from a deposit of Str. 1B-1-2nd in CS 4, consisting of small pieces of carbonized wood, was tested by the Museum Applied Science Center for Archaeology, University Museum (Sample P-2536). Its MASCA-corrected date, using a half-life of 5568 years, was AD 590 ± 50 yr, corresponding to a range from 9.5.10.0.0 to 9.10.10.0.0 in the Maya Long Count. This is a little earlier than expected for a stage immediately preceding Cauac Sky (CS 4), but certainly is well within the range of possibilities. Other samples from the Acropolis are consistent with the stratigraphy as well (see Table 1 and below).

Furthermore, as one would expect from the above hypothesis, there is more continuity in construction techniques at the transition to Quirigua's independence (corresponding to the beginning of CS 2) than there is at the ruler's inaugural date, corresponding to the beginning of CS 3, at which time presumably a previous rulership was replaced. The great western platform which defines the beginning of CS 2 is certainly more grandiose in design and there is a new preference for sandstone, but the individual blocks remain roughly the same in size and shape as before. Also, the multi-room plan and corner masks of Str. 1B-2 (see Sharer et al. 1979) continue in later buildings of the Acropolis—the plan in Strs 1B-4 and -5, the masks in Strs. 1B-1 and -5. That CS 3 is a period of cultural subordination is suggested by the resemblance of the ballcourt (Str. 1B-Sub.4) and its probable markers (Mons. 17 and 18) to those of Copan. As Morley points out (1937-38:IV, 98), the cross-legged seated figures on the markers are like those on contemporary Copan monuments. An additional argument in favor of the hypothesis is the observation that the rear terraces of the Acropolis at the time of the western platform were high steep walls, far more defensible than before or after (Sharer et al. 1979). This concern for the defense of the Acropolis might well be felt by a newly independent political entity at the beginning of CS 2.

Construction Stage 1

Strs 1B-1 and 1B-5. CS 1 began with the building of Str. 1B-1 (Fig. 1:s) followed later by the raising of the Acropolis Court floor by at least one and a half meters to its present level, and the building of Str. 1B-5 (Fig. 1:n; Fig. 7b). The fills of the stairways of this massive building rest directly on the large paving stones of the latest Acropolis Court floor and are abutted by the lime plaster flooring which covers the pavement. Str. 1B-1 has a hieroglyphic frieze and glyphic bench fronts which clearly date the structure to 9.19.0.0.0 (AD 810; Morley 1937-38:IV, 229-241). This date is then taken to mark the beginning of CS 1. Two samples of charcoal from the stairway of Str. 1B-1 were dated to AD 850 ± 50 yr and AD 860 ± 180 yr (MASCA Correction). These dates add some support for the Goodman-Thompson-Martinez correlation.

Str. 1B-1 is built mostly of sandstone blocks and Str. 1B-5 primarily of marble and rhyolite, but the sizes and surface finish of the blocks are similar. Str. 1B-5 once had masks of stucco over roughly-shaped stone, in contrast to the beautifully-cut stone masks of 1B-1. The stone work of Str. 1B-1 is similar to that of the nearby Str. 1B-2 and the stucco-over-stone work of Str 1B-5 is like that in 1B-5-2nd, which it replaced. Since the two earlier structures are also approximately contemporaneous, the two building techniques possibly reflect different attitudes toward the two sides of the Acropolis. Residential/administrative functions as opposed to ceremonial and ownership by separate families come to mind as possible explanations.

At least two more large-scale construction projects took place at Quirigua: a new stairway fronting the platform of Str. 1B-1, and a great stone stairway and platform. The Str. 1B-1 stair was made with beautifully-cut large stair blocks, and included the finely sculptured deep relief figures on the flanking terraces described by Morley. The stones of its sloping terrace faces are flat in front and sharply beveled in back, looking much like the "turtle-back" veneer stones of Puuc architecture.

These two post-9.19.0.0.0 constructions reveal that the economic and political ability to commission large works continued after the last recorded period-ending date. However, since these are the only construction projects known—except for a small, low platform in the Acropolis Court (Str. 1B-19; Fig. 1:y)—it is doubtful that building activity continued beyond the ninth century A. D.

An interesting collection of around sixteen broken and complete storage jars, a censer and a curious duck-shaped pot, along with fragments of bone and a few teeth from a child's skeleton, were found on the floor of the north room of Str. 1B-18, buried under the clay, burnt adobe fragments and stones of the collapsed adobe superstructure. The undisturbed positions of the vessels and the presence of the child suggest a sudden collapse of the room, calling to mind, of course, the high death toll from collapse of adobe structures during the 1976 Guatemalan earthquake (cf. *Quirigua Paper No. 12*, this volume). The vessel forms and types also argue for a residential ("kitchen") use of the room, although no hearth areas could be found.

General Remarks

During the 1977 season, Kevin Gray and John Weeks completed a systematic record of the ground plans, interior and exterior elevations, additions, masonry and all noticable architectural features and techniques in the Acropolis. The study was intended to improve upon the earlier record of this architecture, to make a record of its state before restoration and to gather evidence for the function of the buildings and of the Acropolis. Strs. 1B-2, 1B-3, 1B-4 and 1B-5 seem best described as "palaces," an old but still useful term distinguishing a building designed for residential and administrative uses from a "temple" suitable for ritual or ceremonial uses (cf. Pollock 1965:409-410). For formal definitions of the two sets, one begins with extremes, such as the high, single-doorwayed Great Temples of Tikal with their single enclosed space and lack of windows and benches representing the latter, and the low, many-roomed buildings of Tikal's Central Acropolis, complex in plan and usually possessing benches, many doorways and curtain holders illustrating the palace concept. From this perspective the structures in the Acropolis at Quirigua appear to be somewhat intermediate, but in their general characteristics they do correspond more closely to the Tikal palaces than to the Tikal temples. They all have many rooms, are complex in plan and possess benches, curtain-holders and windows (except for Str. 1B-2). Str. 1B-4 has an interior staircase, perhaps leading to a now-destroyed second story. Str. 1B-1 is also many-roomed and has benches, but its three doorways and non-interconnecting rooms restrict its space and give it more formality than its Acropolis companions. Str. 1B-6 seems to have only one usable room, and thus is more temple-like (cf. Becker 1972). Nevertheless, it does have a secondary bench in the north end of the room. The twin buildings facing north into the Ballcourt Plaza (Strs. 1B-Sub.2 and -Sub.3) are more temple-like, single-roomed, single-doorwayed structures, although Str. 1B-Sub.2 was built with a bench.

Thus, Quirigua had a general overall plan which in some ways is a simplification of the two-part plan of Copan and Tikal: a raised, potentially defensible residential/administrative palace area to the south of a large flat plaza with many monuments, most of which front a large raised construction to the north (Tikal's North Acropolis and Quirigua's Str. 1A-3). In both cases, a ballcourt is found in the south end of the monument plaza. The layout of Quirigua might therefore be derived from a more general Maya concept than just the Copan site-center, with which it is most consistently compared. Quirigua strikes one as a Maya site boiled down to its most basic components, a defensible living and working place for the ruler and his court, and an open, public area in which to impress the visitor, hold public ceremonies, have markets, play the ballgame. The surrounding site-core groups are smaller

THE 1977 SEASON

plaza areas apparently not attached to the main area by pavement. These contain raised, multi-roomed buildings made of the same well-cut masonry as the Acropolis buildings (see below, Site-Periphery Program). One, the South Group, tested in 1975, has a pyramidal structure (Str. 1B-9) and in some ways seems to be a miniature version of the site-core. Since they are so well built, these groups are most easily interpreted as the houses of the wealthy families who supported the ruler. Nevertheless, the huge size of the Acropolis with its adjoining Ballcourt and Great Plazas stands in contrast to anything else at Quirigua and emphasizes the centralization of authority and elite social structure of this provincial, yet apparently independent, Maya community.

THE GREAT PLAZA

Test-Pitting Program

During the 1977 season a systematic test-pit program was conducted in the Great Plaza at Quirigua. This effort was directed by Robert Sharer, assisted by Diane Chase. The objective of the program was to determine the form (extent, composition and thickness) of the prehistoric plaza that supports the massive Quirigua monuments. Beyond this, data bearing upon the plaza's chronological and functional aspects were also sought.

Preliminary probes excavated in 1975 and 1976, together with earlier test pits by Ricketson (1933), indicated that the Quirigua Great Plaza was not of uniform thickness or composition. In 1975 a large pit was excavated by Sharer in the northern portion of the Plaza, between Mons. 3 and 4, immediately south of Str. 1A-3 (see Fig. 3), in order to determine the thickness and composition of the Plaza at that point. This probe revealed that the laja-paved plaza surface capped some 1.65 m of densely packed river-cobble-and-mud fill. This finding corresponded well with Ricketson's 1933 notes describing the two pits excavated some 80 m to the south in the vicinity of Mons. 5 and 7. In contrast to the northern Plaza area, excavations at the southern end of the Plaza in both 1975 and 1976 (on the north side of the Acropolis platform of Str. 1B-17 and around Mons. 15 and 16 in the connecting Ballcourt Plaza; see Coe and Sharer 1979, Sharer et al. 1979) failed to reveal extensive river-cobble construction. Instead, a plaza surface of lajas capped a layer of apparently naturally deposited silt.

While the composition of the Great Plaza appeared to be different in its northern and southern extremities, a similar laja-paved surface appeared to predate (run under) the structures at both its northern and southern extent. However, no formal edge or limit to this prehistoric surface had been found.

The 1977 program comprised 52 test pits, each originally measuring 1 x 1.5 m. Subsequently, six trenches measuring up to 76 m long were opened by connecting test pits, in order to follow the buried plaza surface and associated features (see Fig. 8a). Initially, a north-south line of 21 test pits was placed from Str. 1A-3 in the north to Str. 1B-17 in the south, covering the full length of the Great Plaza, a distance of nearly 400 m. The test pits along this line, corresponding to the original site base-line surveyed in 1975, were placed at 15-m intervals. Intersecting the north-south line of test pits, three east-west lines, usually varying between 10 and 20 m apart, probed each of the major alignments of monuments. The first of these consisted of seven pits in the southern portion of the Plaza, running from Mon. 11 (K) on the east to the north side of Str. 1A-11 on the west. Further north, another line of four pits was placed immediately south of the east-west alignment of Mons. 5 (E) and 6 (F), passing just north of Mon. 7 (G). Furthest to the north, a line of 17 test pits was positioned immediately south of the east-west alignment of Mons. 1, 3, and 4 (A, C and D), intersecting Mon. 2 (B). The remaining three pits were parallel to this latter transect, in line with and to the west of Mon. 4. The majority of these probes were located within the presumed limits of the prehistoric plaza—that is, within the area defined by the monuments. However, the northern east-west transect was extended beyond this area on both the east and west to attempt to find limits to the plaza.

These excavations have documented a great deal about the form of the prehistoric Great Plaza, including verification that it was not a single construction entity (Fig. 3). Rather, the northern portion, supporting the cluster of the largest monuments at Quirigua (Mons. 1 through 7) as well as Str. 1A-3, consists of a massive platform constructed of river-cobble fill within an apparent natural depression, and paved with lajas. The ancient surface of this construction (now designated Platform 1A-1) was some 0.5 m higher in elevation than the plaza to the south. Its extent, as determined by the 1977 excavations, measures 100 m north-south and 85 m east-west. Based upon the four probes that penetrated the full depth of the cobble fill (Ricketson's two test pits, Op. 2H in 1975 and Ops. 17N through 17P in 1977) the thickness of the construction fill varies between 1.0 m (near its southern limits in the vicinity of Mon. 7) and 1.65 m (near its northern limit at the base of Str. 1A-3). Taking the mean thickness (1.3 m) of the cobble fill based upon these four excavations, the total mass of this platform is ca. 11,050 m^3. Although the limits of

Platform 1A-1 were discovered on its southern, eastern and western sides, no formal edge or masonry facing was revealed. Instead, the limits of the platform on these three sides consist of a gradually sloping cobble surface that drops about 0.5 m to the surrounding natural-ground-level surface (paved to the south; see Fig. 8c). No northern limit to the platform has been revealed: the 1977 axial tunnel of Str. 1A-3 verified that the laja-paved surface of the platform underlies this structure, but excavations on the northern side of Str. 1A-3 and the adjacent Str. 1A-2 have failed to find any trace of the platform in these areas. Thus we conclude that the northern limits to this construction lie underneath Str. 1A-3; perhaps they correspond to the northern face of Str.1A-3-B, an earlier construction facing now covered by the bulk of the fill of Str. 1A-3-A. We also conclude that the bulk of the construction fill of Platform 1A-1 was used to level a natural low area, possibly an ancient river channel that may have previously limited site expansion to the north (see Fig. 4).

In constrast to the great northern plaza platform, the southern portion of the Great Plaza consists of a relatively thin cobble and laja paving varying between 8 and 15 cm in thickness, capping an apparently natural deposit of alluvial silt. This surface is not continuous, however, for there are areas revealed in several test pits without any trace of stone surfacing (cf. Fig. 4). The prehistoric plaza level in these areas is represented by the surface of the same silt stratum which was capped elsewhere by cobbles or lajas. It would appear that the paved areas correspond to zones adjacent to structures or monuments. For instance, paving is found adjacent to the terrace fronting the Acropolis in the Ballcourt Plaza (where traces of plaster surfacing were found; see below), and to the north side of Str. 1A-11 on the western side edge of the plaza. Other paved areas appear to be associated with several of the monuments standing in the southern portion of the plaza—these may represent paved aprons that surround the monument platforms, or even access surfaces that interconnect the monuments and adjacent structures. In addition, traces of cobble surfacing were found in association with the remains of a badly ruined construction feature—perhaps a structure or stela platform foundation—located 80 m south of Mon. 7 in the north-south line of test pits (Fig. 3). This feature, designated Platform 1A-3, consists of a single course of masonry, aligned north-south and apparently faced on its west side. Despite considerable excavation to reveal and follow this feature, no corners could be conclusively demonstrated, so that its size and function remain conjectural (cf. Fig. 4; see below). The full extent of the paved areas in the southern plaza is not known: because of the great depth of recent alluvium that overlies the prehistoric plaza level (up to 1.5 m), the cobble surfacing was not followed beyond the confines of the test pits and trenches.

Artifactual remains recovered from the plaza program were sparse. The sherd material found in association with the prehistoric plaza surface (or immediately beneath the surface) was usually badly eroded. However, paste diagnostics indicate typical Quirigua Late Classic wares. In one area south of Plaza Platform 1A-1, sherd density was extremely high, as crushed sherds appeared to be embedded in the plaza surface itself. A broken whole vessel, an *olla* of a "domestic" type, was discovered nearby, lying directly on the plaza surface. These artifacts appear to be associated with use of the plaza, perhaps resulting from prehistoric domestic or market activities carried out in this area (see below).

Str. 1A-3

A new tunnel was begun by Christopher Jones, penetrating Str. 1A-3 three meters west of the axial trench dug in 1975. This new location was based on a more precise determination of the front corners of the structure and the proposition that the tomb of Cauac Sky would most likely be on the axis of the platform. In 1975 it was determined that the structure consists of an original long, thin platform of marble masonry and additional great masses of fill behind the platform. We speculated that the original platform was designed as a backdrop for the monuments fronting it, erected during the later years of the ruler's long reign, from 9.16.10.0.0 to 9.17.15.0.0, and that the additional fill covered the tomb placed on axis with both the mound and Mon. 7. This "zoomorph" has been singled out by Kelley (1962), Shaw (1976) and Jones (1977) as the final monument of Cauac Sky, stating the date and ceremonies of his death and the inauguration of his successor, Sky Xul. The tunnel penetrated 20 m and hit the base of the back wall of the original platform without finding a tomb. We also tunneled 6 m in from the rear on the same axis.

Str. 1A-10

Str. 1A-10, the southernmost of seven small platforms along the east side of the Great Plaza and seemingly in line with Mons. 10 and 11 to the west (see Fig. 3), was a focus of excavation during both the 1976 and 1977 seasons. The 1976 work was undertaken by David Sedat, while the 1977 work was supervised by Diane Chase, assisted by Sedat. The initial research consisted of clearing excavations designed to reveal the present extent and form of the construction. Subsequently, an axial trench penetrated to the core of the structure (see Fig. 9a), while more restricted probes revealed details of superimposed construction.

In these excavations Str. 1A-10 was revealed to be a masonry-faced, terraced, rectangular platform, 11 x 25 m, originally some 4 m high. An 11 m wide staircase projects some 3.5 m on the western face, parallel to the long axis of the structure. The masonry facing consists of cut sandstone blocks, covering a dense cobble and mud construction core. An axially cached owl-effigy pottery vessel(Fig. 9b) was found apparently intruded into the silt beneath the cobble fill, almost exactly at the midpoint of the structure. Two basal terraces, averaging 0.8 m high, with a 0.6 m set-back, are preserved. Given the apparent height of the structure, three additional terraces of this height can be inferred. A low (single course) summit platform is partially preserved on the surface. The projected width (east-west) of this feature is c. 4.5 m; no estimate of length can be made. It is assumed that this summit platform once supported a structure constructed of perishable materials, a conclusion which is reinforced by the presence of collapsed construction debris behind Str. 1A-10, along the eastern basal terrace. Here were found tumbled adobe materials, including at least one intact adobe block (36 x 14 x 10 cm).

The lowest terrace of Str. 1A-10 is abutted by a frontal terrace (Platform 1A-2) that projects some 18 m to the west, extending the full length of the structure (see Fig. 3). The frontal platform covers an area of some 500 m² (20 x 25 m) and is constructed of earthen fill capped by a laja pavement; its limits are defined by a sandstone terrace wall originally about 0.7 m high, but now largely robbed or destroyed. The paving and fill of this platform abut the western basal terrace of Str. 1A-10 north of the staircase. However, the staircase overlies the platform surface. No trace of an earlier staircase of Str. 1A-10 was revealed in the deep axial trench.

The frontal platform of Str. 1A-10 overlies the cobble plaza surface which was 0.1 m thick when penetrated. This plaza surfacing is apparently the same construction revealed some 25 m to the west in association with Mon. 11. In the axial trench, debris released by the destruction of Platform 1A-2's terrace wall sealed an intact rhyolite plaster level capping the cobble plaza surface and abutting the terrace wall. The cobble plaza surface continues eastward under Platform 1A-2 until it ends at a mass of rubble fill that surrounds a remnant of an east-facing terrace wall, also constructed of sandstone blocks. This latter wall survives to a height of about 0.6 m; it is beneath the 1A-10 staircase in the axial trench, and is west of the 1A-10 basal terrace north of the staircase projection. Because of apparent constructional disturbance, the buried terrace wall does not articulate with either the plaza surface or Platform 1A-2.

Two alternative interpretations of constructional sequence may be offered. First, it is possible that this buried terrace wall predates both Str. 1A-10 and its frontal platform (assumed here to be contemporaneous), and thus represents the eastern limit of a now-destroyed early structure. Second, the buried terrace may be contemporaneous with the frontal platform, representing, in fact, its original eastern face. This alternative sees Platform 1A-2 as predating Str. 1A-10. As mentioned above, the fact that the frontal platform appears to abut the basal terrace of Str. 1A-10 might favor the first interpretation: i.e., Platform 1A-2 would appear to be later than Str. 1A-10 and thus could not be a part of the earlier buried terrace wall. On the other hand, the abutment may be connective construction added to link the (earlier) frontal terrace at the time Str. 1A-10 was built. This, together with the fact that the frontal terrace underlies Str. 1A-10's staircase and contains very different fill (earth *vs.* cobbles), appears to favor the second alternative, that is, Platform 1A-2, incorporating the buried wall, predated Str. 1A-10. In either case, it is significant that the eastern limit of the Great Plaza seems to be fixed by the remnants of this buried east-facing terrace wall beneath Str. 1A-10.

THE SITE-PERIPHERY PROGRAM

By the close of the 1976 field season, the reconnaissance and survey aspects of the site-periphery program were considered nearly complete, so that the 1977 season was devoted almost entirely to enlarging the sample of loci tested by excavation. The units chosen for testing were not selected randomly, but, as will be explained for each case below, were picked because they represented the best combinations of specific theoretical interest and logistical practicality, while maintaining a balance within the overall sample for diversity of site location and complexity. In all, eight new loci were tested in 1977 (see Fig. 5 for locations) and one from 1976 was renewed, bringing the total of site-periphery excavations to 15. Each investigation will be discussed briefly below, followed by a short summary.

It should be noted, too, that some data were collected

by means other than excavation. Mapping work included a transit plot of loci on the Quirigua plain, north of the site-core, connecting them to the site-core and to its grid system of labeling. These loci should probably be considered part of a spatially redefined "site" of Quirigua (cf. Fig. 5; see also Ashmore 1977). A transit map was also prepared for Loc. 002, Morley's Group A, refining and adding to the information presented by Morley (1937-38:V, Pl. 215a). As noted in 1975, Morley's map omits a long, low structure, Str. 2, along the west side of the uppermost platform, as well as a probable structure at the end of an apparently natural ridge extending north from the principal (upper) platform. After the site was cleared, the remains of two large-block sandstone stairways were discerned. One leads from the lower, eastern platform, on which the fragments of Mon. 21 are located, up the east side of the upper platform; the other staircase leads up the west side of the upper platform—indeed, along the length and apparently to the summit of Str. 2. Although Mons. 20 and 21 (Stelae T and U) bear early dates (see below), the visible architecture in Loc. 002 is most like that of the latest construction within the site-core (CS 1), suggesting either extended use of the locus throughout the Classic period, or possible re-use during the Terminal Classic (cf. dating of Loc. 025, below).

Information was also recorded concerning a series of unprovenienced artifacts, some of which were donated to the Project, and some of which were only shown, as part of private local collections. The finds were principally figurines, mostly heads, though a few bodies and whole specimens were also recorded, and almost all were characteristically Middle to Late Preclassic. The claimed proveniences of these materials run in a line along the south side of the Motagua River (cf. Schmidt 1883), from Switch Molina to Mixco, and may represent a portion of a more extensive line of occupation. No comparable specimens have been discovered first-hand by Project personnel or seen *in situ*.

Finally, although not part of the site-periphery program proper, the continuation of the valley-wide survey may be noted here. During the final weeks of the 1977 season, Edward Schortman and Patricia Urban began reconnaissance and mapping of sites in the lower valley beyond the limits of the site-periphery program. Building on work begun by Timothy Nowak, they visited several previously reported sites (Las Quebradas, Playitas, Comanche Farm and Oneida) as a feasibility study for an expanded program of reconnaissance, mapping and test excavation in 1978. Though constrained by limited time, bad weather and dense vegetation, Schortman and Urban were able to make or amend maps of nine architectural groups or complexes.

EXCAVATIONS

It should be noted, by way of introduction, that the overall preference for the 1977 excavations was to sample briefly a large number of loci, rather than conduct intensive investigation in a small number of sites. Primary goals of excavation were to relate the peripheral loci to the site-core in time and to seek evidence of the kinds of activities carried on there. Because of constraints on time and personnel, we chose to pursue these goals by limited axial cuts—to reveal construction methods and style, retrieve sealed fill lots and possibly associated primary deposits—supplemented by other shallow excavations as needed. The latter were used principally to discover basic elements of structure plan and interstructural stratigraphy and to clear along occupational surfaces.

Locus 116

The only non-architectural site to be excavated this season was a midden deposit, Locus 116 (Fig. 10a). Located approximately 300 m north of Loc. 025 (Morley's Group B), the deposit was first discovered in 1976 by workmen clearing the Mejia canal in search of exposed archaeological features. Excavation here, supervised by Ashmore, was aimed at recovering ceramics and other artifacts from a stratified deposit, and it was hoped that these artifacts would give evidence of sequential typological change and/or broaden the inventory of materials available for analysis. Two control trenches were excavated to the level of the water table, using arbitrary 20 cm levels. Once the internal stratigraphy was revealed, two pits were excavated in "natural" levels and the matrix from each level of the latter pits was hand-sorted to retrieve small artifacts. Screening, tried on two occasions, was unsuccessful due to the wetness of the matrix, but samples from a number of levels were set aside for flotation and a duplicate series of such samples has been sent to the University of Florida for analysis.

Over 11,000 sherds recovered from this deposit were classified by form and type, but they gave little evidence of change. All seemed to represent the principal Quirigua ceramic complex, a Late to Terminal Classic assemblage. Of interest for functional interpretation, however, were indications that this midden included trash from a ceramic workshop. That

THE 1977 SEASON

is, among the artifacts recovered were a series of ceramic molds for figurines (as well as a few fragmentary mold-made figurines), a concave (curved) stamp, presumably for decorating the side of ceramic vessels, and several bowl sherds with unfired clay still adhering to the interior surface. All these finds suggest that at least the pre-firing aspects of ceramic production were carried out nearby (cf. Adams 1970; Becker 1973). There was also some evidence that an obsidian workshop was located in the immediate area (see *Quirigua Paper No. 10*, this volume).

Plazuela Groups

Two new "plazuela" groups, Loci 039 and 013, were tested in 1977 (see Sharer et al. 1979 and Ashmore 1977 for definitions) and work at a third, Loc. 026, was expanded beyond excavations done in 1976. The two newly tested loci were chosen because they are at the "small" end of the locus size/complexity continuum. Loc. 039 was picked to "represent" the Chapulco-zone plazuelas—in a non-statistical sense—mostly because of its location and accessibility; Loc. 013, on the first bench overlooking the Quirigua floodplain, was of interest because it had an unusual abundance of surface obsidian.

Locus 039. Loc. 039 consists of 11 structures of varying sizes, of which Str. 7 was chosen for investigation (supervised by Ashmore). The latter is a small, apparently trapezoid-shaped structure, with its long axis east-west, situated on the north side of a small court. Although only one corner was surely defined, wall orientations suggest that its overall dimensions were 4.5 m wide by 8.0 m long on the south face, and about 10.5 m long on the north face. Construction consisted of a 0.5 m wide perimeter wall (Fig. 10b), composed of cobbles and rhyolite, laid on a sandy ash surface. The stone wall was preserved to a height of about 0.5 m and may have been the footing for an adobe wall, as lumps of that material were found in debris off the southwest corner of the structure.

Sherds recovered in this excavation were often eroded, but seem to fit within the principal Quirigua complex; forms represented are not inconsistent with an interpretation that this building was residential. The only other artifacts associated with Str. 7 were pieces of obsidian—mostly irregular flakes and debitage, sometimes with cortex—though a fragment of a legless rhyolite metate was found nearby in surface collections in 1976. Loc. 039 is situated near the eastern end of an igneous formation bordering the south side of the Motagua River, and there is a small rhyolite outcrop about 100 m southwest of Str. 7. The occurence, then, of rhyolite artifacts and some construction materials at this unimposing site is not surprising; it does not indicate here the same expenditure of effort in procurement of such raw materials that might be implied by their presence in a site on the floodplain proper.

Locus 013. Loc. 013 was discovered in 1975 and consists of 6 small mounds, divided between two plazuela groups, near the edge of the first river terrace north of the floodplain. Abundant pieces of obsidian—shatter flakes and debitage—were collected here and from the adjacent heavily plowed field (Loc. 014, where no architectural features were detected). Str. 1, a small mound about 5.0 m wide and 10.0 m long, forms the west side of the northen plazuela; the recovery of 2 metate fragments from its surface led us to hope that by digging there we might be able to combine investigation of a possible lithic workshop area with that of a likely domestic locus. Excavation, supervised by Diane Chase and Wendy Ashmore, revealed at least two construction stages, each apparently involving an earthen mound with a basal border of schist slabs. Cobbles, sandstone and schist litter the mound surface, but the site has been plowed and these stones retain no stratigraphic ties to the buried construction; they might simply have formed a summit platform surface on the earthen mound.

Obsidian finds bore out our hopes in terms of abundance, but, with the exception of one projectile point and a handful of flake-blades, all were shatter and debitage pieces or small (ca. 2 cm diameter) pebble nodules. Sherds were eroded but most represent jar forms and seem, again, to fit the main Quirigua ceramic complex. The only other artifacts recovered in these excavations were a piece of chipped red stone (jasper?) and a long cylindrical clay object tentatively labeled as the rod of a compound earplug. For functional interpretation, then, we rely primarily on the size and form of the mound and the two surface metate fragments to identify Str. 1 as part of a residential locus.

Locus 026. The third plazuela investigated in 1977 was Loc. 026, a small group northeast of the site-core where excavations were also carried out in 1976 (see Sharer et al. 1979). In the prior season, work focused on Str. 2C-3, which seems to have been an elite residence. The 1977 excavations, however, supervised by Urban, were directed toward increasing our understanding of the northern structure, 2C-1, and to testing whether Loc. 026 might indeed have been the eastern terminus of the "causeway" feature discovered in 1976 (*Ibid.*). Excavations at the edge of the northwest corner of the

13

court, where the causeway might most logically provide entry, were inconclusive, yielding only a jumble of rough stones which are most easily attributed to collapse debris of Str. 2C-1.

The latter structure has been heavily damaged, especially on the summit and north and west sides, in part at least by a modern drainage ditch. We knew from 1976 work, however, that it had a ruined masonry stairway on its south or front face and that associated artifacts (censers, figurines, lack of jar forms) were seemingly more "ceremonial" and less "domestic" than those from Str. 2C-3 (cf. Sharer et al. 1979). The corners of the basal stair were located this year (Fig. 10c), giving the feature a breadth of about 16.5 m; from general mound form and dimensions we estimate that the overall structure length was not much greater. A number of censer and figurine fragments were recovered along with sherds and obsidian flake-blades, such finds neither contradicting nor supporting in more detail our 1976 imputation of a "ceremonial" function for Str. 2C-1. It might be noted that of the handful of Copador sherds found to date at Quirigua, two came from the area of this structure.

Temporal evaluation of Loc. 026 is based mostly on evidence from Str. 2C-3. Six copper artifacts were recovered in 1976 from a burial in this structure; no other grave goods were associated with the deposit. Use of copper in the southeastern Maya area may have begun at the close of the Late Classic (cf. Stromsvik 1941:71; Kidder 1948; Lothrop 1952; Baudez and Becquelin 1973); bits of this metal have been found with both Copador (Kidder 1948:229; Boggs 1950) and San Juan plumbate pottery (Kidder 1948:229). Since the Str. 2C-3 burial was clearly intruded through the floor, it postdates the original construction. Charcoal found on the step of the structure has yielded a radiocarbon date of AD 850 ± 50 yr (MASCA correction), which is about the beginning of the 10th *baktun* and correlates with Acropolis Construction Stage 1 (see above and Table 1). Another sample found on the pavement in front of the same structure gave a date of AD 530-490 ± 50 yr (MASCA correction). Both samples were "sealed" by alluvium on these terminal occupation surfaces, so that any error in age determination should be toward a more recent date. Possible interpretations of the anomalous early date include use of "scavenged" rather than fresh-cut wood, or redeposition by floodwaters from some disturbed earlier context. At any rate, based on the intrusive burial and the more acceptable, later radiocarbon date, we tentatively assign final occupation of Loc. 026 to a time equivalent to Acropolis CS 1. Original construction of Str. 2C-3 is, however, perhaps assignable to Acropolis CS 2, based on comparison of masonry form and materials. (Table 3 presents a preliminary correlation of non-Acropolis masonry construction, from both site-core and site-periphery, with the Acropolis sequence; unless otherwise noted, the criteria used for comparison are construction style and materials.)

Quadrangles

Particular emphasis was given this season to testing members of the "quadrangle" type in this site-periphery locus typology. The reasons for such emphasis were partly methodological: since part of the definition for the quadrangle locus type depends on access to the central court being cut off at two or more corners, we wanted to test whether this criterion truly represented a regularity of construction, or just similar sequences of collapse, ruination and alluvial burial. But the principal reasons for excavating several quadrangle groups had to do with their apparent importance for understanding large-scale behavior patterns in the Motagua valley. That is, within the site-periphery universe (see Fig. 5), three of the four quadrangles are spaced at regular intervals of 2.5 to 3.0 km in a line across the Chapulco plain; the fourth quadrangle and the easternmost of the first three form parts of the two most imposing sites in the area studied—the "site" of Quirigua (as redefined above) and the Morja site (Loc. 092; see below). (In fact, the Acropolis of the Quirigua site-core might also be considered a quadrangle group.) Thus their specific *and* relative placements suggest both aboriginal importance and deliberate spacing, for such as administrative reasons. Additionally, the form appears to occur elsewhere in the lower Motagua valley, at sites such as Comanche Farm (Stromsvik 1936), Playitas (Nowak 1973; Schortman, personal communication, 1977) and Las Quebradas (*Ibid.*), and might profitably serve as one settlement unit of investigation in a study of valley-wide interaction.

Locus 082. Loc. 082 was the first quadrangle to be excavated, its investigation supervised by Schortman and Urban. This group is just north of the site-core and its principal feature appears on the surface to be a continuous U-shaped entity, open to the east. It was first noted in 1973, when a bulldozer was found razing the eastern end of the southern arm, Str. 3C-6, and it was mapped with a transit in 1976. Excavation, in 1977, centered on Str. 3C-5, the western part of the quadrangle. Disclosed in the trenches was a masonry structure of mixed sandstone and rhyolite blocks, with additional use of schist slabs and adobe. The basal platform measures 27 m north-south and 14 m east-

THE 1977 SEASON

west, and the platform of the superstructure, off-center to the south, is 19.3 m north-south and 5.0 m east-west. The latter is about 1.95 above the level of the plaza surface to the west.

The superstructure featured masonry benches oriented to the north and west (see Fig 11a); no comparable niche-like room was found on the south or east sides. On the west there was also a well-laid, largely intact sandstone and rhyolite block outset stairway, 4.0 m wide and centered on the superstructure (Fig 11b). On the east a series of narrow terraces which also may be interpreted as a stairway stretch possibly the entire length of the substructure and lead down into the central court of the quadrangle; these had been ripped out and buried. It is possible this modification included new terraces/stairs, but the final masonry is gone. A series of secondary wall constructions around the outside of the superstructure suggest increasing compartmentalization of usable space atop the platform, especially on the north and west sides (Fig. 11c). It is not unlikely that the earlier east terrace/stair was buried in order to expand the platform in this direction, thereby to increase the total area on the summit during the later stages of occupation.

TABLE 3

TENTATIVE TEMPORAL PLACEMENTS OF NON-ACROPOLIS MASONRY CONSTRUCTION

Acropolis Construction Stage	Site-Core Structures	Site-Periphery Loci
1		002?*
9.19.0.0.0 (A.D. 810)		
2	Str. 1A-3*** Str. 1A-2 092	025**
		029
		026
	Str. 1B-8 Str. 1A-10 Str. 1A-11 082	006
9.15.6.14.6? (A.D. 737)		
3		
9.14.13.4.17? (A.D. 724)		

*   Placement based on surface examination only; no excavation or clearing
** Placement based on interpretation of setting of Mon. 19 (see above).
*** Placement based partially on inference from dates inscribed on Mons. 1 through 7) (see Coe and Sharer 1979, and Sharer et al. 1979, and above).

The relation of Str. 3C-5 to its neighboring structures is complex. The lowest platform of 3C-5 abuts that of 3C-6 to the south, but a wall resting on the latter platform is built *over* the southern part of the terraces. Counting subsequent burial of the Str. 3C-5 east terraces/stairs, at least four phases of construction are indicated in this area of the quadrangle alone. On the north, the basal platform of Str. 3C-5 abuts that of Str. 3C-4; relations between the upper ranges of these two structures are unknown. In sum, access to the central court of the quadrangle is cut off at these two corners, but it appears that the restriction was gradual, resulting from additional construction rather than part of an original "plan" for the group.

Temporally, Loc. 082 is within the principal occupation of the site-core. Pending more detailed examination, we have observed that its ceramics are like those typical of Late and Terminal Classic Quirigua. The masonry used, however, may allow us to place construction more specifically within this span. The size, shaping and precise manner of the setting of the facing blocks in Str. 3C-5 are virtually identical to those of the masonry from Str. 1B-Sub.1 on the west side of the Acropolis, and on these grounds we tentatively assign the principal construction of Str. 3C-5 as equivalent to early Acropolis CS 2, or ca. 9.15.6.14.6 (AD 737). The basal parts of the two neighboring structures seem to have been built somewhat earlier and the final alterations to 3C-5 are surely later than that date. But the imposing construction of Str. 3C-5 seems to have been undertaken shortly after the newly won independence of Quirigua under Cauac Sky. It is possible that the nearby Loci 006 and 029 (excavated in 1975 and 1976 respectively; see below) may also have been built at or shortly after this time, so that building activities on the floodplain north of the site-core seem to parallel in time those in the Acropolis (cf. Tables 1 and 3).

The functions served by Loc. 082 are tantalizing yet arguable. The excavators observed a differential distribution in artifacts, with more censers ("ceremonial" items) coming from the west side of the structure and more jars (utilitarian/domestic items) from the east. (In fact, more than 40% of the raw count of censer fragments from this operation and locus came from investigation of Str. 3C-7, the small, low platform immediately west of Str. 3C-5.) The east side of the structure faces *into* the quadrangle, while the west faces what appears to be a broad open area, equivalent in size to the Great Plaza of the site-core but without the carved stone monuments. This plaza is "bounded" on the north and west by plazuela groups (Loci 029 and 006, respectively) and on the east, of course, by Loc. 082; it is open to the south. In its southeast corner, about 60 m southwest of Loc. 082, is a possible ballcourt (Loc. 004). Given artifact distributions, structure orientation (including location of the benches) and the fact that the broad eastern terraces or stair into the quadrangle court were destroyed, the final use of Str. 3C-5 appears to be as a building oriented toward public activities. At Copan, on the other hand, structures that are virtually identical to Str. 3C-5 but have fuller artifact assemblages and associated caches and burials have been interpreted as elite residences (Leventhal 1979; cf. Willey and Leventhal 1976). Our tentative functional reconstruction, then, is that Str. 3C-5 and probably all of Loc. 082 were built originally as an elite residential locus, but that in later times 3C-5 was increasingly used to "house" the public duties for which the residents of the group were responsible (see below). Attribution of such a change is supported by the following architectural modifications: (1) the eastward expansion of the summit platform surface, apparently simultaneous with the destruction of the eastern terracing/stairway; (2) the secondary enclosure of northern and western rooms which increased the extent of *enclosed* space but seems to have made passage around the upper platform more difficult; and (3) the apparent channelling of access, from Str. 3C-5 to the quadrangle interior, to a single narrow walkway between the summits of 3C-5 and its southern neighbor, Str. 3C-6.

The excavators suggest that the "public duties" carried on at Str. 3C-5 may have involved mass food processing, as whole or fragmentary remains of perhaps 10 metates were found in terminal-use contexts of this structure. Indeed, as could be suggested for areas of the Great Plaza of the site-core (see above), the plaza area west of Loc. 082 may have served as an open-air market facility. It is open to the south; the Great Plaza is similarly open to the west and Monuments 8 through 11 face west. When the "site" of Quirigua is redefined as suggested above, the two open areas appear as logical traffic destinations for people entering from the southwest. And if, as Jones argues (Jones 1977; cf. Ashmore 1977), the Motagua once flowed closer to Quirigua, the open plazas would have been conveniently adjacent to presumed canoe-docking areas (see *Quirigua Paper No. 8*, this volume).

Locus 089. Loc. 089 is situated midway between the Motagua and Jubuco Rivers, directly south of the Quirigua site-core. It was discovered and mapped (by transit) in 1976 and consists of 13 structures and platforms grouped around three plazas. The quadrangle plaza is the farthest south. Excavations

THE 1977 SEASON

here, directed by Urban and Schortman, centered on Strs. 1 and 2, but also tested the nature of three of the four corners of the quadrangle court.

Structure 1, on the south side of the court, has a masonry substructure, faced principally with rhyolite. Tree roots and modern stone robbing had exposed two buried east-west trending vaulted rooms, the only vaults encountered in the Quirigua site-periphery. The northern one was partially cleared and was found to have been built mostly of rhyolite, schist/gneiss and marble, forming a chamber 1.1 m wide and 1.9 m high. A few sherds and censer fragments were recovered from collapse debris, but there was nothing on the floor of the chamber. While they might have been part of an earlier construction, the two chambers lack an underlying masonry substructure and were more likely built to be contained by Str. 1.

No clear remains of a superstructure were found on this mound, but, as noted above, the summit has been extensively damaged by trees and modern stone-robbing activities. The preserved height of the substructure is 2.1 m.

Structure 2, on the west side of the court, has an L-shaped bench of rhyolite masonry and clay, facing east, and there is evidence that much of the rest of the superstructure consisted of adobe. Most of the stone in the upper reaches of Str. 3 was rhyolite, but the bottom of its basal platform was faced with marble. Unfortunately, the area of the presumed front central stair had been destroyed, and with it the vertical link between zones of rhyolite and marble facings. The height of the substructure from its base to the surface of the summit platform is 1.2 m.

The corner between Strs. 1 and 2 was closed by extending southward the marble wall of Str. 2 with a seal of rhyolite blocks, like those of Str. 1. The seal may have been built at the same time as Str. 1, however, as the abutment pattern seems to be reversed for the slab-footing underlying the juncture of the two structures. As at Loc. 082 and in the Acropolis (between Strs. 1B-4 and 1B-5), the closing of at least this corner seems to have been a secondary aspect of the plan.

The corner between Strs. 2 and 3 also is deliberately closed, as is that between Strs. 3 and 4, but the exact stratigraphic relationships are not clear. It should be noted that Str. 3 is the highest of those bordering this plaza, and, though not tested by excavation, it seems to face into the larger, more open court to the north, toward the largest structure at the site, Str. 11.

Stucture 4 is the lowest and least imposing in the quadrangle, characteristics it shares with the eastern structure both of the court to the north and of the Quirigua Acropolis (Str. 1B-6). A brief clearing operation here revealed an abundance of adobe, very much disturbed, but noteworthy for its evidence of construction methods: some of the pieces were bricks, but others bore impressions of poles and still others of what seems to be stones. The clay was used, then, both as a primary construction element and as a facing for other load-bearing elements.

Although formal analysis had not yet been done by the end of 1977, artifacts from Loc. 089 appear to be within the typical local Late to Terminal Classic range (cross-dating by masonry type will be deferred to a later report). They were not, however, very helpful for assessing function. Circumstantial evidence of function is provided by the relative size and location of the quadrangle: that is, like Loc. 082, the quadrangle of Loc. 089 seems to be a private area linked to an adjacent, more public one (cf. Hammond 1975: Ch.5). On analogy with Loc. 082 and the Copan data, then, we tentatively assert that it was a residential area for members of the (local?) elite who carried out their public business in the neighboring court to the north. Unfortunately, we have no direct material clues as to what, specifically, this business might have been (but cf. above and below, as well as Sharer at al. 1979 and Ashmore 1977).

Locus 092. The third quadrangle examined is in Loc. 092. This site is the most imposing in the site-periphery area. Located near the confluence of the Jubuco, Morja and Motagua Rivers, it is well situated to monitor traffic using these three waterways for passage. The site presently consists of 11 mounds grouped around two plazas and covering an area of about 2 hectares. A third plaza has been destroyed by the Morja River: three of the easternmost structures clearly face onto the area now occupied by the river bed. Old water courses on the northern and southeastern margins of the site have cut into several mounds, obliterating whatever other construction might have existed beyond them.

This may be the site indicated on Seler-Sach's (1925) map; it was located and mapped with Brunton compass and tape by the site-periphery program in 1976. Excavations in this locus in 1977 were divided between the quadrangle area (especially Str. 6) and the easternmost structures (particularly Str. 2).

The Loc. 092 Quadrangle appears closed at its northwest and northeast corners but the southern mound is separated by distances of 14 and 19 m, respectively, from its eastern and western neighbors. Excavation here, therefore, focused on the northern mound, Str. 6. This work, supervised by Schortman with help from Urban, confirmed, first, that the corners were indeed closed. Str. 6 is a platform 1.9 m high, of which the lower 1.3 m are below present ground level. Its northern face has been eroded away by the stream, but the platform was at least 7 m wide and about 50 m long, with a 23 m wide staircase in the center of the south side (Fig 12a). The only suggestions of summit construction were two small raised areas at the east and west ends of the platform. Adobe debris indicated some use of this material, likely in a superstructure.

The final substructure was faced entirely with roughly-dressed marble blocks, but the remains of a buried earlier wall of schist/gneiss, cobbles and marble were encountered immediately north of and running parallel to the stair. Time did not permit extensive clearing of this feature; what details are available will be presented in the final report of this excavation.

Sherds and censers recovered in Str. 6 excavations seemed, on field examination, to be usual types and forms in the principal Quirigua ceramic complex. The obsidian includes remains of a possible workshop from the court surface adjacent to the southwest corner of Str. 6 (see *Quirigua Paper No. 10*, this volume).

Overall, this quadrangle seems rather unlike the other two investigated. Its horizontal dimensions are about twice as large and construction styles are different, although the latter may simply be a function of employment of different, locally available masons and resources. The court area is less private, but can perhaps be argued to be a relatively more private area than one or more adjacent public spaces. The most likely candidates for the latter would be (1) the area east of Str. 8, a large mound, about 3 m high, with long axis north-south, located immediately east of the quadrangle, and (2) a hypothetical, now-destroyed plaza in the stream-effaced area north of Str. 6. The first alternative is possible, but entry from there to the southeast corner of the quadrangle court appears to have been unrestricted; the second alternative must be completely conjectural.

The other investigations in Loc. 092 were concentrated in and around Str. 2 because of its prominence and, compared with the other large constructions of the site, relatively good preservation. The main part of Str. 2 is a marble block construction whose substructure is about 5 m high. Above the basal vertical wall, 0.9 m high, is a sloping apron 1.2 m high. And above the projecting cornice of the latter (Fig. 12b) are remains of one or possibly two successively smaller platforms. A small portion of the rear wall of either a masonry superstructure or a small summit platform is also visible. The summit was reached by a stair, 6.6 m wide, on the north face (Fig. 12c). This stair, as noted above, faced onto a presumed plaza now totally destroyed by the Morja River. Much of the eastern portion of the structure has been similarly destroyed but the stair width is intact and, assuming it was centrally located, the overall length of the structure would have been 23.4 m. Its width is approximately 11.5 m, beyond which the stair projects another 2.6 m to the north.

Logistical and safety reasons prevented trenching in the stair area, but a shallow probe into the opposite (south) side indicated a fill of marble chunks. Other work associated with this structure—supervised by Ashmore with help from Urban—revealed that a marble-surfaced platform had been built against its west side. The space on the platform was enclosed, then or later, by walls joining Str. 2 with Str. 11 to the southwest and a little-understood marble wall to the northwest. The enclosure thus formed was apparently deliberately filled with silt; a stair against its southern wall indicated there was probably some sort of occupation surface on top, but this has not been preserved.

Artifacts recovered in this excavation demonstrate that final use of Str. 2 was contemporary with the main Quirigua occupation. The masonry is most like that of the latter part of CS 2, if the Acropolis sequence can legitimately be extended this far from the site-core. Functionally, interpretation is less clear. Pending formal identification of lot contents, we may note that relatively fine-pasted bowl sherds were frequent in this area; censer fragments were encountered especially around the nothern stairway. Other artifactual material included obsidian and a single (broken) hemispherical spindle whorl. Overall, we tentatively infer that Str. 2 was a high-status area associated primarily with public affairs; the secondary western platform may have been an adjunct service area, for activities using hemispherical bowls and spindle whorls. While a domestic function is not clearly indicated for this area, neither is it ruled out.

The finds associated with Str. 2 seem, subjectively, aesthetically finer than those associated with Str. 6. The architecture of Str. 2 is certainly the more impressive. Assuming relatively minimal destruction of the west end of the site and that construction comparable to that around Str. 6 did not once exist east of Str. 2, we might speculate that the observed "imbalance" in grandeur represents preferential orientation toward the Morja rather than the Jubuco River. It is the Morja route to

Copan that is already known to contain at least one large site (Paraiso; Yde 1938) and, according to local informants, this seems to be the preferred route today. The upper Morja valley also reputedly contains a marble source that might have supplied the construction materials for Loc. 092. Known alternative marble sources are located rather far away to the north, in the Sierra de las Minas, near, from east to west, La Pita, Cerro Tipon and Doña Maria (P. Muller, personal communication, 1977).

Other Groups

The remaining excavations in the 1977 site-periphery program were carried out in two of the three outlying loci with stone monuments, what Morley called Groups B and C. The presence of monuments indicated these groups were important in prehistoric times; excavations there sought to document better the nature of the distinction. Morley's Group A (Loc. 002) was mapped in 1977 (see above), with excavation deferred until 1978 (see *Quirigua Paper No. 7*, this volume).

Locus 025 (Group B). Situated about 1200 m west of Loc. 082, Loc. 025 (Morley's Group B) is the westernmost visible group in the east-west line north of the site-core. In 1923 Morley (1923a, b; 1935; 1937-38) conducted some brief excavations in Str. 7C-1 (his "Substructure II") and in front of Monument 19 (Stela S). His map (1935: Fig. 7; 1937-38:V, Pl. 215b) is over-rectified and places Mon. 19 too far to the south. The area has been plowed probably many times in the interim, most recently in 1976, and his Substructures I and III (Strs. 7A-1 and 7A-2) are today no more than surface scatters of cobble. Str. 7C-1, however, still rises about a meter and a half above the floodplain.

Work in this group in 1977, supervised by Ashmore with the assistance of Diane Chase, centered again on Str. 7C-1 and Mon. 19. In Str. 7C-1 we hoped to gather more details on form and construction. Morley had described the structure as being:

simply a foundation mound, built of river pebbles laid in a mortar of red clay and faced with blocks of dressed stone (1935:55).

It was

composed of three platforms. The lowest and largest is 60 cm.[sic] high with a battered face, about 20 m. long (east and west) and 10 m. wide (north and south); the second, 1.20 m. high with a vertical face; and the third one, 30 cm. high, consisting of a single step. There had originally been a stairway on the south side, but this was in a ruinous condition. On the summit there was not a vestige of the former superstructure, which, it is therefore necessary to assume, had been constructed of some perishable material like thatch and wood (1937-38:IV, 109).

Since he also noted (1923a) that the area of best preservation was the east part of the south or front face, the 1977 trench was placed there. Unfortunately, due to a combination of local agricultural activities and Morley's apparent lack of backfilling, the structure has slumped outward: all we encountered was collapsed debris and what appeared to be Morley's backdirt. Based on the contents of the debris, the faced-block portion of the platform seems indeed to have been built of sandstone, but a few of the blocks are rhyolite. The "rubble" that apparently represents the excavated fill of the basal platform is a mixture of sandstone, rhyolite and a relatively few cobbles. There are also some pieces of schist which might be the remains of a horizontal surfacing.

In terms of artifacts, Morley noted finding only a single spindle whorl and a handful of sherds and obsidian flakes (1935:55; 1923b:270; 1937-38:IV, 109). The 1977 yield was similarly small, containing 6 pieces of obsidian and some potsherds. Although the latter had not been formally identified as to type at the end of the 1977 season, several sherds—from lots thought to represent Morley's backdirt—were recognized as plumbate, suggesting a date after AD 800 for use (if not construction) of Str. 7C-1. This is especially interesting in that the date on Monument 19 is 9.15.15.0.0 or AD 746. Based on the early inscription, Morley considered Loc. 025 an early "settlement," perhaps a second prototype (after Group A/Loc. 002) for the ceremonial center (1935:52-53, 59; 1937-38:IV, 109, 244). In 1975, however, Coe and Sharer (1979) suggested that this monument might be only a fragment, reset in its present position after breakage.

The limited excavations in front of Mon. 19 this year were designed to expose the depth of the monument—to test this idea—as well as to examine the method of setting. A pit was placed directly in front of the monument, as was Morley's in 1923, but going deeper than the latter. Mon. 19 does not seem to be broken, the base of the relatively squat sandstone stela extending approximately 0.9 m below the apparent bottom of the very eroded frontal sculpture. The base is set in sandstone rubble fill, 1.35 m deep, capped with a surface of rhyolite slabs which seem to have abutted the monument at the base of the carving (Fig. 13a). A large rough block near the top of the fill is likely that noted by Morley (1923a). Although the block did not touch the monument in 1977, perhaps the looseness of the soil between the two indicates that the block was partially dislodged by Morley's workmen. If so, it might have served as a brace for the stela butt (cf. Stromsvik 1941). Near the base of the sandstone rubble are what appear, in the space cleared, to be a row of small sandstone slabs, possibly a supporting platform for the monument. Overall, the method of setting for Mon. 19 seems more like that of Mon. 9 (Stela I, which has a date of 9.18.10.0.0 or AD 800; cf. Ibid.: Fig. 25a), than that of Mon. 8 (Stela H), which is the closest to Mon. 19 in date among the monuments in the site-core (9.16.0.0.0 or AD 751). This suggests that although the monument's inscribed date is early, as noted above, it might well have been reset at a later time. It is possible that the ruined Platform 1A-3, discovered between Mons. 7 and 10 in the Great Plaza (see above, and Fig. 3), was the original location of Mon. 19. Such a placement would make it the northern vertex of a triangle with Mons. 8 and 10. The latter are the two earliest sandstone monuments in the site-core and, as noted above, the closest to Mon. 19 in date (9.16.0.0.0 or AD 751, and 9.16.5.0.0 or AD 756 respectively; see Fig. 3) and arrangement of sculptural design (cf. Morley 1937-38:IV, 242-243, Table 99).

Assuming that Mon. 19 was reset as argued above, this would mean that Loc. 025 was in use around 9.18.10.0.0 or AD 800. This is equivalent to the latter part of Acropolis CS 2, the period in which most of the construction in the site-core (including the Acropolis) seems to have taken place. As seen in Table 3, most of the datable masonry construction in the periphery is also tentatively identified as corresponding to this construction stage. Perhaps the resetting of Mon. 19 marks a "redefinition" of the limits of the Quirigua elite precinct, acknowledging the expansion symbolically by moving there the first monument erected after Quirigua's independence. And if, indeed, the Motagua once flowed farther north than it does today, the monument might have served in this new location as a boundary marker, visible to passing river traffic.

Locus 011 (Group C). Morley's description of "Group C" may be read to include all the groups along this part of the first bench north of the Motagua, Mon. 25 (a plain "stela") being situated at the western end of the "chain" of mounds (Morley 1935:43-44; 1937-38:IV, 85). Our definition of Loc. 011, as described in 1975 (Coe and Sharer 1979), includes only the six mounds that appear to be associated with this unsculptured stone shaft (cf. Morley 1937-38:IV, 241). Although the mounds have been cut into in places and the monument toppled, no recorded archaeological excavation had been undertaken there prior to 1977.

Brief excavations in Loc. 011 this season were supervised by Urban with assistance from Schortman. Structure 2, the ca. 2 m high construction west of Mon. 25, was probed on its east face, at the center and corners and on the summit. The core of the mound is a red-brown clay, with overlying tumbled sandstone chunks and adobe probably attesting to previous construction on the summit. Atop the mound a tamped-earth surface was discovered, but in association with modern brass hinges. Other large earthen mounds are known from the site-periphery area, in Loci 024, 057, 122 and perhaps at the north end of 002 (see Fig. 5 for locations).

Mon. 25, standing in Morley's time (1937-38:IV, 241) but since fallen, seems simply to have been set into a layer of reddish clay; cobbles found in the adjacent modern backdirt pile may have been packed about the butt of the shaft as bracing stones. A number of censer fragments, as well as modern glass and metal debris, were also recovered from this backdirt.

Chronological and functional interpretations for Loc. 011 are both difficult to make. Morley (1935:43-44, 1937-38:IV, 241) believed the unsculptured monument was a locally "early" product, based on its form and material which are most similar to early Mon. 20 (see below). Artifacts recovered from excavations here included clearly modern debris as well as apparently **precolumbian** obsidian, censer fragments and potsherds. As this excavation was one of the last of the 1977 season, sherds were not yet recorded by the end of that season as to type or form; the obsidian (flakes, flake-blades and debitage) is like that from other local sites. The location, arrangement and size of the mounds suggest a public function for the group, but more specificity is not possible at this point (cf. Morley 1937-38:IV, 243).

GENERAL REMARKS

In summary, excavations in the site-periphery indicate that all the loci investigated were probably in use, at least in their final form, during the principal occupation span of the site-core. The construction and use of these sites may not have been wholly contemporary, but our most discriminating index, masonry, suggests that all of the more elite loci are, temporally speaking, virtually equivalent to constructions of Acropolis CS 2.

Functionally, most architectural loci may have been at least partially residential. Occupational specializa-

THE 1977 SEASON

tion in or near some of these sites is indicated by the ceramic workshop debris in Loc. 116 and by redeposited remains of an obsidian workshop in the site-core (Str. 1B-Sub.3). Another obsidian-working station may be represented by finds at Str. 6 of Loc. 092; the obsidian of Loc. 013 is less easy to evaluate. Final decisions as to the nature of the latter two deposits await more detailed examination of the remains. With the exception of Loc. 013, all sites involved are at the "elite" end of the continuum; the obsidian found at Loc. 013 seemed, on field examination, to come from smaller (and poorer quality) nodules and may reflect a corresponding lack of wealth and inability to secure choice raw materials (see *Quirigua Paper No. 10*, this volume, for a discussion of the obsidian).

General wealth differentials may be inferred from size and elaborateness of construction which to some extent seem to correlate with proximity to the site-core, though the loci containing quadrangle groups are also architecturally imposing. The activities carried on at the latter sites have been discussed separately above, but in each case are inferred to involve, for the overall site, a combination of public affairs with more secluded private activities. The specific and relative locations of these sites suggest some administrative division of the Quirigua domain.

As a settlement unit, the quadrangle is probably still a useful isolate. The scale, plan and architecture of the quadrangles of Loci 082 amd 089 seem comparable; the quadrangle of Loc. 092 had best be considered separately. The closed-corner aspect of the plan was shown to be truly an architectural feature, rather than a product of post-abandonment slumping. It does seem, however, to be the result of cumulative construction, and not some original plan or template for a large, restricted-access court. Closer comparison with superficially analogous forms elsewhere in the valley and in neighboring areas, such as the Copan valley, will facilitate further interpretation.

As noted elsewhere (Ashmore 1977), there seems a special emphasis in terms of large-scale construction on the Chapulco plain which is the fertile plain cut by two rivers whose valleys provide access into the Honduran sierra toward Copan. A comparable set of sites is clearly lacking to the north, in accord with Voorhies' (1969, 1972) assessments of the occupation of the Lake Izabal area as being of marginal importance in precolumbian times. The most imposing remains in this latter area beyond Loc. 002 are those of Loc. 024, which *is* close to the 19th-century route between Izabal and the Motagua (cf. Haefkens 1969; Stephens 1841).

THE MONUMENT RECORDING PROGRAM

During 1977 an effort was made to strengthen the record of poorly documented monuments. New daylight photographs were taken of the four carved surfaces of Mon. 19 (S) in Group B, showing that the carving has not eroded greatly since Morley's day and that a proper series of night photographs under controlled lighting conditions would result in a greatly improved record. A latex rubber mold was made of the back and sides of Mon. 21 (U) in Group A, from which controlled-lighting photographs can be taken. Daylight shots under good natural light were also taken, giving us a better record of the glyphic inscription on the back as well as the first photographs of what is left of the carving of a human figure on the front and sides (Fig. 13b). Again, Mon. 21 has not suffered much erosion since Morley's photographs were taken. It is hoped that a proper record will not only determine whether or not the monument fits stylistically the clear Initial Series date of 9.2.3.8.0, but also provide us with more information about the early rulers of Quirigua before Cauac Sky. Some new photographs of Mon. 20 (T) were taken, but without turning the monument. Only traces of carving survive, but enough to show the feet and legs of a single figure on the front and glyphs on the reverse similar to those of Mon. 21. A preliminary assessment is that Morley was correct in saying that Mons. 20 and 21 go together with the plain schist stela of Loc. 011 in a group of three roughly contemporaneous monuments. On stylistic grounds, however, it seems likely that these are not of around 9.13.0.0.0, as he suggested, but date from 9.2.0.0.0, the Early Classic, as Mon. 21 states (cf. Thompson 1970:101; Marcus 1976).

THE LABORATORY ANALYSIS PROGRAM

During the 1977 season the field laboratory, under Mary Bullard's direction, continued to process and record all artifacts recovered by the Project. The pottery analysis program, begun during previous seasons, continued under the direction of Bullard and Sharer. In addition, plans were made to initiate the analysis of lithic artifacts, and arrangements were made for Dr. Payson D. Sheets of the University of Colorado to examine and evaluate these collections during the early summer of 1977 (see *Quirigua Paper No. 10*, for the results of Sheets' work). This work has been completed, and Sheets' findings were used to guide the lithic analysis undertaken during the 1978 season.

QUIRIGUA REPORTS

In 1977 the pottery analysis concentrated upon assessing the type and form content of provenience lots, and the recording of descriptive data that will be the basis for the formal definition of type units. Furthermore, several new type and form categories were defined. More significantly, the first clear indications of a pre-Late Classic pottery complex at Quirigua were revealed. This complex has been given a preliminary definition based upon the pottery associated with the earliest constructions known at the site, and appears to correspond to the Middle Classic period (c. AD 550-700).

Most of the day-to-day analysis involved assessing type and form content of lots judged to be significant by excavators. A total of 61 such lots was assessed, representing some 14,000 sherds. The assessments of pottery from a midden (Loc. 116) found in 1976 were of special significance since they provided the first full type and form inventory for the Late and Terminal Classic periods at Quirigua (see above).

This work continued during the 1978 season with the goal of completing the assessments of all significant provenience lots and the recording of the remaining data necessary for the formal definition of pottery type and form units. In addition, analysis of all other artifactual categories was undertaken in 1978 (see *Quirigua Paper No. 7*, this volume).

SUMMARY

The Quirigua Project made substantial progress during the 1977 research season.

Excavations in the site-core completed the documentation of the basic sequence of construction and occupation, both in the Acropolis and in the neighboring Great Plaza and two of its adjacent building platforms. The longest and most complex sequence is that of the Acropolis, now defined according to four provisional construction stages corresponding to the Middle to Terminal Classic periods. With the temporal sequence secure, excavations designed to reveal functional contexts were emphasized during 1977. Preliminary results of this research indicate that the Acropolis served several functions, but that it was used primarily as a residential-administrative complex for Quirigua's ruling elite.

Excavations outside the site-core tested a total of nine sites within the periphery area to determine both temporal position and functional significance. Both these dimensions of prehistoric activity were documented in the excavation of a Late Classic midden containing ceramic-workshop debris, an obsidian workshop site, three elite residential-administrative complexes apparently subordinate to Quirigua and four smaller activity loci.

Progress was made in the other research programs. The Monument Program continued its successful application of microflora retardants (see *Quirigua Paper No. 11*, this volume), as well as recording the hieroglyphic inscriptions. The analysis of pottery continued in the field laboratory, completing the basic typological and form classification, and beginning an intensive effort to assess the temporal and functional range of excavated materials from all areas of the site. A basis for a similar analysis of the lithic artifacts has also been established.

THE 1977 SEASON

REFERENCES CITED

Adams, R. E. W.
    1970   Suggested Classic Period Occupational Specialization in the Southern Maya Lowlands. in *Monographs and Papers in Maya Archaeology*. W. R. Bullard, Jr., ed. pp. 487-502. Harvard University, Peabody Museum, Papers, No. 61.

Ashmore, W.
    1977   Research at Quirigua, Guatemala: The Site-Periphery Program. Paper presented at the 42nd Annual Meeting of the Society for American Archaeology, New Orleans.
    1981   *Settlement at Quirigua, Guatemala: A Functional Definition of the Site and a Taxonomy of Maya Settlement Units*. PhD. Dissertation, Department of Anthroplogy, University of Pennsylvania.

Baudez, C.F. and P. Becquelin
    1973   *Archeologie de los Naranjos, Honduras*. Mexico: Mission Archeologique et Ethnologique Francaise au Mexique.

Becker, M. J.
    1972   Plaza Plans at Quirigua, Guatemala. *Katunob* 8: 47-62.
    1973   Archaeological Evidence for Occupational Specialization among the Classic period Maya at Tikal, Guatemala. *American Antiquity* 38: 396-406.

Boggs, S.
    1950   Archaeological Investigations in El Salvador. in *For the Dean*, E. K. Reed and D. S. King eds., pp. 259-276. Santa Fe: Hohokam Museums Association and the Southwestern Monuments Association.

Coe, W. R. and R. J. Sharer
    1979   The Quirigua Project: 1975 Season. *Quirigua Reports I* (No. 2). Museum Monographs, No. 37. Philadelphia: University Museum.

Haefkens, J.
    1969   *Viaje a Guatemala y Centroamerica*. (orig. 1827) Sociedad de Geografia e Historia de Guatemala, Serie Viajero 1.

Hammond, N.
    1975   *Lubaantun: A Classic Maya Realm*. Harvard University, Peabody Museum, Monographs, No. 2.

Hatch, M. P.
    1975   *A Study of Hieroglyphic Texts at the Classic Maya Site of Quirigua, Guatemala*. PhD. Dissertation, Department of Anthropology, University of California, Berkeley.

Jones, C.
    1977   Research at Quirigua, Guatemala: The Site-Core Program. Paper Presented at the 42nd Annual Meeting of the Society for American Archaeology, New Orleans.

Kelley, D. H.
    1962   Glyphic Evidence for a Dynastic Sequence at Quirigua, Guatemala. *American Antiquity* 27: 323-335.

Kidder, A. V.
    1948   *Kaminaljuyu, Guatemala: Addenda and Corrigenda*. Carnegie Institution of Washington, Notes on Middle American Archaeology and Ethnology, No. 89, Washington, D. C.

Lothrop, S. K.
    1952   *Metals from the Cenote of Sacrifice, Chichen Itza, Yucatan*. Harvard University, Peabody Museum Memoirs, Vol. 10, No. 2.

Marcus, J.
    1976   *Emblem and State in the Classic Maya Lowlands*. Washington, D. C.: Dumbarton Oaks.

QUIRIGUA REPORTS

Morley, S. G.
- 1923a Unpublished Field Notes.
- 1923b Archaeology. *Carnegie Institution of Washington, Yearbook, No.* 22: 267-273.
- 1935 *Guide Book to the Ruins of Quirigua.* Carnegie Institution of Washington, Supplementary Publication 16,Washington, D. C.
- 1937-38 *The Inscriptions of Peten.* 5 vols. Carnegie Institution of Washington, Publication 437, Washington, D. C.

Nowak, T. R.
- 1973 Mercantilism and Colonization: A Study Of Prehistoric Regional Community Patterning and Cultural Change in the Lower Motagua Valley, Guatemala. Harvard University, Peabody Museum, Manuscript.

Pollock, H. E. D.
- 1965 Architecture of the Maya Lowlands. in *Handbook of Middle American Indians.* Vol 3: 378-440. Austin: University of Texas Press.

Proskouriakoff, T.
- 1973 The Hand-Grasping-Fish and Associated Glyphs on Classic Maya Monuments. in *Mesoamerican Writing Systems.* E. P. Benson ed. pp. 165-178. Washington D. C.:Dumbarton Oaks.

Ricketson, O. G., Jr.
- 1933 Unpublished Field Notes.

Satterthwaite, L.
- 1979 Quirigua Altar L (Monument 12). *Quirigua Reports I* (No. 4). Museum Monographs, No.37. Philadelphia: University Museum.

Schmidt, J.
- 1883 *The Stone Sculpture of Copan and Quirigua.* A. D. Savage trans. New York:Dodd, Mead and Co.

Seler, E.
- 1900 Auf Alten Wegen in Mexiko und Guatemala. *Reiseerinnerungen und eindruche aus der Jahren 1895-1897,* pp. 327-380. Berlin.

Sharer, R. J., C. Jones, W. Ashmore and E. M. Schortman
- 1979 The Quirigua Project: 1976 Season. *Quirigua Reports I* (No. 5). Museum Monographs, No. 37. Philadelphia: University Museum.

Shaw, T. J.
- 1976 Notes on Historical Data in the Inscriptions of Quirigua and Palenque. *Katunob* 9 (1): 8-15.

Stephens, J. L.
- 1841 *Incidents of Travel in Central America, Chiapas and Yucatan.* New York.

Stromsvik, G.
- 1936 The Ruins on the "Comanche Farm" in the Motagua Valley. *Maya Research* 3 (1): 107-109.
- 1941 *Substela Caches and Stela Foundations at Copan and Quirigua.* Carnegie Institution of Washington, Publication 528, Contributions to American Anthropology and History, No. 37, Washington, D. C.
- 1952 *The Ball Courts at Copan; with Notes on the Courts at La Union, Quirigua, San Pedro Pinula and Asuncion Mita.* Carnegie Institution of Washington, Publication 596, Contributions to American Anthropology and History, No. 55, Washington, D. C.

Thompson, J. E. S.
- 1970 *Maya History and Religion.* Norman: University of Oklahoma Press.

Voorhies, B.
- 1969 *San Felipe: A Prehistoric Settlement in Eastern Guatemala.* PhD. Dissertation, Department of Anthropology, Yale University.
- 1972 Settlement Patterns in Two Regions of the Southern Maya Lowlands. *American Antiquity* 37: 115-126.

Willey, G.R. and R. M. Leventhal
    1976   A Preliminary Report on Prehistoric Maya Settlements in the Copan Valley. Harvard University, Peabody Museum, Manuscript.

Yde, J.
    1938   *An Archaeological Reconnaissance of Northwestern Honduras.* Tulane University, Middle American Research Institute, Publication 9, New Orleans, Louisiana

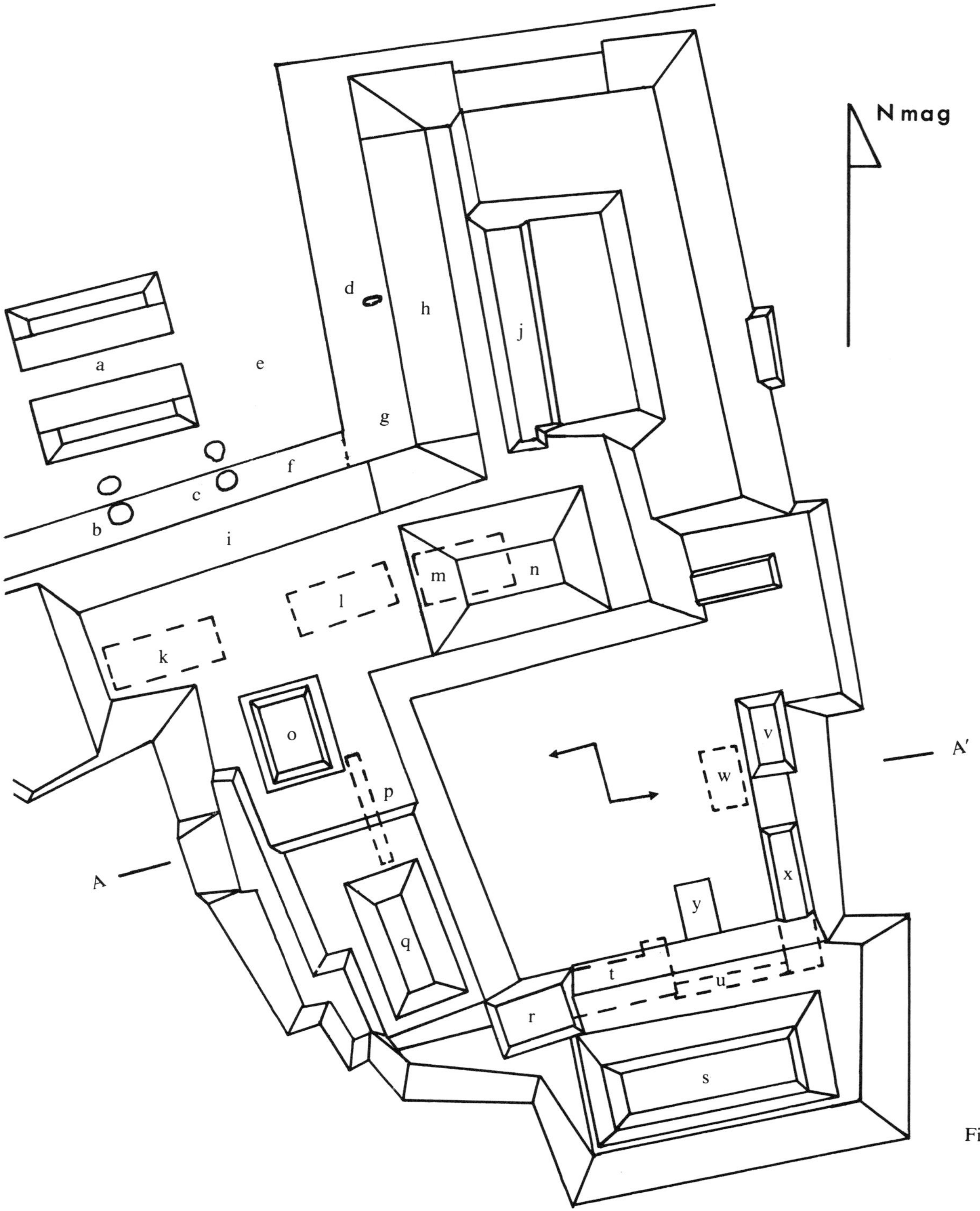

Key

a. Str. 1B-7.
b. Monuments 16 and 24.
c. Monuments 15 and 23.
d. Pedestal stone, probably for Monument 14.
e. Ballcourt Plaza.
f. Terrace.
g. Terrace.
h. Stairway.
i. Stairway.
j. Str. 1B-17.
k. Str. 1B-Sub. 2.
l. Str. 1B-Sub. 3.
m. Str. 1B-5-2nd.
n. Str. 1B-5-1st.
o. Str. 1B-4.
p. Str. 1B-Sub. 1.
q. Str. 1B-3-1st (overlies Str. 1B-3-2nd).
r. Str. 1B-2.
s. Str. 1B-1-1st.
t. Str. 1B-1-2nd.
u. Wall.
v. Str. 1B-6-1st.
w. Str. 1B-6-2nd.
x. Str 1B-18-1st (overlies Str. 1B-18-2nd).
y. Str. 1B-19.
(A-A' East-West section shown in Figure 6.2).

Figure 6.1. Schematic plan of the Quirigua Acropolis (scale: 1:1000).

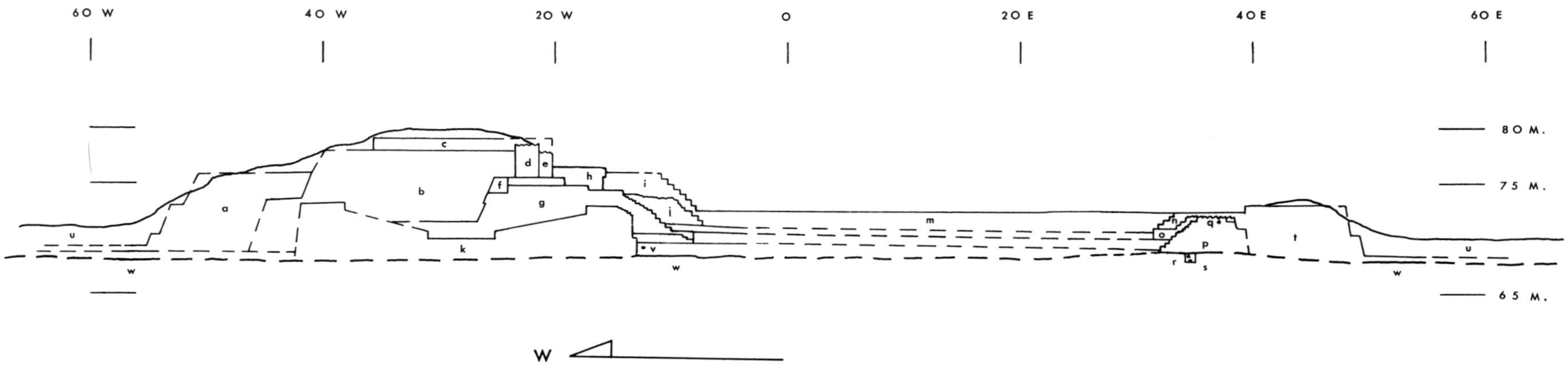

Figure 6.2. Schematic east-west section of the Quirigua Acropolis (A-A' in Figure 6.1). Approximate scale: 1:600.

Key

CONSTRUCTION STAGE 1
u. Post-Construction Silt.
i. Western Stairway.
m. Uppermost Plaza Floor.

CONSTRUCTION STAGE 2
g. Western Platform.
d. Str. 1B-Sub. 1.
f. Addition to West Edge of Platform.
b. Addition to Platform at Time of Str. 1B-3.
a, c, e. Later Additions to Platform.
h, j. Renovations to East Side of Platform.
o. Renovation of Str. 1B-6-2nd.
q. Special Deposit 12.
t. Str. 1B-18.
n. Platform for Str. 1B-18.

CONSTRUCTION STAGE 3
k. Early Ballcourt (Str. 1B-Sub. 4).
v. Special Deposit 8 (Cache).

CONSTRUCTION STAGE 4
p. Str. 1B-6-2nd.
r. Special Deposit 13 (Cache).
s. Special Deposit 14 (Burial).
w. Pre-Construction Silt Surface.

27

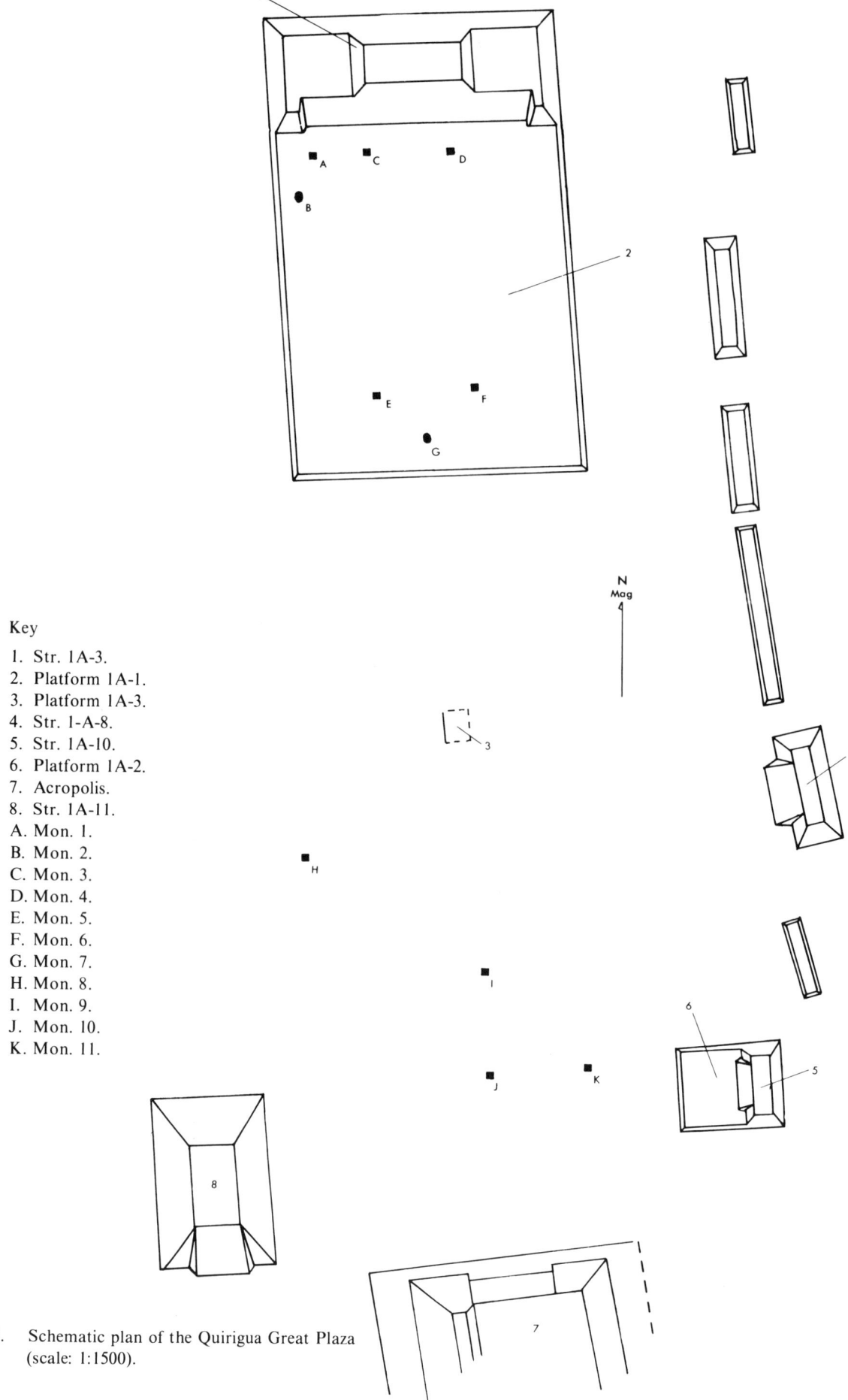

Key

1. Str. 1A-3.
2. Platform 1A-1.
3. Platform 1A-3.
4. Str. 1-A-8.
5. Str. 1A-10.
6. Platform 1A-2.
7. Acropolis.
8. Str. 1A-11.
A. Mon. 1.
B. Mon. 2.
C. Mon. 3.
D. Mon. 4.
E. Mon. 5.
F. Mon. 6.
G. Mon. 7.
H. Mon. 8.
I. Mon. 9.
J. Mon. 10.
K. Mon. 11.

Figure 6.3. Schematic plan of the Quirigua Great Plaza (scale: 1:1500).

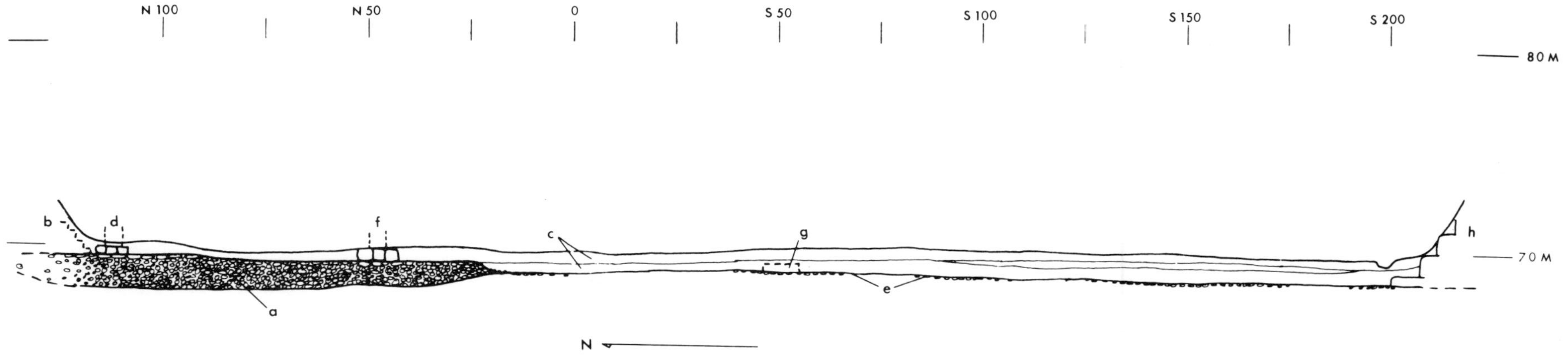

Figure 6.4. Schematic north-south section of the Quirigua Great Plaza (vertical scale 5x horizontal scale).

Key

a. Platform 1A-1.
b. Str. 1A-3.
c. Silt strata overlying plaza.
d. Monument 4 and its platform.
e. Disconginuous cobble stone surface.
f. Monument 6 and its platform.
g. Platform 1A-3.
h. Platform of Str. 1B-17 (Acropolis).

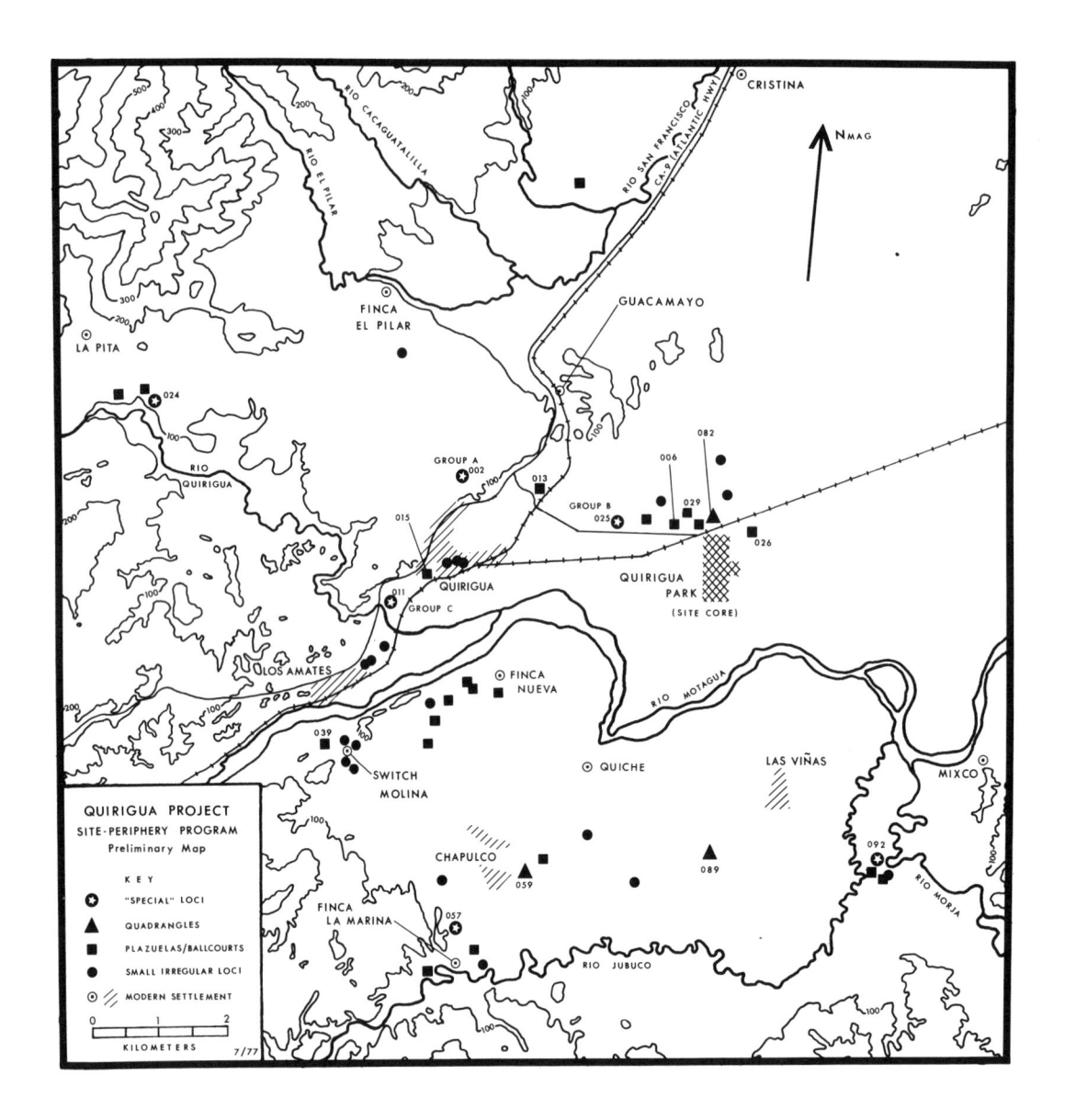

Figure 6.5.

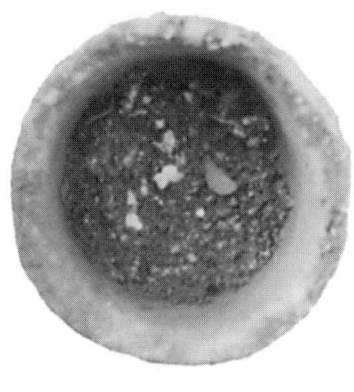

a.

b.

Figure 6.6.
    a. Lower cache vessel (SD 8), after removal of similar covering vessel, from outside the western wall of Str. 1B-Sub 4 (early ballcourt), Acropolis Construction Stage 3.
    b. Decorated wall (Acropolis Construction Stage 3) beneath Str. 1B-4, possibly a portion of the early ballcourt (Str. 1B-Sub 4).

Figure 6.7. Structure 1B-5.
    a. Remnants of Str. 1B-5-2nd masonry beneath later construction.
    b. Str. 1B-5-1st front wall and doorway, from the southwest.

Figure 6.8. Excavations in the Great Plaza.
a. North-south trench during excavation.
b. Trench showing original plaza cobble surface being cleared beneath alluvium.
c. Trench showing southern edge of Platform 1A, just south of Monument 7.

Figure 6.9. Str. 1A-10.
    a. Axial trench showing dedicatory cache (SD 11) in situ.
    b. The two-piece owl effigy found as an axial dedicatory cache (SD 11) beneath Str. 1A-10.

c.

Figure 6.10. Excavations at Loci 116, 039, and 026.
    a. Trench into the midden deposit at Loc. 116.
    b. Excavations at Loc. 039, Str. 7.
    c. Loc. 026, excavation of the basal stairs, Str. 2C-1.

a.

b.

c.

Figure 6.11. Excavations at Loc. 082.
       a. Excavation of masonry benches in Str. 3C-5.
       b. Outset stairway on west side of Str. 3C-5.
       c. Secondary walls and doorway, Str. 3C-5.

Figure 6.12. Excavations at Loc. 092.
    a. Str. 6, remnant of frontal stairway, viewed from the northwest.
    b. Str. 2, preserved section of northern wall of substructure, showing marble masonry forming composite apron-molding profile. Steps of projecting frontal stairway at left.
    c. Str. 2, view from the northwest showing partly cleared frontal stair as well as encroachment of the Morja river.

Figure 6.13. Quirigua monuments.
    a. Excavation at the base of Mon. 19.
    b. Mon. 21, side view of the upper fragment.

PAPER NO. 7

THE QUIRIGUA PROJECT
1978 SEASON

by
Robert J. Sharer, Wendy Ashmore, Edward M. Schortman,
Patricia A. Urban, John L. Seidel and David W. Sedat

INTRODUCTION

1978 marked the final season of research at Quirigua under the provisions of the contract between the Government of Guatemala and the University Museum, University of Pennsylvania. Another season was carried out at Quirigua in 1979, however, to complete the laboratory analyses, floodplain mapping and investigation of sites within the lower Motagua.

The 1978 season lasted a little over three months commencing on 16 January, after a week of preliminary arrangements and meetings in Guatemala City. Although the season closed officially on 31 March, five staff members remained to continue their research until mid-April. Formal inventory of all artifacts recovered by the Project was conducted during the final weeks of the season and these materials, along with the laboratory facilities, were turned over to the Instituto de Antropologia e Historia (IDAEH) on 28 March, 1978.

The archaeological investigations were undertaken by a staff of 12 individuals: Robert J. Sharer was Field Director; Site-Core excavations were supervised by John L. Seidel and David W. Sedat (the latter again serving as Administrative Director); Wendy Ashmore directed the Periphery Program, with assistance from Beth A. Collea; Edward M. Schortman, aided by Patricia A. Urban, directed the Valley Program; Ira L. Fogel undertook geomorphological investigations in conjunction with the Periphery Program; Mary R. Bullard directed the field laboratory, assisted by Julie Benyo (analysis of censers), Andrea Gerstle (analysis of chipped-stone artifacts) and Greta Zuckerkandel (analysis of figurines, ground-stone and miscellaneous artifacts). The last three individuals took time off from their laboratory duties from time to time to help with the work of the Site-Core, Periphery and Valley Programs. The Project camp in Los Amates was again ably and smoothly managed by Rebecca Sedat. The Quirigua Restoration Program continued under the supervision of Enrique Monterroso R., and direction of Arq. Marcelino Gonzalez C.; through the auspices of the IDAEH, Dr. Luis Lujan M., Director.

The research reported herein was conducted under contract between the University Museum, University of Pennsylvania, and the Ministry of Education, Government of Guatemala. We are very grateful to the following agencies and individuals for financial support of the research: the University Museum (especially the Francis Boyer Fund), the National Geographic Society, the Tikal Association, the Ministry of Defense (Guatemala), Mr. Landon T. Clay and Dr. John M. Keshishian. While it is impossible to thank all the individuals who have supported and assisted the Quirigua Project, we would like to express our special appreciation to Dr. Luis Lujan Munoz, Director, IDAEH; Arq. Marcelino Gonzalez C., Jefe, Seccion Proyectos Especificos, IDAEH; Mr. Roy C. Wells, Manager, BANDEGUA (Del Monte Corporation): Ing. Mario Mena, BANDEGUA; Sra. Laura de Garcia Prendes; Sra. Vivian Broman de Morales; and Mr. and Mrs. Frederick Falck.

SITE-CORE PROGRAM

The 1978 investigations in the Quirigua site-core were much reduced from the scale typical of previous seasons. Excavations were limited, for the most part, to probes seeking to resolve questions remaining from previous work. Excavations in the Acropolis were supervised by John Seidel, while continuation of work on Structure 1A-11 was directed by David Sedat. These two investigators also jointly supervised various test pits in the Ballcourt Plaza.

ACROPOLIS

In 1975, a free-standing wall was found buried under the platform of Structure 1B-1; clearing in 1976 indicated that it was joined on the west to Str. 1B-1-2nd (A in Figure 1). This season the wall was traced eastward, and was found to have been demolished immediately west of Str. 1B-18-2nd. It appears that at one time the wall connected Str. 1B-1-2nd and Str. 1B-18-2nd, closing off the intervening space and further emphasizing the access-restrictive architecture of the Acropolis during Construction Stage 3 (*Quirigua Paper No. 6*, this volume).

A second focus of investigation was further excavation in the 1977 trench axial to Str. 1B-6-2nd. Work in 1978 involved deepening the western end of the trench in an effort to understand better the depositional sequence and dating of the earlier construction strata. Excavation was carried down to an elevation of 68.00 m., 4.03 m below the present Acropolis Plaza elevation and the same depth at which a burial was found in the eastern end in 1977. At 68.27 m, the silt fill of Str. 1B-6-2nd gave way to a sandy silt, containing only one, probably intrusive, sherd. Sand and gravel were encountered at 68.04 m, exhibiting the sorting characteristics of water-laid deposits. This would appear to be a pre-construction level upon which was laid the silt fill for Str. 1B-6-2nd. Further excavation was precluded, however, by the water table. A carbon sample was obtained from the charcoal lens which had sealed the 1977 burial.

Subsequent Acropolis excavations concentrated upon the northeast corner of the Acropolis Plaza, the only portion not bounded by platforms, buildings or stairways (Fig. 1:B). These investigations were planned principally to delineate the stratigraphic links between Str. 1B-5 and Str. 1B-6, or the northern and eastern sides of the Acropolis. Furthermore, since this area probably provided access to the Acropolis Plaza during the final stage of occupation, it was hypothesized that the same may have been true during earlier times, and excavations were aimed specifically at clarifying this issue.

Excavations within the Acropolis Plaza at this point revealed the same penultimate compacted gray surface found in other plaza probes during earlier years, laid over river-cobble fill. This surface appears to be contemporary with the stairs and platform of Str. 1B-6-1st, the north edge of which was also uncovered this year. Str. 1B-6-1st and this plaza surface have been placed chronologically in late Construction Stage 2 or early Construction Stage 1 (*Quirigua Paper No. 6*, this volume). Renewed filling later raised the plaza surface approximately 1.5 m, and a small access stairway was built, descending to the east. The stairs were constructed primarily of small marble blocks capped with small schist slabs. In places, however, the construction consisted only of cobbles and small stones, raising the question of whether this was simply a construction stairway, or the result of rip-outs and shoddy repair. Evidence for resurfacing of the plaza at the bottom of the stairs argues for a long period of use and against a short-term (construction) function. This plaza staircase abuts the stairs of Str. 1B-6, to the south, and runs under the Str. 1B-5 stairs on the north.

Some time before construction of the Str. 1B-5 staircase, however, the Acropolis Plaza was extended eastward: the aforementioned plaza stairs were covered with fill and surfaced in the same manner as the rest of the latest plaza surface, i.e., a schist paving, which here runs under—and thus predates—the Str. 1B-5 stairway. Associated with this extension of the final Acropolis Plaza surface was a scatter of censers and other ceramics, broken in place at the foot of the Str. 1B-5 stairs, along with broken eccentric flints and a small, ground-obsidian disc.

Another trench was placed northeast of Str. 1B-6, to intersect the eastern limit of the elevated Acropolis Plaza. Sterile silt was encountered at 67.05 m, the deepest point of this excavation. Above this was a deposit of silt, containing cultural debris, that apparently represents a silt mound comparable to that underlying Str. 1B-6-2nd. At the base of this were found four superimposed layers of ceramic debris.

Resting on these ceramic-bearing levels was a wall 1.2 m high. It was constructed in seven courses, primarily of sandstone blocks, with some marble. Stratigraphically, this wall seems contemporary with the penultimate Acropolis Plaza surface (CS 1; see above), and evidently functioned as a terrace wall. Later, two steps

THE 1978 SEASON

were constructed below the wall (abutting it) and four more were added above, thus converting the vertical terracing to a final stairway, leading east from the Acropolis Plaza down to ground level outside.

The last phase of construction in this area recalls the curious situation found elsewhere in the site-core, particularly the rear of Str. 1A-3 and on top of Str. 1B-17. The above-mentioned final Acropolis stairway was covered over with cobbles in a deposit two and one half meters deep, extending the Acropolis Plaza some nine meters farther to the east. There is no surviving masonry facing for this cobble fill, nor is there any evidence that such existed. We do not know whether this was simply an unfinished Acropolis extension, or a finished addition which was later robbed of its facing stones.

The 1978 excavations reveal the northeast corner of the Acropolis Plaza as the site of successive access staircases, all built during the final stage of Acropolis construction (CS 1). Each successive staircase grew wider and was extended farther to the east. Except for the period of use of the 1.2 m terrace wall, the lateral and vertical expansion of the Acropolis was accomplished by increasingly open access from the east.

BALLCOURT PLAZA

Excavations in the Ballcourt Plaza sought to discover and define a terrace fronting the western platform (Platform 1B-1), hypothesized to exist as an equivalent of the frontal terraces found along the eastern and southern platforms. An excavation in the southwest corner of the court confirmed the existence of this western terrace and its corner with the southern terrace that supports Monuments 15 and 16. An excavation was then placed to the north to trace this feature as it turned to the west, to conform with the end of Platform 1B-1. In fact, however, the terrace continues for an indeterminate distance north, seemingly defining the western limit of both the Ballcourt Plaza and an early version of the Great Plaza beyond.

The ballcourt (Str. 1B-7) was probed to assist IDAEH in evaluating the structure for possible restoration. Stromsvik's (1952) previous excavations were reopened on the western end of the court and new test pits were positioned to reveal the eastern limits of the structure. Only the basal vertical zone facing the playing alley was found to be reasonably intact; no traces of the upper sloping zone could be discovered.

STRUCTURE 1A-11

The 1978 work on Str. 1A-11 began with complete surface clearing and the reopening of the 1976 excavations along its southern base (Sharer et. al. 1979). This year's investigations were intended to define the remaining basal corners of the structure, determine the number of staircases and to probe the interior for traces of earlier construction and possible caches or other interments. Our excavations located the northeast corner, but failed to find a surviving trace of the northwest corner. The three extant corners (the other having been located in 1976) allow an accurate projection of the ultimate size and shape of the structure. Basal terracing was revealed midway on the east side, but no remains of a staircase were found on the face, thus ruling out the possibility of a four-stairwayed platform. More surprisingly, no trace of stairs was found on the outset part of the north face, which has long been assumed to represent a staircase paired with that defined on the south in 1976. If a staircase ever existed on the north side, it must have been unfinished or robbed of masonry. An axial probe here revealed intact masonry terracing beneath the outset, indicating that the latter may be a later addition. Alternatively, this buried terrace may belong to an earlier structure, now encased in later construction.

To test the latter possibility, Maudslay's nineteenth century east-west trench on the summit of Str. 1A-11 was reopened and deepened. The sides of the trench were also cut back to reveal any trace of surviving surfaces, but none could be found. After deepening the excavation a paved surface was encountered, with an apparent step leading down to the south. Collectively, these clues indicate the existence of an earlier platform within Str. 1A-11. Although the end of the season closed our investigations at this point. IDAEH indicated their willingness to provide laborers to continue the Str. 1A-11 excavations in 1979. Accordingly, the Project agreed to conduct limited further investigations of this structure(*Quirigua Paper No. 8*, this volume).

SITE-PERIPHERY PROGRAM

Work in the site-periphery was planned to include two separate operations in 1978: excavations at the hilltop site of Locus 002(Group A) and a systematic test-pitting and coring program to seek further evidence of precolumbian settlement remains buried in the floodplain around the site-core. In conjunction with the latter, a soil coring program was to be undertaken by a consulting geomorphologist, Ira L. Fogel, to document the geomorphological history of the alluvial plain, especially in relation to the sequence and distribution of human occupation. The former operation, excavation in Group A, was carried out as planned, but the scheduled floodplain studies were largely replaced with exploration and recording of an extensive and unanticipated sample of regularly-spaced ditches, exposing both culturally and alluvially deposited materials buried in the floodplain.

GROUP A

Group A proper consists of three structures and two carved-stone monuments perched upon an artificial, bilevel platform at the highest point along the ridge north of the town of Quirigua (Sharer 1978:Fig. 6). The hilltop location, approximately 4 km west of the main ruins, provides a spectacular 360° view, and the site can be seen and recognized from virtually anywhere in this part of the Motagua valley. Previous documented research at Group A was confined to Morley's very brief investigations in 1923 (Morley 1923; 1935; 1937-38:IV, 86-94), which centered on recording the monuments and clearing the principal edifice, Str. 1. Morley (1923:95a; 1937-38:IV, 93-94) also probed about one meter below the floor of Str. 1 in search of a tomb. He was unsuccessful, but someone in more recent years has renewed this or a similar quest, the tangible residue being a large trench from the southeast into the heart of the substructure.

Along with his verbal descriptions, Morley published a sketch map of Group A (Morley 1935:Fig. 6; 1937-38:Pl. 215a). This map is imprecise in a number of respects, most notably that, apparently because of limited time—and consequently limited brush-clearing—Morley missed Str. 2 altogether. Transit readings for a new map of Group A were taken in 1977 (*Quirigua Paper No. 6*, this volume), with excavation deferred until 1978.

The questions to be answered by the 1978 excavations centered on the paradox provided by the two stelae found at this group (Sharer 1978:62). Morley assigned Monuments 20 (T) and 21 (U) dedicatory dates of 9.13.0.0.0 (A.D. 692) and 9.14.0.0.0 (A.D. 711) respectively; Marcus (1976) and Jones (1977; *Quirigua Paper No. 6*, this volume) have more recently argued that the date inscribed on Mon. 21—9.2.3.8.0 or A.D. 478—likely indicates a dedicatory date of 9.2.0.0.0 (A.D. 475). By extension, Mon. 20 was assigned a probable date of 9.3.0.0.0 (A.D. 495). According to either interpretation, these monuments are the earliest in the record of Quirigua inscriptions, and the paradox presented by Group A is that the architecture visible during mapping in 1977 is most similar to the latest construction in the Quirigua Acropolis (CS 1), about A.D. 810 (Jones 1977 and personal communication; *Quirigua Paper No. 6*, this volume). Research was therefore directed to inquire whether (1) Group A was a "prototype" for the main center (cf. Morley 1935, 1937-38), occupied early and either maintained until or reoccupied during later times, or (2) the surface architecture represents an accurate temporal clue, the monuments having perhaps been moved to this new location as part of Quirigua's late expansion (cf. *Quirigua Paper No. 6*, this volume; Sharer 1978).

Excavations concentrated on trenches and lateral clearing in Str. 1 and around the two monuments, supplemented by minor clearing operations in other locations. Little remains of the final superstructure of Str. 1, but there is enough to support Morley's statement that it was a single-roomed building, facing south. Preserved portions of the building platform indicate minimum dimensions of 6 m (east-west) by 5.8 m (north-south), but it was more probably about 6.5 m x 7-7.5 m. Not enough is left of the building walls to reconstruct their width at any point, but Morley describes the south wall as being 1.57 m thick. The substructure on which this building rests is well preserved at the base, where it measures 21.7 m east-west and 16.3 m north-south; the masonry between basal- and building-platform levels is largely gone, as is all but the lowest portion of the central staircase. There is a short pavement extending about 1.6 m south of and abutting Str. 1; as in the site-core (*Quirigua Paper No. 6*, this volume), paved outdoor surfaces pertain to particular structures and monuments, and except for the Acropolis, are not fully continuous within structure groups. Artifact yields in this set of excavations were notably sparse; the eccentric flints to which Morley (1935: 46, Fig. 36; 1937-38: IV, 92-93) attributes a Str. 1 provenience are very equivocal evidence of high-status occupation and/or ritual use of the site (cf. the eccentric flints found in the Acropolis in 1978).

A sequence of construction stages is revealed in the stratigraphic section through Str. 1. The first involved the levelling of the ridge top (perhaps carried out in two phases), with sandy loam deposited toward the ridge center and, nearer the summit edge, a more stable fill of sandstone rubble set in a dense clay. Within this deposit were only two sherds; they have been identified preliminarily as "Middle Classic" in date, consistent with the ceramics of the Mon. 21 cache (see below). The existence of an earlier version of Str. 1 is indicated by a

THE 1978 SEASON

frontal pavement, as well as flooring and masonry units encased within the final construction. A possible period of disuse between construction periods is suggested by a debris line (devoid of sherds) of sandy clay loam and tiny fragments of sandstone, vertically midway between earlier and later pavements.

Str. 2 was little touched by our work, but it appears to be divisible into two distinct summit areas, with sparse indications of a superstructure at only the southern end of the long, low platform. There is a sandstone block staircase running up the west side of the platform, and it seems confined to the area where the superstructure is postulated.

When Morley first saw Mon. 20, in 1922, it was still standing; by the time he returned the following year, it had fallen. Mon. 21, already broken in Morley's day, was found by him on the lower of the two platforms that make up the site. In our visits to Group A over the last few years, we had noted that one of the larger pieces of Mon. 21 had moved downslope. For security reasons, then, the Project requested that IDAEH transport both monuments to the laboratory compound, a move accomplished at the end of 1977, with permanent markers left to record the positions from which the stones were removed.

Excavation this year revealed that both monuments had been set in a soil base adjacent to their recorded positions, and surrounded by a superficial perimeter of stone blocks or slabs. Stone pavements abut the exterior edge of these perimeters, but the surface between perimeter and monument appears unformalized, perhaps simply sediment. Mon. 20 does not seem to have been moved prior to 1977, except, of course, for having fallen. It was set about 30 m south of Str. 1, S20°E from the center of the superstructure. This position falls on a line of sight between the center of the superstructure and Cerro Chino, the most prominent feature in the Serra del Espiritu Santo on the opposite (south) side of the valley. (Sightings relative to the superstructure are approximate because the latter was so badly destroyed; angle measurements were taken from the only surviving midpoint—that is, the back wall of the superstructure.) The Mon. 20 excavations yielded only a few pieces of obsidian, in a dense clay matrix that was difficult to pick through. No dedicatory deposits were encountered, but the excavation was not carried to bedrock.

Since Mon. 21 had the more secure glyphic date, more importance was attached to the excavation of the latter's setting. Excavations at Mon. 21 indicate that it too lay near its Classic siting when recorded in 1922. Morley had confined his definition of Group A to the uppermost level of the ridge, and inferred that Mon. 21 had fallen downhill from a postulated original location near Mon. 20. But excavations in 1978 confirmed Mon. 21's Classic placement on the lower terrace, in front of the stairway connecting upper and lower platforms. The setting was similar to that of Mon. 20—that is, a stone-bordered soil foundation.

An apparent cache was discovered, off-center, in the foundation matrix. The deposit comprised sherds of two broken vessels, eroded but of the same form and ceramic group as the vessels from the two caches pertaining to the earliest construction stages in the Quirigua Acropolis. These vessels have been called "Middle Classic," but a more exact chronological age remains undetermined. Unfortunately, the Mon. 21 cache was disinterred by vandals before it could be fully excavated and recorded; this may be the reason why many fragments of the two vessels were missing. These objects surely contained cinnabar (some of which had turned to mercury) and either held or were associated with shale chips and one small fragment of bone. The deposit lay within 50 cm of the present, somewhat disturbed surface and, while the cache vessels appear to come from a primary deposit, their eroded condition and disinterment by vandals prevents definitive assessment of their context and of whether breakage occurred at the time of deposit. In other words, it is still possible that the cache was disturbed prior to our excavation, by either human or animal activity or as a result of displacement by the falling monument. For the same reasons, redeposition of an earlier cache cannot be ruled out. An undisturbed stratum associated with laying of the stone perimeter of the stela setting contained ceramics which, in preliminary analysis, have been assigned a Middle Classic age; this *terminus post quem* may suggest that the monument was set slightly later than the date inscribed on it, but the non-epigraphic chronological analysis is not fine-grained enough to make any stronger inference.

In sum, the excavations in Group A indicate its use for a period long enough to encompass at least two construction stages in Str. 1, but the archaeological and architectural data encountered do not date the span clearly. Combining the meager artifactual evidence with clues from architectural style noted in 1977 suggests, however, that the principal use of Group A probably fell within the period of major occupation of the site-core (c. A.D. 550-850).

QUIRIGUA REPORTS

FLOODPLAIN INVESTIGATIONS

The major effort of the site-periphery program in 1978 was the exploration and recording of the drainage ditches cut late in 1977 by BANDEGUA (Del Monte Corporation). We are grateful to that company, and especially to Mr. Roy C. Wells, Manager, and Ing. Mario Mena, for providing assistance and information invaluable to our work.

The ditches are evenly spaced, 76.20 m (250 feet) apart, running N24°W—perpendicular to the company rail line—and cut to a variable depth, usually approximately 2 m. Those examined in early 1978 covered an area of approximately 337 ha (3.37 km² or 832 acres) north and east of the site-core (see Fig. 2), revealing more than 50 cobble platforms, as well as other features, including stone pavements, middens, pits and clay-lined wells. A previously unknown, uncarved, altar-like sandstone monument or pedestal stone was also discovered near the South Group of the site-core.

Reconnaissance and surface collections were accompanied by transit recording of all ditches within 0.9 km east of epicentral Quirigua. From this work, it is clear that stone-construction density declines markedly beyond ca. 300 m east of the site-core. Sherds and adobe fragments were found beyond this point, as were a few isolated stone platforms. These data, plus the positive identification of at least one completely earthen platform close to the site-core, suggest that substantial architecture continued beyond these observed boundaries of stone construction. At this preliminary stage of analysis, a *minimum* structure density of ca. 105/km² is indicated for the zone immediately adjacent to the site-core.

The stone features identified from ditch exposures have provided a wealth of detail concerning variability in manner of construction, and one, Str. 3C-11, was cleared to reveal information on plan. It is about 450 m north of the site-core and 150 m north of Loc. 082 (Fig. 2). Excavation revealed a north-facing stone platform, 4.5 m (north-south) by 5.3 m (east-west), with an interior raised area or bench. Artifacts recovered include ceramics, obsidian, figurine fragments and other materials comprising an assemblage suggestive of domestic activities; however, none was recovered from clearly use-related primary context. Although no traces of a hearth were encountered in or immediately adjacent to Str. 3C-11, we hypothesize that there may have been a kitchen-building or -area nearby. Two fragments of grinding stones were recovered from ditch debris in the vicinity.

This particular structure was selected for excavation because of its association with one of four ceramic-lined wells discovered in the ditches. Ricketson (1935) reported finding a well just northwest of the Quirigua site-core, in a plantation-related drainage ditch. His concise but detailed description fits the features we found, except that Ricketson did not note any architectural associations. Of the four wells encountered in 1978, however, three are clearly associated with cobble platforms. The wells consist of ceramic tubes, each at least 1 m long, joined in a column from a cobble pavement at ancient ground level to a large *olla* below the water table. The latter, set in a matrix of gravel and small stones, has one basal and four lateral perforations allowing water to enter. All junctions between tube and *olla* have some overlap between elements and an exterior packing of sherds to prevent dirt from seeping into the well. The elements making up this feature are all of a coarse but well-fired orange clay, approximately 1.5 cm thick, with distinctive diagonal raking on the exterior. The two wells that were cleared yielded abundant artifactual materials, all appearing to be Late Classic in date and including several whole or nearly whole pottery vessels, showing that the wells were also (probably accidentally) trash repositories.

Although all the ditches are approximately 2 m deep, the Late Classic ground surface was found at varying levels within them. This is because the natural levee-building action of the Motagua, in its present course, has deposited more alluvium nearer the river—that is, in the southernmost ditches. Consequently, Late Classic features are exposed at the base of the southern ditches and near the top of those farthest north. The corollary to this is that the northern ditches were the only ones to reach earlier levels and therefore reveal much about settlement predating the principal Late Classic occupation. A cobble "floor" associated with Usulutan-decorated ceramics was discovered at Loc. 029 (Fig. 2) in 1976 (Sharer et. al. 1979) and some possibly Protoclassic materials were recovered form the spoil of the ditch excavations in 1978. The earliest material recorded *in situ* in 1978, however, was Middle Classic in date. As noted in earlier reports, a local Preclassic occupation is hinted at by donations of diagnostically Middle to Late Preclassic figurines. These donations reputedly come from various places near the Motagua, on the Chapulco plain opposite Quirigua; the sources most frequently cited are modern gravesites (i.e., more than 2 m down). Whatever coeval settlement there may have been on the Quirigua plain is buried so deeply in the alluvium that it still eludes detection.

THE 1978 SEASON

A principal thrust of Fogel's geomorphological investigations was the search for ancient river courses. On cultural grounds (i.e., site plan; see *Quirigua Paper No. 6*, this volume) as well as sketchy evidence from old maps, a Late Classic course was postulated flowing east past Locus 025 (Group B) and Loc. 006, but turning south to flow directly by the Great Plaza and the Acropolis before turning eastward again. Given that the canals cut by early 1978 were all north or east of the site-core, this hypothesis could not be tested through the ditches. A coring program, however, was employed to probe the alluvium at 50 m intervals for tell-tale deposits of sand and gravel. One line of tests was made west from the Great Plaza, extending 200 m from the park fence on a line just south of Mon. 8; a second series of samples was taken in a line NW/SE from Mon. 19 in Locus 025 (Group B). Two supplementary (and more widely spaced) series (1) connected the first two sets and (2) probed the area around Loc. 006. The tests reached a maximum depth of 4.85 m below the surface and coarse sand and gravel were encountered in only one sample, ca. 750 m west of the Great Plaza, at a depth of 3 m and more. The data are equivocal concerning the specific hypothetical course; ditches cut in the crucial areas at the end of 1978 would provide more definitive information (*Quirigua Paper No. 8*, this volume).

An apparent ancient channel was revealed in the drainage canals, but it stratigraphically antedates architecture of the Late Classic occupation. This channel seems to follow a bed closely aligned with the Motagua fault zone (*Quirigua Paper No. 12*, this volume), veering several hundred meters north from the site-core. Ditches cut late in 1978, west of Loc. 006 (inspected in October 1978; see below) give further evidence of this channel and allow us to begin to project its course more confidently (see Fig. 2). The cause of the change in course by A.D. 700 is unknown. During the 1979 season we hoped to be able to plot the ancient courses of the Motagua more accurately.

As mentioned above, BANDEGUA cut a second set of drainage channels, west of the site-core, after the close of the 1978 season. The initial ditches, were first recorded in January 1978, after they had been exposed for several months. By that time, they were already eroded along their margins and many had been badly gouged by local treasure seekers. This fact, plus the reports (and some attempted sales) of figurines, jade and other items said to have been encountered, argued that an archaeologist should observe the actual excavation of subsequent canals. Consequently, the Project and the Director of the University Museum, Martin Biddle, sponsored a brief survey by Ashmore during October 1978, to observe and record drainage excavation in progress. Of the 100 new cuts planned, 40 had been or were being dug by this time, at an average rate of 1 every 2.5 to 3 days for each of three draglines. A number of cut platforms were observed, at least two stratigraphically of probable Middle or Early Classic date. Limited artifact collections were made, in part by the guardians employed by IDAEH, and observations recorded about construction form and frequency as well as the aforementioned ancient river channel. A number of functionally significant artifacts were encountered which would surely have been removed by local residents. These materials included finely worked obsidian points, thin blades and cores; basalt pestles; a small basalt palette; *candeleros*; several grinding stones; and three partially reconstructable vessels.

Preliminary estimation suggests a lower structure density in the area to the west of the site-core, observed in October, than in the zone immediately north and east of the site's center. It should be noted, however, that the area between the two large and visible groups, Loci 006 and 082, had not yet been cut. Similarly pending was the area west of the Great Plaza, the hypothesized river bed of the Motagua in Late Classic times. Reports on the data gleaned from these localities are presented in the summary of the 1979 season at Quirigua (*Quirigua Paper No. 8*, this volume).

Another goal of the October reconnaissance was reinforcement of precautions undertaken to safeguard all known archaeological features potentially endangered by the new plantation operations. The preservation of archaeological remains adjacent to epicentral Quirigua has been achieved through the joint efforts of many parties, but the day-to-day diligence of Enrique Monterroso R. of IDAEH has been the key to the success of these efforts. IDAEH has supplied guardians to patrol the new ditches, and signs have been erected, creating small archaeological preserves around known features. Although the first concern of BANDEGUA officials is necessarily the completion of an efficiently engineered plantation, these officials have been consistently sympathetic and cooperative in adapting their plans to accommodate the protection of prehistoric remains. Besides realigning several non-trivial installations, BANDEGUA has moved Mon. 19 from its setting in Group B to protective shelter in the Quirigua laboratory compound (see *Quirigua Paper No. 6*, this volume, concerning Project excavations in Group B). Other groups (Loci 004, 006, 026, 029, 082), imperiled at various points, seem now better assured of protection.

VALLEY PROGRAM

The operational goals of the Valley Program during the 1978 season were to test two sites located in that portion of the valley lying between Quirigua and Morales/Bananera: specifically, Las Quebradas and Choco (Sharer 1978:Fig. 1). These sites were chosen on the basis of the 1977 reconnaissance, which indicated that they were two of the largest and most complex centers known in the target area.

LAS QUEBRADAS

The site of Las Quebradas is located 10.5 km southeast of Morales/Bananera in the *aldeas* of Las Quebradas and Los Cerritos; it may be reached by the Quebradas branch of the local rail system. The site is situated on a spur of the Sierra del Espiritu Santo, at ca. 80 m in altitude, and it overlooks the Rio Bobos and Pablo Creek.

A preliminary map (Nowak 1973) showed a total of 70 structures divided into two major groups, each containing two plazas bounded by monumental structures, and surrounded by smaller attendant constructions. A brief survey by Schortman and Urban in 1977 confirmed this as a conservative estimate of the size and extent of the site, and indicated that more structures would certainly be revealed by clearing operations.

The first objective in 1978 was, therefore, to clear and map Las Quebradas as thoroughly as time and money would permit. The result was the location and recording of ca. 290 structures distributed among three groups: the large East and West Groups, previously noted by Nowak; and the newly discovered and smaller Northwest Group. In total, there are nine sizeable plazas defined by large substructure platforms, with one plaza in the Northwest Group and four each in the East and West Groups. The largest of the three closed plazas in the East Group measures 40 m east-west by 38 m north-south and is enclosed by structures ranging from 2.5 m to 6.5 m in height; its external dimensions are 62 m east-west and 70 m north-south. Seven unsculptured stone monuments were found: two large pecked-stone spheres (ca. 60 cm in diameter) in the Northwest Group plaza (Mons. 2 and 3); a pecked-stone column in the central closed plaza of the West Group (Mon. 1); three large unshaped boulders arranged on a north-south trending line in the center of the East Group closed plaza described above (Mons. 5-7); and an unshaped slab in a smaller closed East Group plaza adjacent to the one noted above. (Mon. 4)

The second focus of activity at Las Quebradas was a series of excavations designed to test each of the three major groups. Within each of these units two different plaza types were examined—closed monumental plazas in which all four corners are joined by construction, apparently designed to limit access to the interior space, and open monumental plazas, in which either all four corners are not joined, or all four sides are not bounded by structures. In addition, the smaller outlying constructions, presumably residential groupings, were also probed, as were the settings of several of the monuments.

In all, 17 excavations were undertaken. Initially, work in the monumental plazas of both types consisted of axial trenches in both long sides of the chosen structures. After it became apparent that the orientations of the large structures were consistently towards the plazas, excavations were confined to the structures' "fronts." Excavation objectives were these: determining methods of construction and locating artifact deposits in use-related primary contexts as well as fill lots for the purpose of dating construction. The smaller structures were also tested by axial trenches: four structures of this kind, scattered among the three groups, were examined, with aims similar to those for the larger structures. The settings of four monuments were studied by means of test pits on one or more of their sides. These pits were located in all three groups—one by the stone sphere in the center of the Northwest Group's major plaza (Mon. 2), one in the West Group (Mon. 1) and, in the East Group, one by the central monument of the north-south line of stones (Mon. 5) and one by the large rock slab in the small closed plaza (Mon. 4).

Excavations in the large substructures revealed a complete lack of cut-stone blocks. Instead, two forms of wall construction were noted, the first all cobble and the second cobble and slab. All large structures examined were terraced or stepped on both front and rear, regardless of construction type. The smaller, presumably residential, structures consisted of low basal cobble retaining walls, backed by earth fill. No prepared floors were detected in any of the constructions examined, although pebble surfaces of limited extent were encountered at the bases of several large structures. Finally, debris from structures of both size groups contained scattered remains of adobe, presumably from former superstructures, although no

THE 1978 SEASON

adobe walls were found intact.

The monument excavations produced no caches, though large quantities of censer fragments were found in association with these features, either broken on their platforms or mixed in with the cobbles and earth in which the monuments were set. In addition, evidence was noted of low (ca. 30 cm high) cobble platforms on at least one side of three of the four monuments studied.

Deep trenching of one large structure revealed at least two earlier construction phases, all made of cobble walls with earth fill. Several of the large structures also produced evidence of secondary alterations and additions, such as superstructure platforms. Unfortunately, it was not possible to investigate structure plan and sequent construction more fully.

On the basis of preliminary ceramic analysis and comparison with materials from Quirigua, all three groups seem to be roughly coeval with the latter settlement's occupation span, in particular the Late Classic. These analyses also suggest that, within this time span, the Northwest and West Groups may be slightly earlier than the East Group.

In summary, there are several particularly interesting aspects of Las Quebradas. First among these are its size and extent—ca. 290 structures covering an area roughly 1.5 km east-west by 0.75 km north-south—both suggestive of its importance within a valley-wide system of interaction. Many of the structures, especially in the East Group, are quite massive. At present, Las Quebradas would appear to have contained more monumental structures per unit area than even the site of Quirigua, previously thought to have been the largest settlement in the valley. Additionally, the seven uncarved monuments are, so far as we know, unique in this valley, as is the construction of such large structures without the use of cut stone.

CHOCO

The site of Choco is located southwest of Morales/Bananera on the *finca* of the same name. In constrast to Las Quebradas' location on the summit of a steep bluff, Choco is situated on the relatively flat floodplain of a tributary of the Rio Motagua, the Rio Encantado, ca. 2.5 km north of where that river issues from the Espiritu Santo range.

The focus of the site seems to have been the two adjoining closed plazas, bounded by monumental structures (ca. 2.6-6.5 m high) and oriented roughly north-south. The more southerly of these plazas possesses by far the largest interior space recognized to date for this portion of the valley, measuring 82 m north-south by 66 m east-west. Surrounding the central group are structures of lesser stature scattered in small, irregular groupings up to a distance of 400-450 m to the north, west and south. Unfortunately, heavy vegetation to the east of the central two plazas pre-empted effective clearing and mapping in this portion of the site. Despite this limitation, 75 structures were mapped in 1978 at Choco and another 10 noted but not located precisely on the finished map.

Due to the unexpectedly large size of Las Quebradas, comprehensive mapping there took longer than expected and only 25 days could be alotted to the work at Choco. As at Quebradas, the twin research emphases encompassed mapping and test excavation of both monumental and small structures.

In all, 13 excavation sub-operations were defined at Choco. Four of these concentrated on the intensive investigation of a small structure located ca. 250 m south of the central double plaza; five more were in the monumental structures on the main closed plazas and followed the format established at Las Quebradas, i.e., axial trenching of at least the plaza-face of the structure to recover material from fill for tentative dating and to expose construction techniques. The final four were excavated to determine the extent of the pavement in the southern closed plaza, as the stone surfacing did not appear to extend over the totality of this space, and to examine the nature of the interior corner junction between the northern and western structures of that plaza.

The excavations in the large structures revealed that, in what appears to be final stages of construction, cobble and stone-slab terracing similar to that noted at Las Quebradas was used. This, however, is not the only style of construction found at Choco. In an earlier building stage of a structure shared by the northern and southern closed plazas, and in the small structure, standing walls of coursed cobbles packed with chinking stones were noted. In the former instance, one such wall was preserved to the height of at least 2.9 m. In addition, some fragments of adobe from both the monumental and "residential" structures suggest the use of this material in construction, though it was not found here in the abundance noted at Las Quebradas. Finally, plaza excavations revealed that roughly the western three-fourths of the southern plaza was surfaced with stones in the terminal phase of occupation, while the eastern quarter was left unpaved.

On the basis of a very cursory ceramic analysis, all of the structures excavated at Choco seem to date to the Late Classic period, approximately contemporary with the principal occupation at Quirigua.

QUIRIGUA REPORTS

LABORATORY PROGRAM

A large part of the Project's effort in 1978 was directed toward laboratory analyses. In addition to the usual processing of newly recovered materials, all categories of artifacts underwent specialized studies. Pottery analysis, formally begun in 1976, had increased in scope and volume annually. In 1978, 614 pottery lots were assessed as to their form and type-variety content, and type descriptions were almost all completed. This work was performed by Mary Bullard and Robert Sharer, with assistance from Greta Zuckerkandel. In general, the findings summarized for previous years (Sharer 1978; Sharer et al. 1979; *Quirigua Paper No. 6*, this volume) were further substantiated. The major influx of new materials consisted of the greatly increased sample of relatively early (Early to Middle Classic) pottery gained from the periphery ditches. Detailed reports on content and distribution will be presented at a later time.

The importance of obsidian in the Quirigua collections was recognized in the first seasons of the project. In 1977, Payson D. Sheets of the University of Colorado performed a preliminary analysis of Quirigua obsidian in order "to derive a general impression of patterns and diversity in artifacts, to see if production and distribution information can be derived from analysis of artifacts when combined with provenience-context data, and to try to determine the source(s) of Quirigua obsidian" (*Quirigua Paper No. 10*, this volume contains Sheets' detailed report).

As part of the preliminary study, Sheets selected 30 samples for source analysis, five specimens each from six proveniences. The specimens were submitted to Frank Asaro and Fred Stross at the Lawrence Berkeley Laboratory of the University of California. Their findings indicate that 24 pieces were from the Ixtepeque source; four more were from El Chayal (La Joya); the other two could not be assigned a source.

Matching geological sources with Quirigua proveniences, we note that all the material from the site-core was from the Ixtepeque source. The proveniences represented were the Ballcourt Plaza, Str. 1B-Sub.3 and Str. 1B-8. One of the Chayal pieces had been found in an apparent workshop context at Loc. 092; the other specimens from the lot containing this piece were from the Ixtepeque source. The other three Chayal specimens, plus the two unassigned ones, were from a cobble-percussion locale (Loc. 014).

Sheets notes that straightline distance from Quirigua to Ixtepeque is 115 km; to El Chayal, it is 145 km. We had previously anticipated, in accordance with this fact, and with Hammond's (1972) model, that the majority of Quirigua finds would be attributable to the Ixtepeque source. On the basis of this first round of analysis, we propose a model that reiterates belief in control of Ixtepeque trade by Quirigua elite. The occupants of Loc. 092 participated in this trade also. The apparent contrast between the occurrence of El Chayal material in site-core *vs.* Loc. 092 may be an artifact of sampling. It may also, however, reflect interaction of 092 residents with more than one network of supply; Sheets comments on the more "miserly" production of blades (a higher cutting edge per unit mass ratio) at the latter site, suggesting to him that obsidian was a rather more precious commodity at Loc. 092. Finally, the occurrence of El Chayal and unassigned specimens at Loc. 014 may reflect haphazard selection by local residents from available river cobbles, which had been borne down the Motagua from varied sources along tributaries of that river.

The study of obsidian was continued in 1978 by Andrea Gerstle, who completed a technical analysis of the extant Quirigua collection. Samples of all artifact categories were selected for further detailed examination in the United States. A form classification for censers was established as a result of the work of Julie Benyo. Descriptive data pertaining to the remaining artifact categories was recorded by Greta Zuckerkandel. The results of these artifactual studies will be reported as papers in the *QUIRIGUA REPORTS* series.

THE 1978 SEASON

REFERENCES CITED

Ashmore, W.
    1977   Research At Quirigua, Guatemala: The Site-Periphery Program. Paper presented at the 42nd Annual Meeting of the Society for American Archaeology, New Orleans.

Hammond, N.
    1972   Obsidian Trade Routes in the Mayan Area. *Science* 178: 1092-1093.

Jones, C.
    1977   Research at Quirigua, Guatemala: The Site-Core Program. Paper presented at the 42nd Annual Meeting of the Society for American Archaeology, New Orleans.

Marcus, J.
    1976   *Emblem and State in the Classic Maya Lowlands.* Washington D.C.: Dumbarton Oaks.

Morley, S. G.
    1923   Unpublished Field Notes.
    1935   *Guide Book to the Ruins of Quirigua.* Carnegie Institution of Washington, Supplementary Publication 16, Washington, D. C.
    1937-38   *The Inscriptions of Peten.* 5 vols. Carnegie Institution of Washington, Publication 437, Washington D.C.

Nowak, T. R.
    1973   Mercantilism and Colonization: A Study of Prehistoric Regional Community Patterning and Culture Change in the Lower Motagua Valley, Guatemala. Harvard University, Peabody Museum, Manuscript.

Ricketson, O.G., Jr.
    1935   Maya Pottery Well from Quirigua Farm, Guatemala. *Maya Research* 2 (2): 103-105.

Sharer, R. J.
    1978   Archaeology and History at Quirigua, Guatemala. *Journal of Field Archaeology* 5: 51-70.

Sharer, R. J., C. Jones, W. Ashmore and E. M. Schortman
    1979   The Quirigua Project: 1976 Season. *Quirigua Reports I* (No. 5). Museum Monographs, No. 37. Philadelphia: University Museum.

Stromsvik, G.
    1952   *The Ball Courts at Copan; with Notes on Courts at La Union, Quirigua, San Pedro Pinula and Asuncion Mita.* Carnegie Institution of Washington, Publication 596, Contributions to American Anthropology and History, No. 55, Washington, D. C.

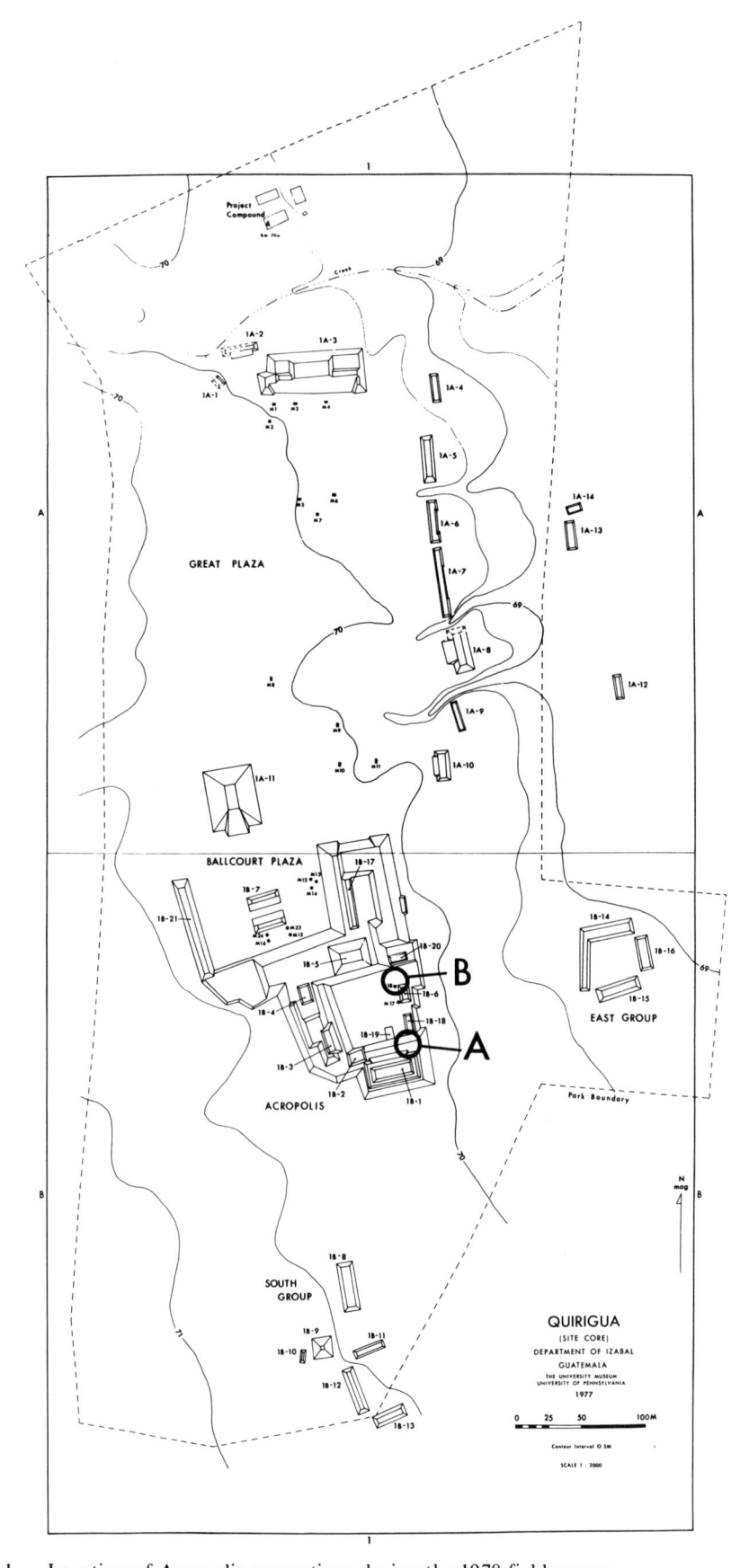

Figure 7.1. Location of Acropolis excavations during the 1978 field season.
A. Wall connecting Strs. 1B-12nd and 1B-18-2nd.
B. Northeast corner of the plaza (link between Strs. 1B-5 and 1B-6).

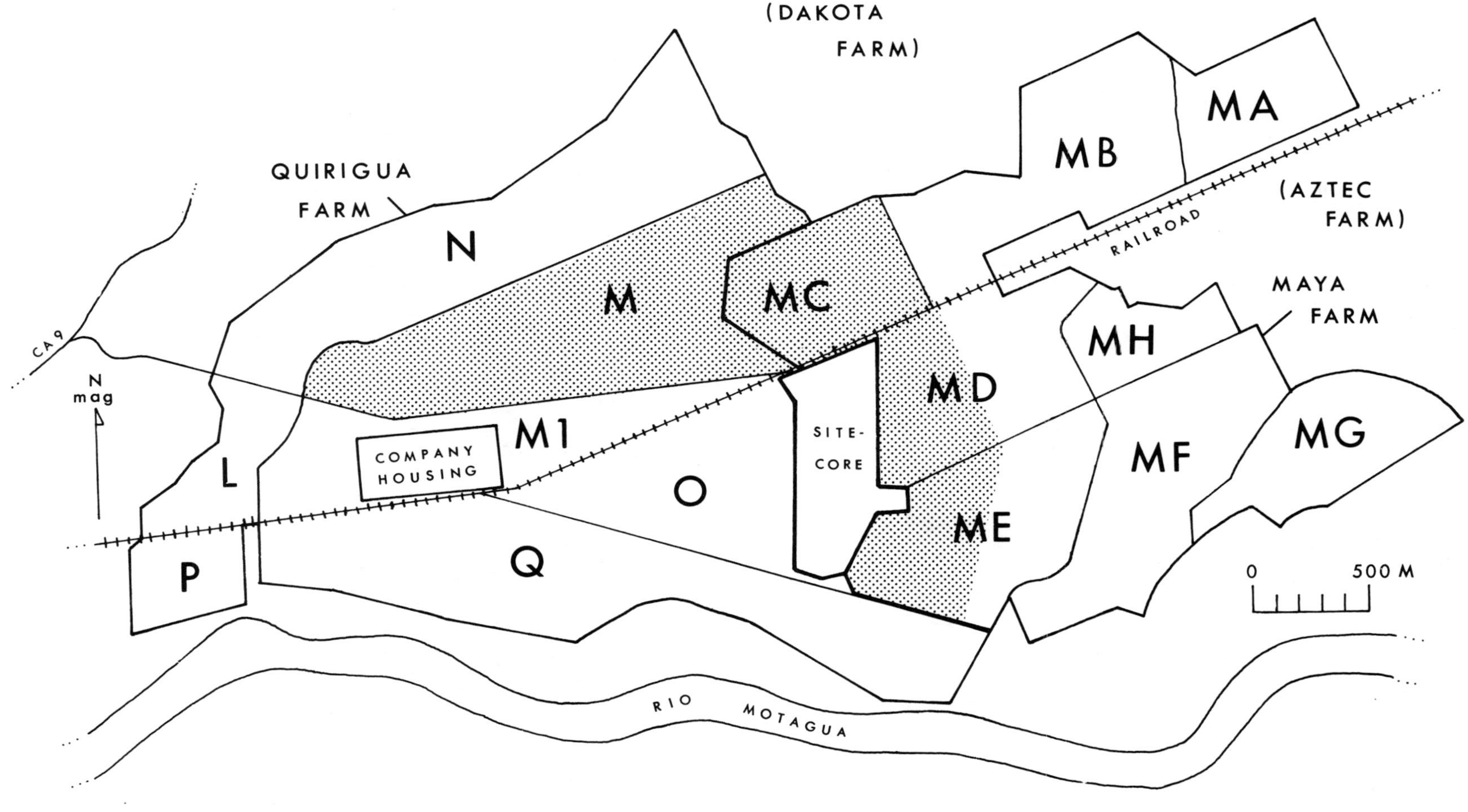

Figure 7.2. Map of the Quirigua floodplain periphery (areas covered by drainage ditches): Shaded area corresponds to portion mapped by transit.

a.

b.

c.

d.

Figure 7.3. Excavations in the Site Core and Group A.
    a. Excavation in the northeast corner of the Acropolis Plaza, revealing an early staircase covered by the Construction Stage 1 plaza surface.
    b. Summit excavation into the fill of Str. 1A-11.
    c. Locus 002 (Group A), Str. 1, view from south after clearing but before Project excavations. Deep, non-axially oriented pit, left by previous illicit excavation, can be seen clearly.
    d. Locus 002 (Group A), Str. 1, axial excavation from south, showing preserved remnants of central stair and frontal pavement. Old illicit excavation still visible in background.

Figure 7.4. Site Periphery investigations.
a. Quirigua Monument 28, uncarved sandstone slab discovered in drainage ditch at Terminal Classic elevation. This view to the northwest also shows the proximity of the site-core, marked by the dense stand of trees just beyond the ditch.
b. Str. 3C-22, Late Classic cobble structure exposed in commercial drainage ditch.
c. Str. 3C-11 after clearing, view to the east along the front of the structure. The excavation at Well 3C-1 was on the far side of the commercial drainage ditch that cuts across the top of the photograph.
d. Well 3C-1 during clearing, from the west. Part of preserved ceramic well tube can be seen within the excavation, and at the top, a fragment of the cobble pavement that originally encircled the mouth of the well is also visible.

Figure 7.5. Periphery and Valley Program investigations.
  a. Geomorphologist Ira L. Fogel drilling for soil samples west of the site-core.
  b. Northeast corner of the Choco Southern Court after clearing, view from above. This corner of the court was closed by a juncture of the step terraces from the adjoining structures (Strs. 212-4 and 3).
  c. Str. 212-4-3rd, buried construction at the site of Choco illustrating the use of a high, steeply battered wall in monumental construction. View from the south.
  d. Monument 1, Las Quebradas, viewed from the north.

PAPER NO. 8

THE QUIRIGUA PROJECT
1979 SEASON

by
Wendy Ashmore, Edward M. Schortman, and Robert J. Sharer
Appendix by Bruce Bevan

INTRODUCTION

Although the 1978 season was the final period of archaeological fieldwork covered by the original contract, personnel of both the University Museum and the Instituto de Antropologia e Historia, Guatemala (IDAEH), believed an additional season in 1979 would be necessary and desirable to complete laboratory analyses, excavation at Structure 1A-11, floodplain mapping and investigation of more distant sites within the lower Motagua valley. Through the cooperation and assistance of IDAEH, the research staff was both permitted and encouraged to pursue these concluding operations.

After some initial meetings and arrangements in Guatemala City, research commenced on 29 January. The different programs required varying lengths of time for completion, but all field studies ended by 17 April. Commensurate with the smaller scale of operations in 1979, the research staff was limited to 7 persons: Robert J. Sharer was Field Director and conducted ceramic analyses on site-core and periphery collections; David W. Sedat was responsible for completing the investigation of Str. 1A-11 as well as continuing duties as Administrative Director; Rebecca Sedat again served as Camp Manager, and also did much to further laboratory processing. In the site-periphery program Wendy Ashmore carried out reconnaissance and mapping in the floodplain ditches and excavations at Str. 3C-14. Edward M. Schortman, assisted by Patricia A. Urban, directed operations in the valley at large, including extensive reconnaissance, intensive survey and excavations at Playitas, and analysis of ceramics from all Valley Program collections. Bruce Bevan (Geosight and consultant for MASCA) conducted a ground-penetrating radar survey and assisted in floodplain ditch exploration. Restoration in the site-core continued under the direction of Arq. Marcelino Gonzalez C., Jefe, Seccion de Proyectos Especificos, IDAEH. Arq. Gonzalez also furthered the Project's research by kindly making additional labor available for the excavation of Str. 1A-11.

The research reported herein was conducted under an extension of the original contract (1974-1978) between the University Museum, University of Pennsylvania, and the Ministry of Education, Government of Guatemala. We are very grateful to the following agencies and individuals for financial support of the investigations: the University Museum, University of Pennsylvania (especially the Francis Boyer Fund); the National Geographic Society; the Tikal Association (Guatemala), Mr. Landon T. Clay; and Dr. John M. Keshishian. While it is impossible to thank all the individuals who have supported and assisted the Quirigua Project, we would like to express our special appreciation to Lic. Francis Polo Sifontes, Director, Instituto de Antropologia e Historia, Guatemala; Arq. Marcelino Gonzalez C., Jefe, Seccion de Proyectos Especificos, IDAEH; Licda. Dora G. de Gonzalez, Directora, Museo Nacional de Arqueologia e Etnologia, IDAEH; Sr. Enrique Monterroso R., IDAEH; Mr. Roy C. Wells, Manager, BANDEGUA (Del Monte Corporation); Ing. Mario Mena, BANDEGUA; Dr. John M. Keshishian; Sra. Laura de Garcia Prendes; Sr. Rafael y Sra. Vivian B. de Morales; and Mr. and Mrs. Frederick Falck.

SITE-CORE PROGRAM

The 1979 investigations in the Quirigua site-core were limited to an expansion of the original trench that exposed the *Kinich Ahau* wall in 1975 (Coe and Sharer 1979), a survey of two areas with the ground penetrating radar unit by Bevan and completion of the Str. 1A-11 investigations, supervised by Sedat (see Figure 1, *Quirigua Paper No. 6*, this volume).

The *Kinich Ahau* work was undertaken at the request of IDAEH in order to facilitate the consolidation and conservation of this elaborately decorated wall. The original 1975 trench was extended several meters to the west along the front of the wall. No features or significant materials, other than the usual Late Classic artifactual fragments, were encountered in this operation.

The radar survey was conducted in the Great Plaza around Monument 7 (Zoomorph G) and in the Ballcourt Plaza. Both of these surveys were essentially experimental applications of the ground penetrating radar unit, prior to its being deployed in the site-periphery (see below). The survey in the vicinity of Mon. 7 detected known shallow buried features, such as the monument platforms, but produced only faint traces of more deeply buried items such as the sloping edge of the northern plaza platform discovered in the 1977 excavations (Platform 1A-1; *Quirigua Paper No. 6*, this volume). Similar limitations were apparent as a result of the Ballcourt Plaza survey, since the radar unit failed to consistently detect the northern edge of the plaza platform revealed this season by excavation (see below and appendix).

The probing of Str. 1A-11, begun in 1976 (Sharer et al. 1979) and continued in 1978, was completed in 1979. Work began on 5 February and lasted for some nine weeks until early April 1979. Two areas were investigated: the summit probe, begun in 1978, was continued; and the previously untested west side of the structure was investigated by a single excavation placed midway along the base. A series of test pits and trenches was also opened to explore the connections between Str. 1A-11 and the adjacent northern edge of the Ballcourt Plaza.

The summit excavation cleared and penetrated the floor and southward facing stairs of a buried platform discovered in the previous year. A layer of burned material, including Late Classic sherds, was encountered in the fill beneath this floor. Apart from fill retaining walls, no other significant features were found and the excavation was halted due to danger of collapse from the surrounding fill (despite the use of extensive bracing).

The western probe of Str. 1A-11 revealed a poorly preserved basal course of sandstone masonry. Above this, only the face of the construction core was preserved, the original masonry having fallen or been removed anciently. As a result it was impossible to determine with certainty whether the west side of 1A-11 was once terraced, or, as had been suspected, once supported a staircase. The staircase option thus remains a possibility. A special deposit (SD 20) was found in the lower zone of debris from the disintegration of 1A-11's west side, consisting of a rubble-lined cyst containing a single undecorated pottery vessel and poorly preserved bone fragments.

The series of excavations along the north side of the Ballcourt Plaza revealed that this feature consists of a cobble-filled platform, at least 0.88 m thick in the excavated portion. The edge of this plaza-platform appears to run from the northwest corner of Platform 1B-1 (the stepped "reviewing stand" forming the western limit to the Ballcourt Plaza) in a northeastern direction towards the northwest corner of Str. 1A-11. Along this west edge the plaza surface plunges 2.3 m into a deep cobble-surfaced depression, now filled with silt. The extent of the depression to the north and west remains unknown. Based upon the identification of alluvial deposits of clay and fine sand at the base of the silt in the feature, it is concluded that it once held standing water; perhaps it once functioned as an embayment connected to the main channel of the Motagua River during the period when the river's course lay immediately west of the site-core (see below, under site-periphery program). A small projection along the plaza-platform edge located immediately west of the midline of Str. 1A-11 may have been a jetty or docking facility for this embayment. Two large sandstone monoliths, similar in size and shape to either small unsculptured stelae or pedestal stones for a monument were found lying on the laja pavement of this "jetty." Given their location, it might be suggested that these monoliths were transported by water from their quarry, were off-loaded onto the "jetty," but for reasons unknown were never moved to their intended location. A single grooved clay object, perhaps a fishline weight, was also found on this surface, as were sherds which appear to belong to the Early Postclassic period. The existence of an embayment immediately to the west of the site-core, together with the possible jetty or docking area, would obviously furnish support for the supposition that Quirigua once functioned as a riverine port (Sharer 1978; Ashmore and Sharer 1978; *Quirigua Paper No. 6*, this volume).

SITE-PERIPHERY PROGRAM

The unparalleled opportunity provided by continued commercial excavation of regularly-spaced drainage canals in the site-periphery area led to the extension of the periphery program through a 1979 season, in order to record remains exposed in all areas transected by the ditches. The principal objective for 1979 was to be reconnaissance and surface survey of a maximum number of ditches, seeking both traces of precolumbian settlement and evidence of ancient courses of the Motagua River (see *Quirigua Paper No. 7*, this volume). Limited excavation, to clear some features (as in 1978) was also anticipated. In November 1978, however, the commercial dragline operations recovered two large fragments of an Early Classic stela, and the National Geographic Society generously provided additional funds to allow expansion of the periphery program in 1979, with the aims of seeking further fragments of this important monument and exploring apparently associated architecture. The site-periphery fieldwork accomplished in 1979 will be summarized under three headings: monument area operations; ditch survey—cultural data; and ditch survey—geomorphological data. The radar reconnaissance is described in Bevan's appendix to this report, and Christopher Jones has prepared a preliminary epigraphic analysis of the new stela, Monument 26 in the Quirigua Project nomenclature (*Quirigua Paper No. 13*, this volume).

MONUMENT AREA OPERATIONS

The most intensive work in the periphery in 1979 consisted of excavations in the vicinity of the monument discovery site. The discovery was first reported to us, independently, by Arq. Marcelino Gonzalez C., Jefe, Seccion de Proyectos Especificos, IDAEH, and David W. Sedat, Administrative Director of the Quirigua Project. Both reports indicated that, while only the dragline crew was on hand when the stela fragments were recovered, the approximate horizontal provenience was fairly secure, and there was some evidence of construction in that vicinity at a depth of more than 1.0 m below present ground surface. The stela itself is represented by two large fragments with a figure on the front and sides and a well preserved inscription on the back. More specific information is given in Jones' report; what is important here is the similarity of Mon. 26 in style, material (schist) and inscribed Early Classic date to the two stelae (Mons. 20 and 21) associated with the hilltop site of Group A. The latter two stelae have been interpreted as having dedicatory dates of 9.2.0.0.0 and 9.3.0.0.0 (A.D. 475 and 495, respectively); the nearly complete Initial Series date of Mon. 26 is tentatively read as 9.2.18.0.? (*kin* missing).

Morley (1935, 1937-38) had long ago suggested that Group A was the prototypical Quirigua, the earliest siting of a local elite center. Our excavations in 1978 suggested that Group A was in use during the height of Quirigua's power, in the late eighth and early ninth centuries A.D., but we could neither confirm nor refute definitively an earlier founding date (*Quirigua Paper No. 7*, this volume). What Mon. 26 offered, however, was likely evidence of Maya elite occupation on the floodplain itself in the fifth century about 1 km north of the Acropolis, the later epicenter of elite activities. Moreover, the asserted provenience of the stela fragments suggested strongly their association with construction features visibly cut by the drainage ditch. Relative elevation of these features supported an Early Classic date and so clearing the architectural remains became important both for their monument association and because local architecture of this time period is rarely encountered and therefore poorly known. The ditch exposure revealed a floor line of crushed rhyolite on an earthen platform (Platform 3C-1), with a short northern stair of rhyolite blocks. On this floor, just south of the stair, lay a flat, circular, uncarved slab of schist (Mon. 27), protruding from the west wall of the ditch (Fig. 3a).

The generous loan of a BANDEGUA dragline allowed us to dig three shallow ditches west of the original ditch, radiating from the location of Mon. 27. The heavy equipment was used to remove most of the overburden which, from the original ditch exposure, was seen to contain a Late Classic trash lens but no construction features (Fig. 3b). Clearing of Platform 3C-1 then proceeded by hand. The platform was found to support a single, nearly rectangular structure (Str. 3C-14; Fig. 3c), built of rhyolite-block masonry, 9.5 m long (north-south) and 5.0 m wide (east-west). The structure was oriented approximately to what are now cardinal magnetic directions, and has small outsets on all four sides. Its northwest corner is about 8 m directly south of Mon. 27.

Platform 3C-1 itself was revealed to be more than 32 m north-south, greater than 24 m east-west and about 1 m high. Horizontal dimensions cannot be specified more precisely because the south and east sides of the platform could not be located. In fact, the crushed-rhyolite flooring disappears to the southeast in a manner which, with associated stratigraphy, suggests that this part of the platform was destroyed by flooding.

The summit of Str. 3C-14 was disturbed in antiquity, but bore no clear trace of either superstructure or a stela pit. West of the structure, however, on the east-west axis, was an enigmatic feature which is our only candidate for a stela setting. The feature consisted solely of 8 schist slabs, set in pairs which formed upright "X's" outlining a rough square (Fig. 4a). The area thus enclosed is almost twice the lateral breadth and more than double the back-to-front width of the butt of Mon. 26. The feature does not resemble other known stela foundations at Quirigua, but since the other two Early Classic monuments (Mons. 20 and 21) may well have been re-set in Late Classic times, this observation is not in itself conclusive. The "stone-lined pit" had no detected contents. While the excavator concludes that this "pit" feature seems unlikely to have been the setting for Mon. 26, more categorical assertations are inappropriate.

A trench across the shorter axis (east-west) of Str. 3C-14 did reveal an intact cache (SD 21) of six plain red, everted-rim bowls, placed lip-to-lip in three pairs along the east wall of a well-built rhyolite masonry chamber (Fig. 4b). The bowls are of the same general type (Seneca Red) as in other structure caches found in the Acropolis (SD 8 and SD 13; *Quirigua Paper No. 6*, this volume) and in the cache associated with Mon. 21 in Group A (SD 16; *Quirigua Paper No. 7*, this volume). Similar vessels are also known from Copan (Longyear 1952:Fig. 39, described as "cache jars"). The most striking differences between SD 21 and similar deposits are the larger size of the vessels, their numbers (three pairs, as opposed to one), and their contents.

The two Quirigua Acropolis caches contained a different variety of Seneca Red vessels from those found in SD 21. One of these caches (SD 8; probably early eighth century A.D.) contained shell, two pieces of worked jadeite, about 1700 small fragments of jadeite and about 100 pieces of pyrite. Another cache (SD 13) is stratigraphically earlier but as yet without a clear calendar age. SD 13 held no artifacts. In the cache from Group A (SD 16), associated with Mon. 21, the vessel is the same typological variety as those in SD 21. SD 16 had been badly disturbed (*Quirigua Paper No. 7*, this volume), but contained at least some shale (possibly a broken backing for a pyrite plaque or mirror; cf. Kidder, Jennings and Shook 1946:126—hereafter cited as KJS), bone fragments and streaks of cinnabar, along with its derivative, liquid mercury. Mercury has also been found in ritual contexts at Kaminaljuyu (KJS:145). Lake Amatitlan (Borhegyi 1959; Brown 1977a), Copan (KJS:145; Maudslay 1889-1902; Gann 1925), and Paraiso (KJS), a site in the Honduran sierra between Copan and Quirigua. In SD 21, the cache from Str. 3C-14, all three vessel pairs contained large amounts of cinnabar and some mercury, as well as bits of pyrite, and the central pair held at least one bird bone and what is possibly an armadillo palate. Most spectacular, however, and probably most informative, were six pieces of worked light green jadeite (formal mineralogical identification has yet to be made) weighing altogether some 5.5 pounds. All were placed in or atop the cinnabar, centered or toward the west edges of their respective vessels (Fig. 4c).

In the central bowl were two large jadeite cobbles (Figs. 5 and 6), roughly trapezoidal in outline, reminiscent of the "half pebbles" illustrated from Tomb B-I at Kaminaljuyu (KJS:Fig. 150). These pieces appear to be unfinished earflares, consistent with Kidder's (KJS:Fig. 50) and Digby's (1972:Fig. 4) reconstruction of the technology used to make jadeite earplugs. Each has a completed central perforation and one has a circular groove surrounding and concentric with its perforation. Under the perforation of each jadeite cobble lay a small carved fist, also in jadeite. Each of the latter portrays a clenched right human hand, resembling quite closely two fragments from the Cenote of Sacrifice at Chichen Itza, pieces described and illustrated by Proskouriakoff (1974:Fig. 11; cf. Rands 1965:Fig. 30 for a similar theme executed in a different style).

A jadeite pendant was found in each of the two smaller, flanking vessel pairs, showing the same motif of a seated figure, perhaps a hunchback, portrayed in right profile (Fig.7). These are similar in motif to a pendant from the Cenote at Chichen Itza (Proskouriakoff 1974:93-94, Fig. 51b, Color Plate III, f), an incised jadeite bead from Kaminaljuyu (KJS:Fig. 47, p. 113, summit cache in Str. A-7), a piece of "black, fine-grained stone" from Asuncion Mita (Kidder 1942:37, Fig. 39b), and possibly finds at Nebaj (Smith and Kidder 1951:Fig. 55a) and an unspecified site in the western highlands of Guatemala (Kidder 1949:Fig 4n). The closest comparison, however, is with four or five of the "incised pebbles" from a cache at Copan (Longyear 1952:Fig. 91, esp. m, n, r, s; cf. Digby 1972:Plates XII,

XIII, esp. XIIa, XIIIa, b and d). These "acrobat" pebbles were associated, in the Copan cache, with another jadeite figurine, a seated person shown in frontal view. It should be noted that Proskouriakoff suggests that many of the Chichen Itza pieces derive from areas to the south of that site.

Reasoning from stratigraphy and ceramic evidence, as well as provisional linkage with Mon. 26, we would tentatively assign SD 21 a date in the late fifth century A.D. Chronological placement of most of the above comparative jadeite materials is compatible with such a date. The one apparent exception would be the Copan set, to which Longyear (1952:107) tentatively ascribed a Full (i.e., Late) Classic date on comparative stylistic grounds. Detailed stylistic and technological studies of Maya jadeworking, however (Kidder 1951; Easby 1961; Digby 1972; Proskouriakoff 1974), would indicate an Early Classic date. It is also worth noting in this regard that the provenience of the Copan Cache is "The Mound of Stela 7," a mound in Copan pueblo which was apparently associated with a great number of carved monuments (Morley 1920). Although Stela 7 itself has a dedicatory date of 9.9.0.0.0 (A.D. 613), four of the other monuments found on the same mound ("nearer" the cache provenience, but admittedly disturbed; Morley 1920) are among the earliest at Copan, ranging in date from 9.1.10.0.0 (A.D. 465) to 9.4.10.0.0 (A.D. 524). The Copan jades too, then, may well be of an age compatible with the date provisionally ascribed to the Quirigua examples.

Analysis of the jadeite pieces as well as other attributes of the cache (arrangement, location and so on) suggest that the cache may be a manifestation of the same ritual complex exemplified by the Esperanza-phase tombs of Kaminaljuyu (see below). This "complex" (some of whose constituent elements will be discussed presently) has a distribution of presently unknown limits, but seems to be a highland Maya trait (cf. Brown 1977a, b). The known distribution of the Seneca Red pottery type (associated with SD 21) is limited to Copan and Quirigua; the known occurrence of mercury is linked to the same region plus the Valley of Guatemala. The carved pendants have analogues that may span the Maya highlands (see above), and Proskouriakoff (1974:95) observes that

Hunchback figures in stone have a wide distribution in Mesoamerica and immediately to the south. In the Maya area they occur only in the highlands.

It seems likely that the Quirigua pieces do represent hunchback figures, but perhaps equally important is their seated posture and portrayal in profile. The excavator suggests that they are effigies for the attendants or servitors found in the Kaminaljuyu tombs. In the Esperanza-phase tombs at Kaminaljuyu, it appears that, ideally, the "principal personage" was accompanied by one or more attendants to either side. All but one of the whole or nearly whole skeletons were buried in a seated posture. The principal occupant in five of the six relevant tombs (A-III, A-IV, A-V, B-I, A-VI, B-II; cf. the Pattern 2/Mode B category in Cheek 1977:Fig. 62, p. 154) had at least one pair of jadeite earplugs. In none of these did an attendant have any earplugs; in a later tomb (B-IV) one did, but these were slate, not jadeite. These interments were originally described by the excavators (KJS), but have been reconsidered and discussed more recently by members of the Pennsylvania State University Kaminaljuyu Project (Cheek 1977; Brown 1977a, b). Attention is drawn to the observation that while the tombs in question include Teotihuacan-imported or -inspired goods among their contents, and while they are associated with structures that copy characteristically Teotihuacan architecture, the overall nature of the tombs themselves seems to reflect a Maya highland pattern or complex (cf. Brown 1977a:299-302, 348, 355, 358; 1977b:426).

Suggested here is that the Early Classic Quirigua cache, SD 21, was a "symbolic tomb." Like the tombs at Kaminaljuyu, the Quirigua cache is dedicatory to a structure. In the cache, the "earflares" represent the principal personage and are accordingly placed in the central position. To either side are the effigy "attendants." (It is possible that the aforementioned Copan cache may have consisted of a "principal personage"—the jadeite figurine shown in frontal view—accompanied by multiple servitors; cf. Longyear 1952:107, Figs. 91k and l-s). Unexplained are, among other things, the two carved fists underlying the "earflares" (not to mention another Copan cache containing multiple frontal-figure jadeite plaques; Longyear 1952:106-107, Fig. 90a, c, e-k; cf. Digby 1972). Nonetheless, the preliminary comparisons seem provocative enough to warrant further study.

All materials in the Quirigua cache showed evidence of intense burning, and discoloration of the east wall of the cache chamber suggests that at least some of the burning took place *in situ*. Burning of the cinnabar in the cache probably explains the presence of the liquid mercury in the bottom of the vessels. The floor of the chamber was an orange clay, underlain by a layer of charcoal, from which a sample was collected for radiocarbon assay.

East of Str. 3C-14, in the original drainage ditch

(ditch M-27 in the BANDEGUA system), debris from a blade-core obsidian workshop was found associated with the crushed rhyolite surface of Platform 3C-1. A controlled-volume sample of debitage from this deposit is being studied by Andrea Gerstle of the University of California, Santa Barbara. Several cores and large blades (cf. Sheets 1975) were recovered in dragline backdirt collections from ditch M-27. These important collections were made between November 1978 and January 1979 by IDAEH employees under the supervision of Enrique Monterroso R. No further such pieces were recovered *in situ* after January and our interpretation is complicated by the fact that ditch M-27 cuts through at least two Late Classic middens as well as Early Classic features. The cited finds, therefore, either add to the Early Classic workshop evidence from Str. 3C-14 or attest to the continuity of obsidian-working in the vicinity.

Along with architectural excavations, a search was instituted to locate more fragments—and therefore more of the well-preserved inscription—of Mon. 26. The principal means used on this search was ground-penetrating radar (see Appendix). With funds made available by the National Geographic Society, Bruce Bevan conducted a radar survey along both banks of ditch M-27 as well as within and around our ongoing excavations. Additional probes into ditch balks were made with a hand-held auger. Unfortunately, as Bevan reports, local soil conditions greatly reduced the ability of the radar to detect any differences or anomalies in subsurface materials, and neither radar nor auger probes located any further stela fragments.

Although we shall never know the exact provenience of Mon. 26, the large earthen platform supporting Mon. 27 and Str. 3C-14, which includes the most elaborate cache found to date at Quirigua, all apparently of Early Classic date, offer strong circumstantial support for the Early Classic stela's having come from on, within or near Platform 3C-1. In combination, these data provide convincing evidence for the presence of an elite center on the Quirigua floodplain in Early Classic times.

Also intriguing is the apparent broad association of Maya highland (and/or specifically southeastern) remains—the cache—with a small, highland-style pedestal sculpture and other fragments of sculpted schist, as well as Peten-affiliated materials (the stela and Tzakol-like polychrome bowls). The juxtaposition suggests a situation perhaps similar to that described by Kenneth Brown for the Valley of Guatemala, as a "port-of-trade" where parties representing equal-status foreign polities could meet on neutral ground (Brown 1977a, b; cf. Rathje and Sabloff 1973; Sabloff and Rathje 1975). In fact, if the analogy is an apt one, the contemporaneity of this Quirigua center with the "Middle Classic" florescence of Kaminaljuyu and its neighbors, Solano and San Antonio Frutal, might be coupled with Brown's (op. cit.) interpretation of Frutal as the "meeting ground" of Peten, Copan-related and general Maya highland groups, to further suggest the possibility that the rise of Quirigua's own importance during this period was directly stimulated by, and linked to, the "profitability" of exchange networks that came together in the Valley of Guatemala. Interestingly enough, a similar interpretation of Quirigua's role in the Early Classic was arrived at independently by Schortman on the basis of his understanding of the lower Motagua valley materials and certain theoretical considerations.

DITCH SURVEY

Cultural Data

The ditches studied in 1979 spanned an area of approximately 475 ha (4.75 km^2 or ca. 1190 acres), 138 ha larger than the area investigated in 1978 (Fig. 7.2). As in 1978, reconnaissance and survey were accomplished by examination within and alongside ditches, with transit mapping over as wide an area as time permitted. Detailed analysis of recorded features is now underway. These features include more than 40 previously-undetected Late Classic constructions as well as Late Classic trash deposits, two ceramic wells (cf. *Quirigua Paper No. 7*, this volume) and a small number of Early Classic features. Except for Str. 3C-14, we have little clear evidence regarding construction technology in Early Classic times; Late Classic construction consisted, as has been noted in previous reports, primarily of cobbles, often as a "veneer" over an earthen core, and sometimes with a final casing of masonry blocks. Because of the nature of the sample, the existence of undetected perishable structures remains a problem (*Quirigua Paper No. 7*, this volume).

While the distribution of Early Classic settlement cannot be specified in any detail, the limits of Late Classic settlement seem secure. The distribution of occupation in the latter period extends at least 150 m west of Group B, the western limit of previously detected settlement. Mon. 19 (moved from Group B to the Quirigua laboratory compound in late 1978) was argued in 1977 to have been a western boundary marker for the Late Classic settlement (*Quirigua Paper No. 6*, this volume; Sharer 1978; Ashmore and Sharer 1978). Despite sporadic construction beyond this point, some of it moderately impressive, we still believe Mon. 19

THE 1979 SEASON

functioned as a symbolic western boundary for the main elite areas of Late Classic Quirigua.

From the ditch survey, Late Classic occupation west of the site-core appears to have been densest within 650 m north of the modern site access road, although a large above-ground mound group exists slightly more than 1 km north of this modern road, about 800 m west of the western boundary of the site-core. Other construction was found up to 300 m south of the site-core, making the extent of revealed settlement slightly greater than 2 km north-south and a similar span east-west, with the Acropolis near the southeast corner of this area. Settlement was not, however, evenly distributed throughout the implied rough 2 km by 2 km square, and it is to the culturally "empty" southwest quarter that we turn now.

Geomorphological Data

In 1977, we hypothesized that the Motagua had a different course in Late Classic times from the one observed today (*Quirigua Paper No. 6*, this volume; Sharer 1978; Ashmore and Sharer 1978). Specifically, the combined evidence of site layout, including individual structure and monument orientations, and of recent documented channel shifts suggested that the Motagua once flowed east just south of Locus 025 (Group B), making a southward bend somewhere west of Str. 1A-3, then flowing south past the Great Plaza, Str. 1A-11, providing a visual climax for river travellers at the Acropolis. The BANDEGUA ditches, excavated in 1978-1979 afforded us the opportunity to test this hypothesis via the deposits exposed in the ditches west of the site-core.

Not surprisingly, the evidence for channel shifts is rather complicated, but there does appear to be support for our contention. Gravel deposits are moderately plentiful in the critical area and the project is particularly grateful to Bruce Bevan for invaluable help in recording these deposits in 1979. The most important problem concerns dating the sand and gravel strata. There are a few instances of sand and gravels being sealed by demonstrably Late Classic construction. But of the deposits west of Loc. 025 (Group B) or south of the modern site-access road, a few have rare, isolated Late Classic/Postclassic artifacts overlying them and most are overlain by no cultural materials at all. It is, of course, possible that some Late Classic (or even Postclassic) features have been destroyed by Postclassic or Post-Conquest northward meanders of the Motagua. But overall, the most parsimonious model for incorporating the observed stratigraphy as well as the horizontal distribution and orientation of precolumbian cultural remains seems to be one which posits the existence of a Late Classic channel in approximately the course predicted. Questions concerning still earlier channels and other river-related events, such as flooding, cannot be surely answered at this time.

VALLEY PROGRAM

The final field season of the Lower Motagua Valley Survey Program, under the direction of Edward Schortman and assisted by Patricia Urban, came to an end in late March 1979. The goals of this last phase of field research were three: to continue the reconnaissance, locating and recording additional sites within the survey area; to map and conduct test excavations at the site of Playitas, one of the largest centers in the survey region (the other two, Las Quebradas and Choco, were tested in 1978); and to undertake analysis of all ceramic materials recovered by the valley program from 1977 to date (see Laboratory Program, below).

RECONNAISSANCE AND SURVEY

As in previous years, work in 1979 was restricted to the south side of the Rio Motagua, concentrating on the zone immediately adjacent to the Espiritu Santo mountains which mark the southern limits of the lower Motagua valley. Eight sites previously unrecorded by this survey were located and described while one which had been visited in the previous year was more fully explored. Of these eight, four are of particular interest.

Quebrada Grande, situated on the floodplain of the Quebrada Grande (a tributary of the Rio Motagua) within the *aldea* of the same name, is ca. 4.25 km NNE of the site of Las Quebradas. During our initial investigations here in 1978 two large plazas surrounded by monumental structures were found and recorded. In 1979 we discovered that this site was much larger than anticipated, consisting of a total of four such plaza groups or quadrangles extending along a rough north-south line for approximately 640 m. Structure heights in these plazas vary from ca. 1 to 7 m with the average height between 3-4 m, while the quadrangles themselves range in size from 60 x 70 m to 65 x 100 m, measured along their exterior sides. An interesting feature of this site area is that, despite the large number of monumental quadrangles, very few subsidiary structures were noted: only 43 structures were discovered at Quebrada Grande, of which 22 were incorporated into the aforementioned plazas. The possibility that many smaller constructions have been buried by the floods of the Quebrada Grande must, of course, be considered.

The site of Bobos, possibly first located by Nowak (1973), is situated on the north bank of the Rio Bobos approximately 200-300 m southeast of the junction of that river with the Rio Motagua. At least 28 structures arranged in small plaza groups and scattered over an area roughly 200-300 m east-west by 600 m north-south were recorded at this site. The structures range in size from ca. 0.5-1.5 m, although most are 1.0 m or less in height. The one exception to this generalization is a group of five structures located in the northern portion of the site which together form a small quadrangle similar in form to those noted at the larger sites. The range of structure sizes in this group is 0.75-2.5 m with an average of about 1.5 m, while the largest structure measures ca. 55 x 27 m along its base. The court enclosed by these structures is 15 x 27 m. The location of Bobos on the floodplain of the river of the same name and so close to the Motagua raises the possibility that many structures here may have been buried by alluvium.

The site of Arapahoe Viejo was originally noted by Heinrich Berlin (1952) and later refound and preliminarily mapped by T. Nowak (1973). We remapped this center in 1979 with compass and tape. Arapahoe Viejo, about 2.75 km southwest of the site of Choco, differs from both Quebrada Grande and Bobos in being situated in the foothills of the Espiritu Santo mountains and not on the valley flats. In total, 22 structures were found covering an area of roughly 310 m northwest-southeast by 80 m northeast-southwest. Structures range in size from 0.1 to 5.5 m in height with the average falling at about 1.5 to 2.5 m. As at Bobos, most of the structures were arranged in loose plaza groups though there was one small enclosed court, ca. 27 x 42 m on the interior, which is similar in form to the larger quadrangles which dominate other valley centers. In addition, two unusual features were noted here. First, a small pecked stone sphere, roughly 0.5 m in diameter, was found situated almost precisely in the center of the court of the small quadrangle. This sphere is reminiscent in form and location of Mons. 2 and 3 found in 1978 at the site of Las Quebradas, Northwest Group (*Quirigua Paper No. 7*, this volume). The second feature consists of three roughly rectangular stone-lined depressions built into the summit of a large platform in the southern portion of the site. These northwest-southeast trending features range in size from 6 x 9 m to 9 x 33 m and are c. 1.5 to 2.0 m deep. Their regularity suggests that they were purposefully constructed, though only a program of excavation could even begin to answer questions of function.

The site of Juyama, straddling the river of the same name, was first reported by Sapper (1895) and was subsequently rediscovered by Nowak (1975). It is located ca. 13 km northeast of Quirigua and ca. 4 km southwest of Arapahoe Viejo. It shares with the latter site an unusual location, being situated along the tops of three roughly north-south trending ridges which extend out from the main body of the Espiritu Santo range toward the Rio Motagua; the ranges are moreover separated from eachother by the fast-flowing Rio Juyama and an unnamed *quebrada*. The site itself consists of, at minimum, 90 structures arranged in groups of 1-11 constructions, though most contain between 3-6. Each of the groups usually contains one larger structure that dominates the rest of the locus. Structure sizes range between 0.5-9.0 m, though most are 1-2 m in height. This site is unusual in that it does not appear to possess the quadrangle arrangement of structures which is so common at other valley sites, although one large group which could not be examined in detail because of the dense overgrowth may have had this form. Juyama is also one of the few sites to produce evidence of pre-Late Classic occupation in the valley outside of Quirigua. A brief series of excavations conducted by Nowak in 1974 recovered possible Protoclassic or Early Classic material from a deep deposit in the northeastern part of the site (Nowak 1975:17-18). Unfortunately, construction associated with this earlier occupation was not clearly exposed by this work. The bulk of the visible structures would appear to be Late Classic in date.

Of the remaining four sites investigated this year, three were found along the west bank of the Rio Chinamita and one of its tributaries where they extend SSE into the Espiritu Santo mountains towards Honduras. Each of these loci occupies a small pocket valley within these mountains and is situated close by the extant trail system which runs from the railhead at the town of Playitas to at least the *aldea* of Mojanales about 2 km from the Honduran border. Of these centers, Mojanales, located within the aforementioned *aldea* ca. 7.5 km from Playitas, would appear to have been the largest, though our rapid survey permitted us time to examine only two plaza groups consisting of 3-4 structures each. The size of these remains, averaging 2-4 m in height, and the reports of many more constructions

THE 1979 SEASON

in the area lead us to believe that this center may have been quite large. A petroglyph is also reported to have been found somewhere in this zone, though we were unable to determine its exact nature and location. The remaining two sites, Los Vitales and Los Limones, were found ca. 4.25 and 3.0 km SSE of Playitas respectively and were quite small. Of the 10-11 structures at Los Vitales and the 5 at Los Limones, most were between 0.5-1.5 m in height.

The last site visited in 1979 was that of La Coroza approximately 1.75 km southwest of Playitas in the low foothills of the Espiritu Santo mountains. Material reported to have come from the area of the La Coroza *aldea* suggested an occupation there prior to the Late Classic, possibly within the Protoclassic or Early Classic. Because of the rarity of such finds within the valley we attempted to locate their source here. Unfortunately, while a small site was found, consisting of three low structures 0.5-1.0 m in height arranged around a rough plaza, the associated sherds suggested a date well within the Late Classic. Ultimately, we were unable to locate the source of the earlier material.

The work this year brings to 19 the total number of sites visited and recorded by the Lower Motagua Valley Survey Project since 1977. While this certainly does not constitute a complete inventory of all sites within the defined survey zone, it does include, we believe, all those of primary interest to this project, i.e. those containing monumental architecture.

PLAYITAS OPERATIONS (Figs. 8 & 9)

The site of Playitas is located on the west bank of the Rio Chinamita at the point where the latter issues from the Espiritu Santo mountains to the south. This floodplain site, situated within and to the north of the *aldea* of the same name, is approximately 4.75 km northeast of Choco and 7.5 km southwest of Las Quebradas, the two large sites excavated in 1978 (*Quirigua Paper No. 7*, this volume). Nowak originally mapped and excavated in at least the southernmost Playitas group in 1974 (Nowak 1975). The purpose of our work in 1979 was to extend the existing map of the southern group to cover the rest of the site and to carry out excavations in at least two of the other three groups.

In total, 185 additional structures were transit-mapped this season, bringing to nearly 200 the number of constructions presently known from this site. It was also discovered that Playitas covers an area approximately 2.65 km north-south by 1.0 km east-west. As at Las Quebradas and Choco, this site is dominated by large court groups or quadrangles, here numbering four, whose court dimensions range in size between 25 x 45 m and 50 x 71 m. These courts are enclosed by large structures whose heights vary from 1.5 to 8.0 m. Around these larger units are scattered, mostly in small groups of 3-8, the other structures which compose the site.

As in the 1978 work, the excavations at Playitas were primarily designed to determine the age of the site; if all of the quadrangles and associated structures dated to the same period; and whether any functionally identifiable work areas could be discovered. To do this, 17 test excavations in all were placed in two of the previously untested groups. These trenches were usually located along the axial lines of the major structures comprising the quadrangles in order to recover not only terminal occupation debris but to penetrate these structures to some degree to recover evidence of earlier construction. In addition to these excavations, 6 trenches were opened in one of the smaller groups surrounding the northernmost quadrangle to determine the basal plan of a presumed domestic structure as well as to penetrate it in search of earlier deposits. One previously untested group was avoided because it had been heavily disturbed by mechanized plowing. Surface collections were made from this area to obtain some idea of its chronological placement.

In general, all of the excavations and surface collections produced essentially the same materials. Even in those cases where sherds were recovered from buried deposits there was no noticeable difference which would suggest temporally distinct occupations. The materials recovered in 1979 all suggest a Late Classic date, approximately contemporaneous with the period of florescence at Quirigua. A possible exception to this generalization came to light when Nowak's excavated material from the southernmost quadrangle was reexamined. While there were some similarities in ceramic types between his excavations and ours, there were also some major differences. Whether these differences can be attributed chronological significance is still under study.

Architectural details were very similar to those noted in 1978 at Las Quebradas and Choco. Unfaced river cobbles overlain by large stone slabs were arranged in long, low and narrow terraces to form the high substructures which are so common at this site. Finds of pieces of adobe from excavations suggest that this material may have functioned prominently in superstructure construction. No clear evidence of functional differentiation was uncovered, though the possibility that an obsidian blade workshop was found in the area of the peripheral structure excavated is presently under study.

LABORATORY PROGRAM

1979 saw the completion of pottery studies in the field laboratory. This work included the final type-variety and form assessments of excavated and surface lots, definition of several new type-variety and form units, and the refinement of the ceramic descriptions. The 1979 work was carried out by Sharer, Ashmore, Schortman and Urban. Assessments of pottery from the site-periphery resulted in a firmer and more complete definition of the Early Classic ceramic complex at Quirigua. A total of 140 pottery lots were examined from site-core or site-periphery proveniences, though the bulk of the laboratory activity was focused upon the Valley Program.

VALLEY PROGRAM

Approximately 15,000 sherds from the Valley Program were analyzed during the 1979 season. Most derived from the three excavated sites of Las Quebradas, Choco and Playitas, though a sizeable surface collection from the site of Comanche Farm also contributed to this number. The remainder of the sherds came from small surface collections obtained from various valley sites. All of these sherds were classified according to a type-variety system that included types and forms derived from Quirigua along with some newly created taxa. In addition to this study, those sherds recovered by Nowak from his Playitas excavations for which we had definite provenience data were re-examined and compared to the types created this year. Finally, because of the previously noted unusual nature of Juyama, Nowak's material from his excavations there were also briefly reviewed.

While it is still too early to supply precise results, the most striking feature of this analysis is the similarity in pottery types among the different valley sites. Las Quebradas, Choco, Playitas and, to a certain extent, Comanche Farm all produced material which, although differing in details from that found at Quirigua, could easily be related to the last phases of occupation at that site. Outside of the aforementioned distinctiveness of Nowak's Playitas material, little evidence suggestive of any considerable time depth was noted among the major sites in the lower Motagua valley, with one exception. The sherds from the deep deposit uncovered by Nowak at Juyama constituted quite a strikingly different array of ceramics, including Usulutan-decorated sherds, suggestive of a Protoclassic or Early Classic date. This evidence, taken together with collections containing similar material made by Nowak in irrigation ditches in the Motagua floodplain northwest of Arapahoe Viejo, as well as the sherds reported to have come from La Coroza, all suggest that there definitely was a pre-Late Classic occupation in the survey area, but we are unable at this time to establish the location of these finds in a more precise manner.

COMPARISONS WITH OTHER SOUTHEAST MAYA SITES

Following the field studies, discussions were held with Dr. G. R. Willey of Harvard University, representing the recently completed Copan Valley Project, as to how to facilitate meaningful ceramic comparisons between Quirigua and Copan. Later the same issue was raised with investigators from several other projects currently working with pottery from sites in the southeastern Maya area, including Copan proper (Proyecto Copan) and the Zapotitan Basin of El Salvador (Proyecto Protoclasico). Two complementary approaches were agreed upon: first, to undertake direct side-by-side comparisons of pottery samples from southeastern sites; and, second, following the lead of the Copan Valley Project, to attempt to identify pottery manufacturing zones from neutron activation analysis of samples from these same sites.

At Willey's invitation, the first in a series of ceramic conferences was held at the Peabody Museum, Harvard University in mid-April 1979, at which pottery samples from Quirigua were compared with samples from the Copan valley, as well as examples from Chalchuapa, El Salvador. In mid-June, 1979, the second conference was held at the University Museum, University of Pennsylvania, to continue and expand these comparisons. Because of the success of these meetings, further conferences are planned involving larger samples from additional sites. At the same time, the second component of these studies is being pursued in conjunction with the Lowland Maya Ceramic Survey under the direction of Dr. Ronald Bishop and sponsored by the Research Laboratory, Museum of Fine Arts, Boston, in collaboration with the Brookhaven National Laboratory. Samples of Quirigua pottery have been submitted to Brookhaven for neutron activation analysis and are compared with the results being obtained by the same technique from Copan and other southeastern Maya sites. The first results of these comparitive studies will be reported in the near future.

THE 1979 SEASON

REFERENCES CITED

Ashmore, W. and R. J. Sharer
    1978   Excavations at Quirigua, Guatemala: The Ascent of an Elite Maya Center. *Archaeology* 31 (6): 10-19.

Berlin, H.
    1952   Novedades Arqueologicas. *Antropologia e Historia de Guatemala* 4 (2): 41-46.

Borhegyi, S. F. de
    1959   Underwater Archaeology in the Maya Highlands. *Scientific American* 200 (3): 100-113.

Brown, K. L.
    1977a   The Valley of Guatemala: A Highland Port of Trade. *Teotihuacan and Kaminaljuyu: A Study in Prehistoric Culture Contact*. W. T. Sanders and J. W. Michels, eds., pp.205-395. University Park: The Pennsylvania State University Press.

    1977b   Toward a Systematic Explanation of Culture Change within the Middle Classic Period of the Valley of Guatemala. *Teotihuacan and Kaminaljuyu: A Study of Prehistoric Culture Contact*. W. T. Sanders and J. W. Michels, eds., pp. 411-440. University Park: The Pennsylvania State University Press.

Cheek, C. D.
    1977   Excavations at the Palangana and the Acropolis, Kaminaljuyu. *Teotihuacan and Kaminaljuyu: A Study in Prehistoric Culture Contact*. W. T. Sanders and J. W. Michels, eds., pp. 1-204. University Park: The Pennsylvania State University Press.

Coe, W. R. and R. J. Sharer
    1979   The Quirigua Project: 1975 Season. *Quirigua Reports* I (Paper No. 2). Museum Monographs, No. 37. Philadelphia: University Museum.

Digby, A.
    1972   *Maya Jades*. Revised ed. London: British Museum.

Easby, E. K.
    1961   The Squier Jades from Tonina, Chiapas. *Essays in Pre-Columbian Art and Archaeology*. S. K. Lothrop et. al., pp. 60-80. Cambridge Mass.: Harvard University Press.

Gann, T. W. F.
    1925   Maya Jades. *21st International Congress of Americanists, Proceedings*: 273-282.

Kidder, A.V.
    1942   Archaeological Specimens from Yucatan and Guatemala. *Notes on Middle American Archaeology and Ethnology* I (No. 9): 35-40. Carnegie Institution of Washington.

    1949   Jades from Guatemala. *Notes on Middle American Archaeology and Ethnology*. IV (No. 91): 1-8. Carnegie Institution of Washington.

    1951   Artifacts. *Excavations at Nebaj, Guatemala*. A.L. Smith and A. V. Kidder, pp. 32-76. Carnegie Institution of Washington, Publication 594, Washington, D. C.

Kidder, A. V., J. D. Jennings and E. M. Shook
    1946   *Excavations at Kaminaljuyu, Guatemala*. Carnegie Institution of Washington, Publication 561, Washington, D. C.

Longyear, J. M., III
    1952   *Copan Ceramics: A Study of Southeastern Maya Pottery*. Carnegie Institution of Washington, Publication 597, Washington, D. C.

Maudslay, A. P.
    1889-
    1902   *Archaeology. Biologia Centrali-Americana*. 5 vols. London: Porter.

QUIRIGUA REPORTS

Morley, S. G.
    1920   *The Inscriptions at Copan.* Carnegie Institution of Washington, Publication 219, Washington, D.C.
    1935   *Guide Book to the Ruins of Quirigua.* Carnegie Institution of Washington, Supplementary Publication 16, Washington, D. C.
    1937-38   *The Inscriptions of Peten.* 5 vols. Carnegie Institution of Washington, Publication 437, Washington, D.C.

Nowak, T. R.
    1973   The Lower Motagua Valley Survey Project: First Preliminary Report. Manuscript, American Section, University Museum, University of Pennsylvania.
    1975   Prehistoric Settlement and Interaction Networks in the Lower Motagua Valley, Guatemala: A Regional Analysis. Manuscript, American Section, University Museum, University of Pennsylvania.

Proskouriakoff, T.
    1974   *Jades from the Cenote of Sacrifice, Chichen Itza, Yucatan.* Memoirs of the Peabody Museum of Archaeology and Ethnology, Vol. 10, No. 1. Cambridge Mass.: Harvard University.

Rands, R. L.
    1965   Jades of the Maya Lowlands. *Handbook of Middle American Indians* 3: 561-580.

Rathje, W. L. and J. A. Sabloff
    1973   Ancient Maya Commercial Systems: A Research Design for the Island of Cozumel, Mexico. *World Archaeology* 5(2): 221-231.

Sabloff, J. A. and W. L. Rathje
    1975   *Changing Pre-Columbian Commercial Systems. The 1972-1973 Seasons at Cozumel, Mexico.* Monographs of the Peabody Museum, No. 3, Cambridge, Mass.: Harvard University.

Sapper, K.
    1895   Altindianische ansiedlungen in Guatemala und Chiapas *Katalog einer Sammlung von Idolem, Fetischen und Priesterlichen Ausruestungsgegenstaenden derZuni-Oder Ashuir Indianer von Neu Mexiko.*J. H. Cushing. pp. 13-20.

Sharer, R. J.
    1978   Archaeology and History at Quirigua, Guatemala. *Journal of Field Archaeology* 5: 51-70.

Sharer, R. J., C. Jones, W. Ashmore and E. M. Schortman
    1979   The Quirigua Project: 1976 Season. *Quirigua Reports* I (Paper No. 5). Museum Monographs, No. 37. Philadelphia: University Museum.

Sheets, P. D.
    1975   Behavioral Analysis and the Structure of a Prehistoric Industry. *Current Anthropology* 16: 369-391.

Smith, A. L. and A. V. Kidder
    1951   *Excavations at Nebaj, Guatemala.* Carnegie Institution of Washington, Publication 594, Washington, D. C.

THE 1979 SEASON

APPENDIX

GROUND-PENETRATING RADAR AT QUIRIGUA

by Bruce Bevan

During the 1979 season at Quirigua, a ground-penetrating radar was employed in the search for the missing fragments of a schist stela (Mon. 26, see *Quirigua Paper No.6*, this volume), about two-thirds of which was found in drag-line ditch M-27 (Quirigua Farm, BANDEGUA). This search was unsuccessful, primarily because the unexpectedly high attenuation of the soil at the site did not allow radar echoes to be received from deep enough underground. The unfound fragment is believed to lie between 2 and 3 m below ground surface; reliable radar returns were not received from below about 1 m. However, in the Great Plaza area of the site-core, the buried cobble platform 1A-1 (*Quirigua Paper No. 6*, this volume) is within this detection range and its undulations relative to the present land surface could be mapped.

The ground-penetrating radar is analogous to airborne radar. Rather than having its signal beamed into the air, it is transmitted into the earth; underground discontinuities such as stone or metal cause a fraction of the radar pulse to be reflected back to the receiver. In operation, the radar antenna, mounted on a low cart, is slowly pulled along the ground. An electrical cable connects this antenna to bulky recording and display instruments which remain at a fixed point. The graphic display illustrates the buried structures as a profile map made along the line of traverse of the radar antenna. An example of one of these profiles is shown in Fig. 10.

In Fig. 10, the horizontal axis represents a traverse distance of 50 m; calibration of the vertical axis indicates that the bottom of this profile marks a depth of about 1.5 m. There is a large horizontal compression of this profile. The undulations of the black bands reveal several buried structures, all less than about 1 m deep.

This profile results from a traverse made up the bottom of shallow dragline excavations just west of ditch M-27. Shortly before this traverse was made, several schist slabs were found at the 17 m point along the traverse; these were temporarily covered again with earth. The radar profile indicates their position by the dip in the black bands near the surface at this point. Later, deeper, excavation along this trench revealed several other features which appear on the radar profile. A very rough sketch of the location of these is enclosed (Fig. 11); this interpretation profile is made at the same horizontal compression and scale as the radar profile. Correlation between these figures indicates that the dipping upper surface of the structure (Str. 3C-14) on the mound Platform 3C-1) is detectable at the 12 m point along the traverse. It appears that the stairs on the north side of the structure are also detectable, although only faintly. The sand lens farther north yielded a very strong echo; it is evidently natural, although possibly related to stream flow sedimentation of the structure.

The radar was later operated at it's greatest amplification for maximum detection of deeper echoes. This made the antenna very sensitive to surface roughness. A traverse made in the Great Plaza near Mon. 7 indicated a deep, and therefore interesting, echo. This, however, proved to be spurious, since a brief test excavation on the east side of Mon. 7 failed to reveal a source for the echo. Later work indicated the likelihood that this echo was caused by the antenna lifting slightly off the ground as it was pulled over a concavity.

While ground-penetrating radar was unsuccessful at Quirigua, it has been successful at many other archaeological sites, locating stone and earth structures which cannot be detected with any other geophysical instruments. This test at Quirigua has, however, furnished a good calibration reference for radar attenuation. Simple electrical tests done before a survey at a site can now more accurately predict the success of a subsequent radar survey.

Financial support from the National Geographic Society made this geophysical survey possible, and their help is gratefully acknowledged.

Figure 8.1. Pulse radar unit in use at Quirigua.
    a. Radar antenna unit immediately east of Monument 7 (Monument 5 in background).
    b. Pulse radar system in use during the excavation of Str. 3C-14.

Figure 8.2. Excavation immediately west of Str. 1A-11 (background), showing the western edge of the cobble-filled plaza and *in situ* monumental sandstone blocks on its surface overlooking the silt-filled basin in the foreground.

Figure 8.3. Excavations at the discovery site of Monument 26.
a. Quirigua Monument 27, originally exposed in the west slope of the drainage ditch, as first seen by project staff in 1979. The schist slab rests on the crushed rhyolite surface Pl. 3C-1.
b. Project-commissioned dragline excavation at Pl. 3C-1 and Str. 3C-14, view to the southeast. Workmen in commercial ditch, left, are standing by an area of dense obsidian blade-manufacturing debris associated with the surface of Pl. 3C-1.
c. Str. 3C-14, partially cleared, from the northwest, showing ruined rhyolite-block construction and, on the summit, schist slabs under which SD 21 was found.

Figure 8.4. Excavation of Str. 3C-14.
    a. Slab-lined pit west of Str. 3C-14, viewed from the east after clearing. Successive surfaces of Pl. 3C-1 can be seen in excavated section.
    b. Cache vessels of SD 21 (Str. 3C-14), in places within rhyolite-block chamber. View from the west.
    c. SD 21 partially reassembled in Project laboratory compound, showing position of jadeite before removal from vessels.

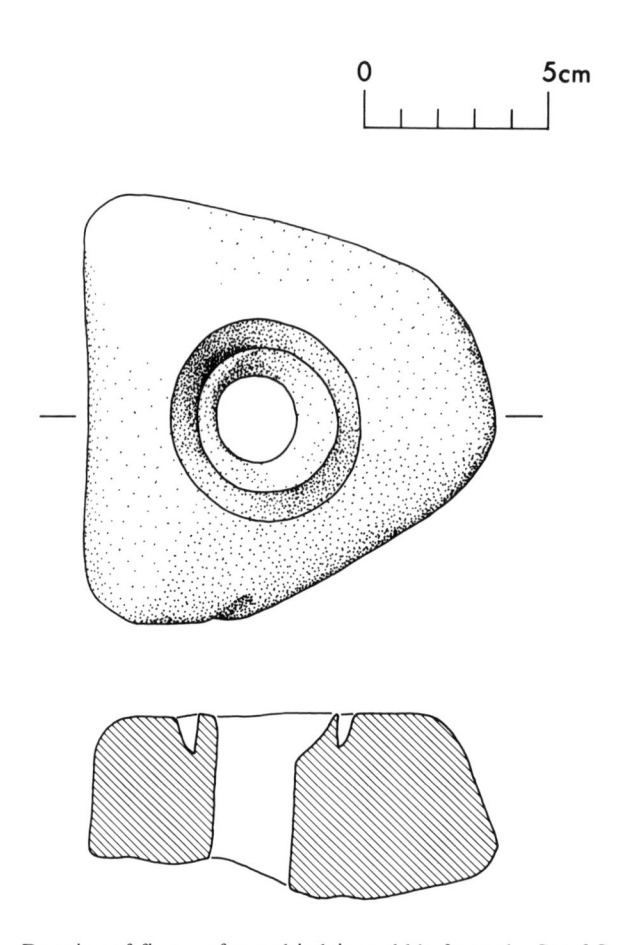

Figure 8.5. Drawing of first perforated jadeite cobble from the Str. 3C-14 cache.

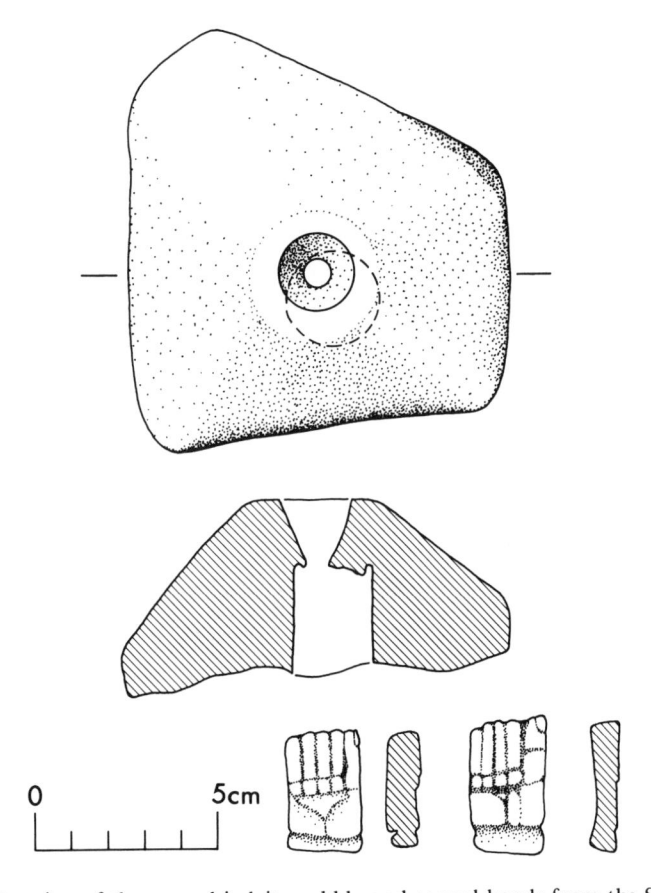

Figure 8.6. Drawing of the second jadeite cobble and carved hands from the Str. 3C-14 cache.

73

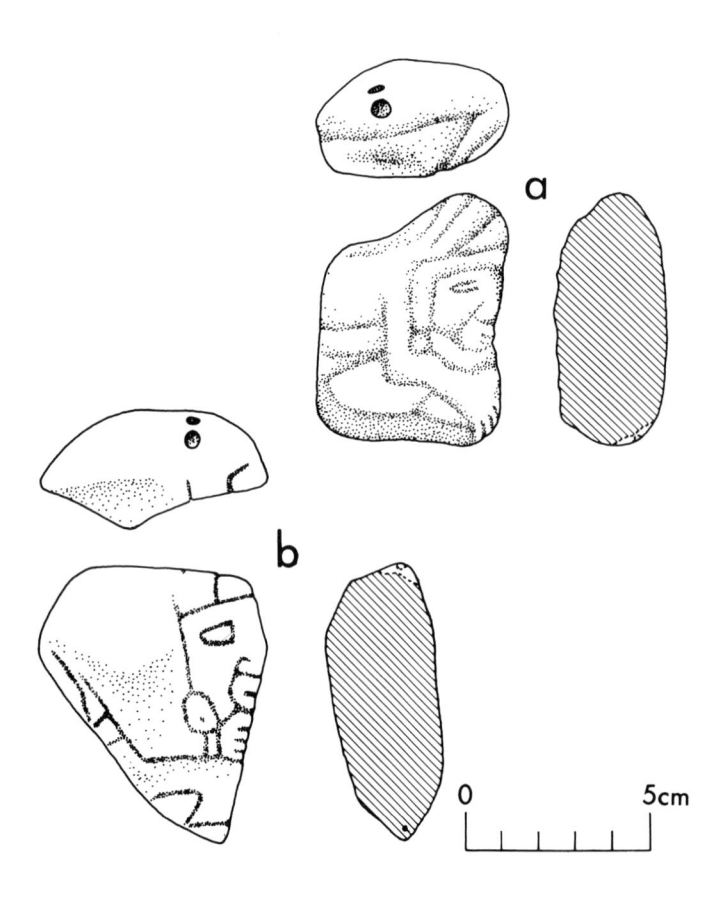

Figure 8.7. Jadeite figures from the Str. 3C-14 cache.

Figure 8.8. Playitas Group I as viewed from the air; the outlines of the three adjoining quadrangles which comprise the architectural core of this group are visible in this photograph. View from the southeast.

Figure 8.9. Excavations at Playitas.
    a. Str. 200-23, Playitas, showing the step-terrace mode of construction in section. View from the east.
    b. Str. 200-16, eastern basal wall, viewed from the east, after it had been cleared and partially cut through.

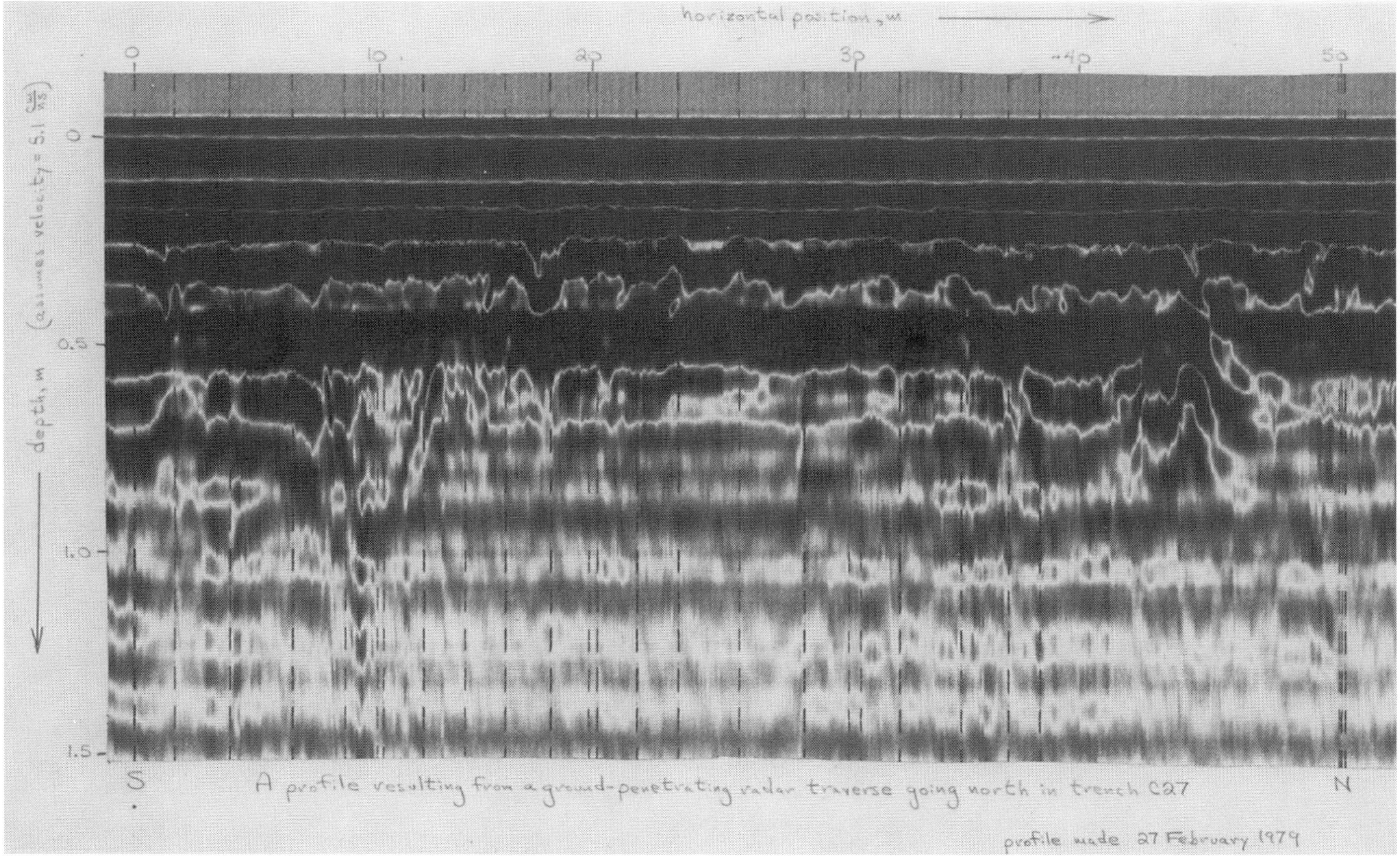

Figure 8.10. Ground-penetrating radar profile from traverse over Str. 3C-14 and its supporting platform.

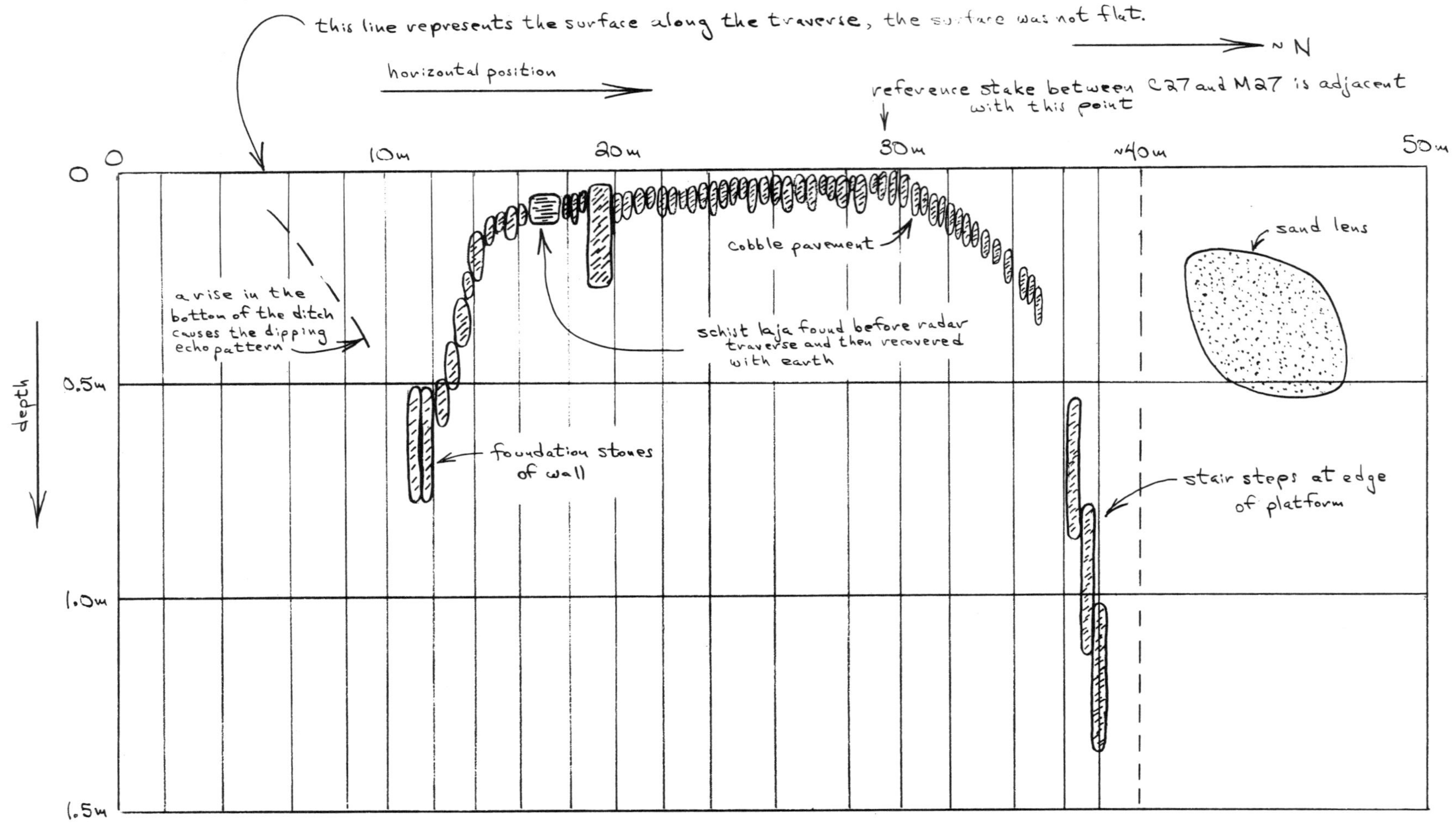

Figure 8.11   Interpretation of the radar profile in Figure 8.10.

PAPER NO. 9

A MAGNETIC SURVEY AT QUIRIGUA

by
Bruce Bevan

INTRODUCTION

During March of the 1976 season, a magnetic survey was undertaken at Quirigua which covered territory both within and without the park boundaries. Due to the magnetic properties of much of the site's cobble construction fill, recognized as anomalies on magnetic maps, it was hoped that such a survey would aid in the detection of buried features. This report discusses the 1976 survey and covers the methods and results of the investigation.

The idea for this survey originated with Robert Sharer and Wendy Ashmore. Maintenance was provided by the Quirigua Project, and travel by Ashmore's National Science Foundation grant BNS76-03283. My salary and part of the upkeep of the magnetometers was provided by NSF grant SOC-75-04203.

THE SURVEY

Equipment

A cesium magnetometer was used to make point-by-point measurements of the total intensity of the earth's magnetic field. The Varian Associates cesium sensor model 49-544 was combined with their digital readout model 49-116. Rechargeable batteries furnished the power for the equipment.

Field Operations

Rectangular grids, usually 30 m square, were staked at their four corners and cloth tape measures were run along two parallel sides. A rope, marked at one meter intervals with paint and black tape, was laid perpendicular to the tapes to define each line of traverse. A serpentine pattern three measurements wide was centered on the rope for reference.

The cesium sensor staff was carried by one individual over this traverse pattern, stopping at each measurement point momentarily for a magnetic reading. A short coaxial cable connected the sensor to the digital readout carried by another individual. This person carried the batteries in a harness and was responsible for recording the magnetic intensity values in a notebook. Later in the survey another person was added to help speed the survey by keeping the coaxial cables from snagging and by carrying the batteries.

Total magnetic field intensity was measured and recorded in gammas (γ) which are equivalent to the S.I. units nanotesla (nT). A difference magnetometer arrangement was not used to correct for diurnal fluctuations since the temporal change in the magnetic field was small. For the same reason, repetitive measurements at one reference station were not made since correction was unnecessary. However, as magnetic maps were measured on different days, slow changes in the earth's magnetic field, over large areas, did cause discontinuities in the values of magnetic intensity between any two adjacent grids. While the trend of the contour lines can be followed from grid to grid, the numerical match can be improved by adding or subtracting a constant value to all numbers on one grid of an adjacent pair.

The magnetic survey grids were plotted using a Suunto compass and cloth tape. Wooden stakes marked the corners of all the grids exterior to the plaza. Their tops and bottoms were painted red and their location descriptions were written on the middle band. On the east traverse, Grids 3-9, and the northwest cluster, Grids 20-22 and 25, stakes were left at each 30 m point along the lines. The position of these stakes is only accurate to about 1% (points 100 m apart on the grids may have a measurement error of 1 m). This level of accuracy was judged sufficient for the preliminary survey, although more precise location of the stakes may be necessary later.

The crew was composed of Bruce Bevan (MASCA, University Museum) with help from Efrain Hernandes and Arturo Velazquez.

ANALYTIC PROCEDURES

The matrix of point magnetic measurements was contoured with isointensity lines to show the patterns of changes in the magnetic field. Some materials, iron in particular, are good magnetic "conductors": the natural magnetic field originating deep within the earth is somewhat concentrated by them causing a magnetic pattern above a small object (Fig. 2). The observed "dipole" pattern is caused by the addition and subtraction of the magnetic field by the two "poles" of the magnetic material. Many archaeological materials also contain iron; most detectable is the mineral magnetite in clays and rocks. Fired clays and many dark igneous rocks (called basic or mafic) have an added effect in that the magnetite has remnant magnetization and is a permanent magnet. A single fired brick or basalt stone will give a magnetic anomaly like that shown in Fig. 2, but because it is a permanent magnet the dipole low may not be north of the high if the item has been moved from its place of magnetization. In a cluster of magnetic stones or bricks random orientation of the many small magnets can cause their permanent magnet effects to be neutralized, leaving only the magnetic "conductor" effect (also called induced magnetization); this effect can still be quite strong.

The total magnetic intensity at the site is about $41{,}400\gamma$. Typical changes from this average were only several tens of gammas. To simplify recording in the field, only changes from 41,400 were usually entered in the notebooks; for example, the number 43 indicates 41,443, while 387 indicates 41,387.

The magnetic properties of a pair of stones were measured; these two magnetic rocks were from the test pit in Grid 2 at coordinates SW 14, SE 10 (see Fig. 1). These properties were measured by rotating the rocks at a fixed distance from the sensor and noting the maximum and minimum values of magnetic intensity.

One stone was an unidentified black metamorphic cobble with a wavy and striated fracture surface on its almost-platey interior crystallites. Inside, it had a vitreous luster while the weathered exterior rind (ca. 2 mm thick) was a brownish cream color. The induced magnetic moment for this rock was about zero while the remnant component was about $0.3\gamma \cdot m^3/\text{liter}$.

The other magnetic stone was an igneous rock (between basalt and gabbro in texture) composed apparently of magnetite, olivine and feldspar phenocrysts (ca. 4 mm in diameter). The phenocrysts weathered to give an external surface which was pitted and bluish-grey in color. The magnetic properties were:

$$\text{Mr (remanant moment)} \sim 0.6 \frac{\gamma_6 m^3}{\text{liter}}$$

$$\text{Mi (induced moment)} \sim 0.06 \frac{\gamma_6 m^3}{\text{liter}}$$

These magnetic moment values can be used to estimate the quantity of material causing an anomaly with the formula:

$$V = \frac{Ad^3}{M} = \text{volume of source of anomaly}$$

where A = anomaly amplitude, the maximum change in the field relative to the surrounding (background) field.

Example:

high → 527

                        431 ← actually 41,431

low → 375   ← surrounding background

anomaly amplitude = 527-431 = 96γ

MAGNETIC SURVEY

d = estimated depth to source = h+U; note that d is cubed
   h = sensor height ca. 0.75 m above ground
   U = underground depth, often ca. 1 m here

M = magnetic moment, Mi, or Mi+Mr as appropriate
   For an *in situ* magnetized object (e.g. kiln) choose Mi+Mr
   For a cluster of magnetic stones choose Mi (Mr cancels out)

For a cluster of igneous stones as measured above, the formula is:

$$V = \frac{A(0.75+1.0)^3}{0.06}$$

for object 1 m underground
~90A in liters (a typical cobble is 0.5-1.0 liter in volume)

This implies that a 50γ anomaly might be caused by about 450-900 magnetic cobbles, which seems reasonable. However, there will be considerable variability in the magnetic moments between rocks. Another factor is the change with weathering: there are indications that some weathered rocks might be more magnetic than their originals.

GRID ANALYSIS

Causeway Area

Early in the season a posthole dug about 300 m northwest of the plaza area revealed parts of three stones at a depth of approximately 1 m (the usual thickness of river alluvium accumulated on the site in the last 1100 years). This evidence combined with a literary reference to a causeway uncovered north of the plaza (Villa Rojas 1934) led Wendy Ashmore to suggest that the posthole stones did indicate this feature. A magnetic map was made of the area around the posthole (Grid 2, Fig. 3); it revealed a strong dipole anomaly at the edge of the posthole. This anomaly had a suggested east-west orientation (and a weaker magnetic high and low along the same line) which differs from the orientation given by Villa Rojas.

A 2 by 2 m test pit on the southwest side of Grid 2 revealed cut blocks of schist (with average dimensions of c. 0.5 m) at a depth of about 1 m. While these large blocks are essentially nonmagnetic, they are underlain by a stratum ca. 0.35 m thick of river-rounded cobbles, averaging 15 cm in diameter. Many of these cobbles are nonmagnetic quartz or sandstone, but possibly 20-40% are highly magnetic (a mafic igneous rock with a pitted bluish-grey exterior is particularly magnetic). It is easy to identify individual magnetic cobbles since they have a high enough magnetite content that a small magnet dangling from a string will stick to them slightly or strongly.

A later test pit dug toward the center of the grid showed the continuation of the stone blocks and cobbles in the predicted east-west direction. Both pits revealed only the southern side of the line of stones; the anomalies suggest a width of around 2.5 to 4.0 m.

Five additional grids were later made following the line of the possible causeway. A length of about 90 m has been traced and the anomalous patterns are summarized in Fig. 3. Further testing to the west is difficult because of the thick concentration of modern iron refuse for a distance of several hundred meters. To the east, in Grid 15, the course of the anomaly becomes more ambiguous. A very pronounced and uniform magnetic high is directed at an angle of about 74°; since the general trend of the anomaly is 95°, this either implies a change in direction or that this major anomaly in Grid 15 does not indicate the causeway. While slightly undulating terrain in the region of the anomaly indicates the possibility of a soil change (perhaps a natural drainage channel), this anomaly should be tested by excavation. A uniformly diffuse, but moderately weak, magnetic source can give a magnetic high like this without a magnetic low being associated with it; the lineament through Grid 26 is almost identical to that in Grid 15. The southwest side of Grid 14 is disturbed by iron refuse (?) in a modern drainage ditch which obliterates the course of the anomaly there. The anomaly might be indicated by the spotty dipoles in Grids 14 and 15. The northwest edge of Grids 10 and 13 may be disturbed by modern iron from the fence and railroad.

Northwest Cluster

Grids 20 through 22 and also 25 extend between Loc. 004 and Loc. 006. The line of the traverse, 260° (magnetic), begins at the former and leads toward the latter.

An interesting magnetic low is in front of the ballcourt (Loc. 004) at N 8 W 10. The strong magnetic lineament centered at N 15 W 228 is probably due to a small or highly rusted iron pipe buried at a shallow depth (<0.5 m).

The most interesting features in this area are two magnetic lineaments. One magnetic high goes from S 28

W 60 to N 8 W 160. Since this lineament is along the side of a slight slope (to the south, to a broad, possibly natural, drainage ditch) the likelihood of a soil change causing the anomaly must be considered. The soil in the area of these grids is extremely hard; penetration tests with a knife blade indicated differences in soil hardness but no correlation with this anomaly. The other magnetic high, from N 6 W 88 to N 26 W 102 is bounded on the east by a magnetic low. It is on more level ground and is less likely to be due to changes in soil. A strong dipole on its northern end is near a small mound which could be recent. This lineament is directed at an angle of about 135°, roughly toward the main site, while the longer lineament is directed at about 105° which is neither toward the main site nor toward the Grid 2 "causeway" lineament.

A weaker lineament located at N 6 W 204 is less certain. A building was probably located at N 18 W 140 and the magnetic high at N 30 W 154 is probably related and unimportant.

Plaza Area

A series of separate test pits had already defined the position of a sandstone terrace wall near the Acropolis. A magnetic grid between two pits (Grid 23) showed a tendency for a magnetic low (expected with nonmagnetic rock in slightly magnetic soil) to be along the interpolated line of the terrace wall. However, the pattern is much too weak to be a reliable indicator.

Grids 24 and 27 attempted to locate the edge of the thick cobble fill which underlies the plaza. In neither grid were definite patterns found, and the magnetic gradient in Grid 27 going west from N 143 E 29 is the only possible indicator. Four other grids (16-19) were also unsuccessful. In these grids the line of dipoles going north from S 165 E 62 might be interesting to test. Excavation of the mound bisected by Grids 17 and 19 was begun after the survey was completed. The sandstone ledge found to the west of that mound is not indicated on the maps; however, the anomaly at S 39 E 74 is on the edge of a test pit there. The magnetic high at S 109 E 96 could be much like the "causeway," a bed of magnetic cobbles.

East Traverse

Grids 3 through 9 extend east from the park nearly to the canal. A sizeable number of drainage ditches trend northeast-southwest through the grids and many of them are apparently thick with iron refuse, for strong magnetic clustered lineaments follow them. This region was grazed by cattle at the time of this study but formerly was planted with bananas, and over the years many machinery parts were likely to have been lost in the fields; several iron fragments found within the grid appear to be exhaust pipes, and near E 472 an apparent railroad rail is at the surface.

The presence of these many magnetic disturbances makes the search for small buried living mounds in this area quite difficult, although a good accumulation of magnetic cobbles only one meter underground might still be detectable.

Miscellaneous Grids

Grids 11 and 12 were mapped to try to extend the "causeway" alignment across the railroad tracks; but the high concentration of modern iron there makes interpretation of the maps impossible.

Grid 1 was over a known cobble mound; and while some structure within the mound might be indicated, topographic relief is the primary cause of the major anomaly.

SUMMARY

The cobble fill underlying some archaeological structures is partly composed of magnetic stones; a concentration of these stones gives a recognizable and anomalous pattern in magnetic maps. In contrast, the monuments at the site are composed of sandstone which has no magnetic distinctions with respect to the surrounding soil. The masonry blocks which have been squared for construction are often schist or marble or other nonmagnetic rock and are also undetectable. This study was undertaken in 1976 in hopes that the magnetic properties of the fill would lead to the disclosure of features not visible on the surface.

Very distinct magnetic lineaments were found in the grids northwest of the site; while they may be caused by soil changes, they are worthy of test excavation.

The drainage ditches in the fields are usually thick with intense magnetic anomalies, probably caused by recent iron refuse. Many discarded railroad rails and thin iron pipes are found in some areas and iron pipes for watering cattle are found in others. However, some anomalies are distinctly different from the ones caused by modern iron; one of these different anomalies, upon excavation, proved to be a structure of prehistoric origin (the "causeway") and others might merit further testing.

MAGNETIC SURVEY

REFERENCES CITED

Villa Rojas, A.
   1934   *The Yaxuna-Coba Causeway.* Carnegie Institution of Washington, Publication 436, Contribution 9, Washington, D. C.

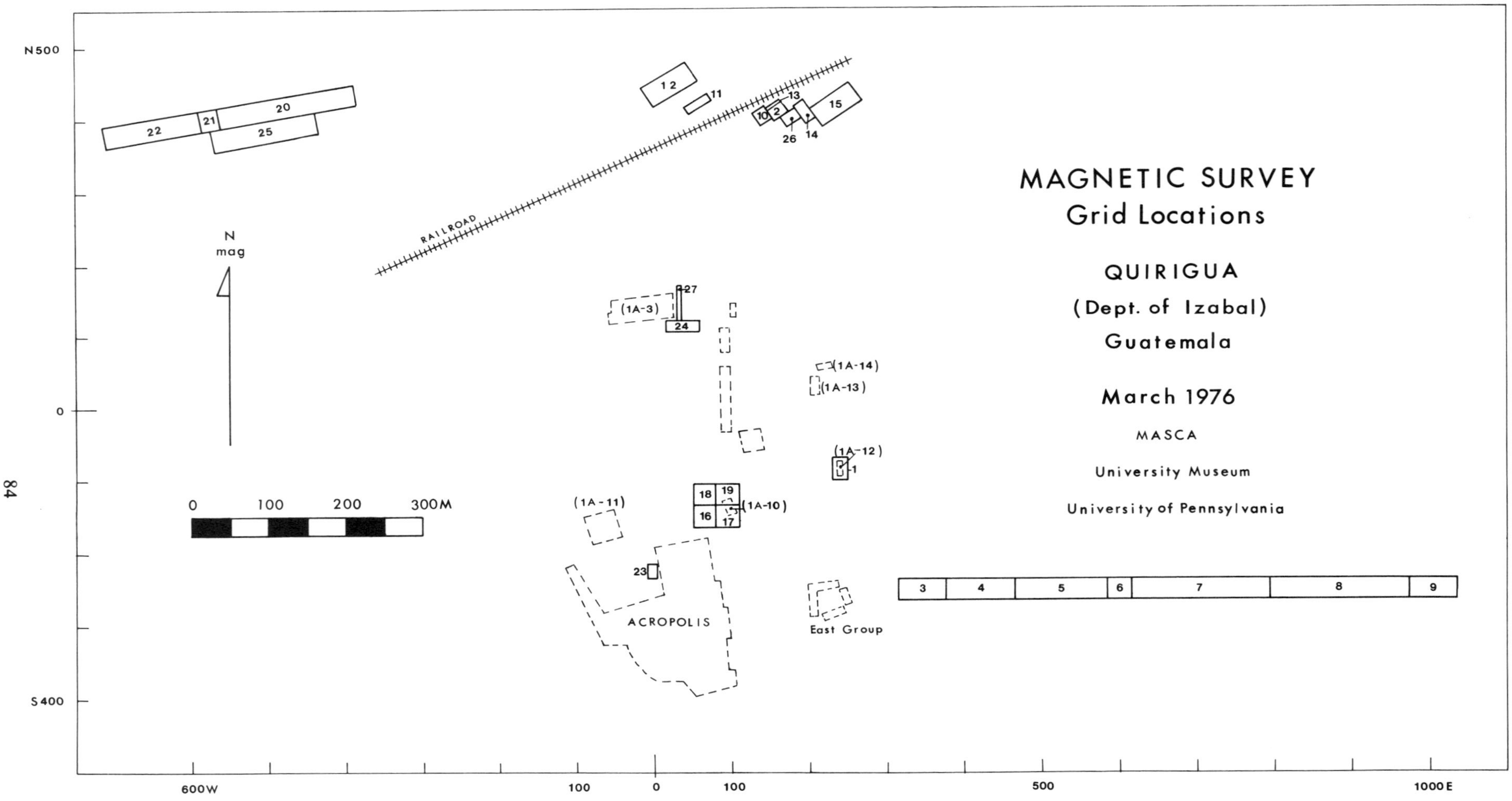

Figure 9.1.

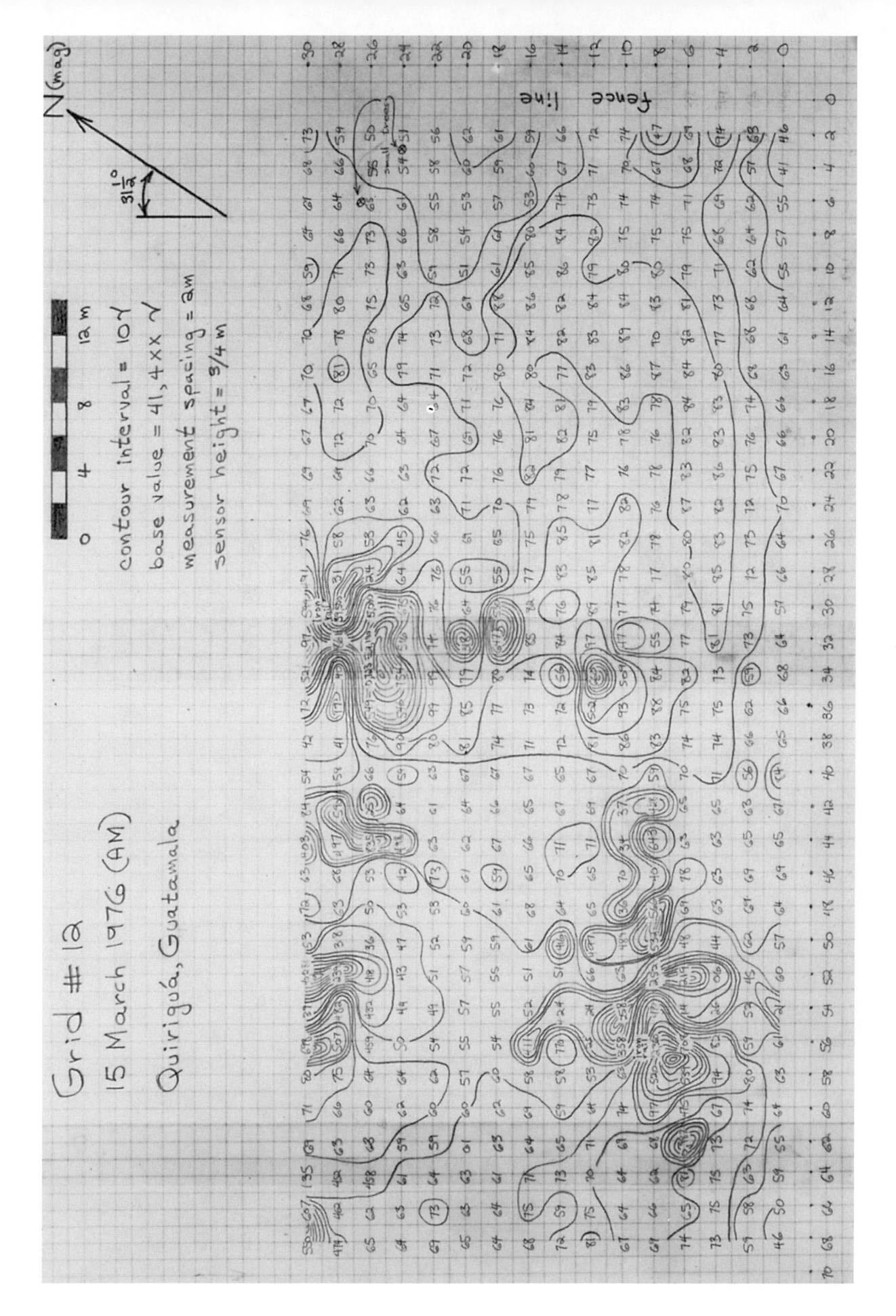

Figure 9.2. Magnetic contour map of Grid 12 (see Figure 9.1 for location).

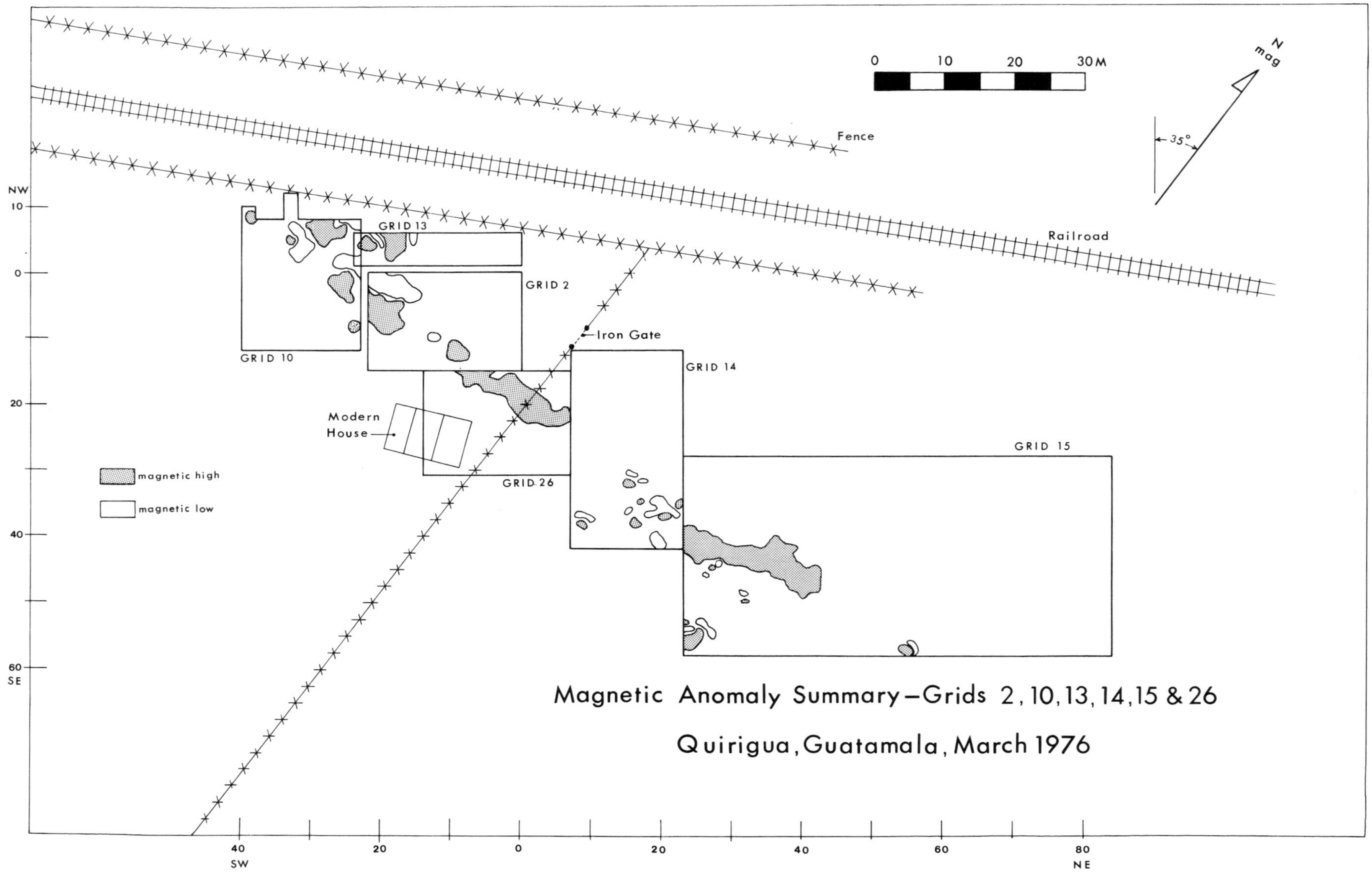

Figure 9.3. Summary of magnetic anomaly northeast of the main group (see Figure 9.1 for location).

PAPER NO. 10

GUATEMALAN OBSIDIAN: A PRELIMINARY STUDY OF SOURCES AND QUIRIGUA ARTIFACTS

by
Payson D. Sheets

INTRODUCTION

This report gives the results of both an extensive survey of obsidian sources and associated sites in the highlands of Guatemala and a more detailed analysis of the obsidian artifacts excavated, as of May 1977, from the lowland Maya site of Quirigua. Our knowledge of the lithic technologies of Precolumbian Mesoamerica, once one of the most thoroughly ignored topics in this field, has been expanding rapidly in recent years. Despite this quantum increase in interest and work, much still remains to be learned. This paper will focus primarily on two aspects of the problem: the location and nature of obsidian sources; and the recognition and means of integration of different technologies using the same basic material within a particular region. The social implications of this latter problem are very tantalizing and, though not dealt with in detail here, would repay further examination from a number of different perspectives. The Quirigua Project has continued its investigations in the Lower Motagua Valley for two seasons subsequent to the writing of this paper; and the analysis of the chipped stone recovered from all seasons' work is in the hands of Andrea Gerstle. This paper does not, therefore, present substantive answers to the questions it poses; rather, it provides suggestions and working hypotheses which can be tested as the analysis is carried forward.

GUATEMALAN OBSIDIAN SOURCES, OUTCROPS AND ASSOCIATED SITES

A total of twelve natural obsidian outcrops was collected during the last week in June and the first week in July of 1977. An attempt was made to focus on lesser-known outcrops, for the huge sources of El Chayal and Ixtepeque often have been collected, described and analyzed. In cases where workshop debris was found near outcrops, artifacts are described in terms of abundance and technology to give at least a hint of the nature of aboriginal exploitation. For clarity, the terminology proposed by Sidrys et al. (1976:1) in their overview of Maya highland sources is used. They define an *outcrop* as a single location where obsidian occurs naturally, and which may or may not have been a *quarry*, that is, have been utilized. Often several outcrops may occur in one general area, and this is termed a *source area*. The term "source area" is potentially misleading: it does not imply aboriginal use. An area where debitage and implements indicate lithic manufacture is called a *workshop*.

It struck me while conducting this research that our ignorance of indigenous obsidian technology far outweighs our knowledge. The need for systematic, regionally-oriented research is becoming more clear. Earlier quick visits to sources and processing localities have contributed basic information, but research into exploitation and distribution of obsidian, either on the synchronic or diachronic plane, now must begin to be more comprehensive. For example, Luis Hurtado de Mendoza has been performing innovative, regionally-oriented analyses of obsidian from the perspective of the Valley of Guatemala.

A problem with most of the earlier source collection studies is the inadequacy of locational information. Therefore, each location is specified to within 100 m by reference to the excellent series of 1:50,000 topographic maps available from the Instituto Geografico Nacional in Guatemala City. The abbreviated Universal Transverse Mercator grid system is used for pinpointing locations: the first grid number is the vertical coordinate, while the second is the horizontal.

AMATITLAN (#1A, 1B)

Howel Williams (1960:51-52) encountered perlite and obsidian along the southern shore of Lake Amatitlan, some 25 km south of Guatemala City. These deposits have not been collected and analyzed previously. Two of Williams' localities were visited and collected but neither yielded a sufficiently isotropic obsidian to allow for controlled fracture. Both outcrops were along the southwest shore of the lake and both produced highly weathered obsidian from a white tephra matrix. No evidence of aboriginal utilization was encountered during a brief survey of both locales, and none would be expected unless outcrops of a far superior obsidian exist in places not visited by this survey.

A few Preclassic prismatic blades (as judged from platform attributes) observed at the Amatitlan archaeological site are fairly large and thick. Their cutting edge/mass ratio (CE/M) is 2.43 (76.6 cm/41.5 g on 17 specimens), probably indicating their source of obsidian to be within a few dozen kilometers.

SAN MARTIN JILOTEPEQUE SOURCE AREA

The San Martin Jilotepeque source area is poorly understood, although obsidian outcrops are known to exist at numerous localities in this large area of well over 100 km². Many sources were exploited aboriginally. It appears probable that they represent more than one geological event, so a chemical or petrographic characterization of one outcrop cannot be assumed to represent the entire source area. While observations and collections have been made here by Williams (1960:20), Heizer et al. (1965), Cobean et al. (1971), Sidrys et al. (1976:8-9) and by Hurtado de Mendoza (personal communication 1977), no systematic regional sampling of either source or artifactual specimens has been conducted. That this brief survey encountered three previously unreported outcrops—Dulce Nombre, Sauces and Las Burras—underscores the limited knowledge of this source area. Whether in composite it rivaled El Chayal or Ixtepeque, or if exploitation and distribution were more limited, is not known.

In June 1977 approximately a ton of large sized and excellent quality obsidian had been hauled in and dumped for use in roads in the town of San Martin Jilotepeque. Informants were not certain of the specific source, but most agreed that it was quarried quite a few kilometers north of the town, toward the Motagua River. Alternatively, it might have come from Chuisac, where informants mentioned seeing much obsidian. Chuisac is 2 km west of San Martin Jilotepeque. All observed items had a rounded, abraded cortex. This is a lead which needs to be investigated, for it is possible that a sizeable outcrop and a quarry may be in the vicinity.

BUENA VISTA OUTCROP (#2)

The Buena Vista area is 3 km northwest of Chimaltenango, only 0.5 km north of the Panamerican Highway (cf. Table 1). Although the flaking quality is quite good, most cobbles are very small. A habitation site is located here, as indicated by a few ceramic and lithic artifacts, and it is likely that the residents were exploiting this local outcrop, particularly if they were able to obtain larger cobbles. Only a few scattered prismatic blades (CE/M ratio = 2.0 cm/g) and debitage flakes were observed within the category of lithic artifacts.

RIO PIXCAYA 'OUTCROP' (#3)

That obsidian cobbles occur in the Rio Pixcaya alluvium is not surprising, for the Pixcaya is the principal river draining the San Martin Jilotepeque-Comalapa-Chimaltenango area. Samples were collected near the bridge on departmental route 1 between Chimaltenango and San Martin Jilotepeque. Cobbles ranged in size from a few centimeters in diameter up to one which was 80 cm in diameter. Cortex, of course, was that of a stream cobble. Analysis of cortex types on artifactual obsidian sourced to the San Martin Jilotepeque area could help determine how much exploitation there was of alluvial versus *in situ* obsidian from this area.

A small collection of artifacts was made at the Finca El Durazno site 3.5 km northeast of Chimaltenango (373x239 on the Tecpan Quadrangle). Platform morphology of prismatic blades indicates a date of the Middle or Late Preclassic, and the CE/M ratio (50.8 cm/25.0 g = 2.0 cm/g) on a very small sample of 15 specimens indicates a nearby source.

TABLE 1
GUATEMALAN OBSIDIAN OUTCROPS COLLECTED

Outcrop Name	Number	Quad Name	Grid No.	Elevation	Workshop Debris
Amatitlan	1A	Amatitlan	582 × 004	1370m	None
Amatitlan	1B	Amatitlan	593 × 013	1120m	None
San Martin Jilotepeque Source Area:					
Buena Vista	2	Tecpan	312 × 228	1900m	Slight
R. Pixcaya	3	Tecpan	382 × 302	1420m	None
Dulce Nombre	4	Tecpan	379 × 371	1810m	Moderate
Sauces	5	Tecpan	386 × 378	1820m	Moderate
Las Burras	6	Granados	438 × 412	1640m	Slight
El Chayal Source Area:					
El Chayal (K25)	7	San Pedro Ayampuc	845 × 300	990m	Extensive
La Joya	8	San Pedro Ayampuc	843 × 323	989m	Extensive
Media Cuesta	9	L. de Ayarza	105 × 975	1480m	Moderate
Jalapa	10	Sanarate	183 × 287	1265m	Slight
Ixtepeque Source Area:					
Obrajuelo	11	Asuncion Mita	152 × 999	925m	Extensive
Agua Blanca	12	Asuncion Mita	153 × 044	980m	Moderate

DULCE NOMBRE OUTCROPS (#4)

Between 2 and 3 km north of the town of San Martin Jilotepeque is a previously uncollected extensive outcrop of obsidian as well as evidence of aboriginal utilization. The obsidian is of excellent quality for controlled fracture, although the sizes of the cobbles observed are rather small: most are under 8 cm in diameter. The cobbles are found eroding out of a red clay matrix, perhaps a weathered volcanic ash. The cortex is characteristically very rough and some is of a perlitic nature.

The artifactual material associated with the Dulce Nombre outcrops is a mixture of Mesoamerican core-blade technology with a rural percussion flake industry. The prismatic blades, with the lowest CE/M ratio yet recorded, only 1.47 cm/g (6 specimens), were apparently made from the immediately available obsidian. The percussion flake industry is an informal one involving the removal of various-sized flakes from the core. Numerous errors were made, as shown by the commonality of hinge fractures in the debitage.

SAUCES OUTCROP (#5)

Near the Dulce Nombre outcrops is a road cut exposing *in situ* obsidian nodules interbedded with white volcanic tephra and associated with porphyritic basalt. The cortex is very smooth and faceted. The cortex differs from Dulce Nombre obsidian indicating the possibility that this is a different obsidian deposit.

LAS BURRAS OUTCROP (#6)

The Las Burras outcrop is located some 11.5 km from San Martin Jilotepeque along the rough, 4-wheel drive road to Mixco Viejo. Exposed along the south bank of the Quebrada Las Burras are cobbles ranging in size from a few millimeters to over a meter in diameter. Flaking quality is only fair, for numerous small xenoliths averaging 1 mm in diameter are scattered throughout the obsidian. Only a few flakes were encountered which gave evidence of aboriginal usage, but the survey was not conducted farther than 20 m from the road. Cortex is smooth to lightly frosted and is irregular (not faceted).

EL CHAYAL SOURCE AREA

So much has been written about El Chayal during the past two decades, and source characterizations are so extensive, that this brief research project did not attempt to add to this body of information. What is needed for the El Chayal area is an intensive and extensive study of lithic technology through time; little more can be learned from the sporadic short visits to which the area has been subjected to date. Beyond the extensive description of one locality by Coe and Flannery (1964), a short overview by Cobean et al. (1971) and a good summation by Sidrys et al. (1976), I shall add only a few comments.

Cortex, varying considerably from one outcrop to another in this huge source area, might, with systematic study, prove valuable in making distinctions as to derivation of samples from specific outcrops. For example, some cortex from the kilometer 25 area is so smooth and fresh-appearing that it could be mistaken for human-induced fracture in an archaeological collection. In contrast, the El Chayal *outcrop* (at the northeastern edge of the El Chayal *source area*) tends to have a frosted, micro-bubbley, and very largely faceted conformation. The La Joya outcrop, some 4 km to the northwest and still within the El Chayal *source area*, generally has a more bubbley, almost frothy cortex, and is often more opaque and laminated than El Chayal or the kilometer 25 outcrop along highway CA9.

Detailed trace element analyses, or petrographic analyses, may detect systematic variation in specimens from the various outcrops sufficient to distinguish among them.

The El Chayal area outcrops and workshops are massive but, as noted by Sidrys et al. (1976:1), insufficient evidence is available to determine whether El Chayal was utilized more or for a longer time than was Ixtepeque. The latter probably is larger in terms of the sheer volume of obsidian available at the surface.

The predominant debitage found in the El Chayal area workshops is derived from the early stages of core-blade technology, indicating that the primary focus of lithic activity here was the shaping of macrocores for shipment. The principal objective of the El Chayal area obsidian industry was not, as some have supposed, the manufacture of prismatic blades which were then shipped ready-made to the consuming sites.

MEDIA CUESTA OUTCROP (#9)

The Media Cuesta outcrop was visited by Cobean, who collected and had analyzed two samples (Cobean et al. 1971). The last 6 km of the 'road' from San Rafael Las Flores to the Laguna de Ayarza are for 4-wheel drive vehicles only. The road fords the river sixteen times—the river is aptly named Rio Los Vados—and fords side streams 3 times. For a stretch the canyon walls leave insufficient room for a river and a road, so the river *is* the road. The water was generally less than 0.5 m deep in early July, and much more water would have rendered the road impassable to wheeled transport.

Some scattered natural obsidian occurs as far west as San Rafaelito (5 km west of Media Cuesta), but the primary outcrop is just south of the town of Media Cuesta and half-way down the caldera slope toward the lake in the area known locally as 'El Chayal', after *chay*, the common name for obsidian.

Much of the Media Cuesta obsidian is an opaque gray color, lacking the black translucency of most Guatemalan obsidian. It has a micro-grainy appearance somewhat like a very fine-grained quartzite. The cortex ranges from a faceted frosty look to a slightly frothy kind of surface. Flakeability is quite good, for xenoliths are rare, and some specimens show fine laminations. The obsidian is available extensively in the ground surface, making quarrying operations unnecessary.

Artifactual material is scattered around the town and caldera slope at Media Cuesta. The predominant artifact is the percussion flake, many of which appear to be ends in themselves, that is, results of a percussion core-flake industry, rather than debitage from the early stages of core-blade technology. Only two prismatic blade fragments were encountered, along with a section of a bifacially-flaked knife and a few biface trimming flakes. These latter probably indicate exploitation at least during the Late Classic and Postclassic. One-half kilometer west of the town is a prehistoric site which, although much destroyed (local people recount tales of mound destruction for agricultural and looting purposes), retains at least one plazuela unit. The mounds here were constructed of uncut lava as facing for earthen fill. Both on the plaza surface and in mound fill there is a striking lack of ceramic or lithic artifacts. Lithic workshops may have existed nearby, but no workshops were found in the site center.

JALAPA OUTCROP (#10)

Twelve kilometers northwest of Jalapa, on Ruta Nacional 19 toward Sansare, is a road cut in the hill known as Cerro Chayal. There excellent quality obsidian, in nodular form from 1 to 30 cm in diameter, is weathering out of a clay and volcanic ash matrix. Cortex, generally, is non-faceted and quite frothy, with some development of perlitic surfaces. For reasons discussed below, I suspect it was not utilized in the Preclassic, and only slightly during the Classic and Postclassic.

A brief survey of the north and west sides of Cerro Chayal recovered two fragments of bifacially-flaked implements. One is of the same type as the 'pointed stem, ovate blade' biface from Chalchuapa (Sheets 1978:Fig. 2b3). Also, a large percussion flake and a small piece of debitage were observed, making notable the paucity of workshop debris.

If the Jalapa quarry were exploited heavily, then nearby sites should show an abundance of obsidian (barring colonial exploitation and exclusive ownership from afar) and low CE/M ratios among prismatic blades. With this in mind, the El Sare site, 10 km southeast of the outcrop and 1.5 km north of the town of Jalapa, was visited. El Sare is a moderately large site containing sizeable mounds arranged around plazas. These plazas and their surrounding areas are densely covered with ceramic and groundstone debris, but very little obsidian is observable. Only seven chipped stone artifacts including one prismatic blade (CE/M ratio of 4.5 cm/g) and five small pieces of debitage. Artifactual evidence from the outcrop does indicate some exploitation during the Late Classic or Postclassic and I suspect that the El Sare site may have been occupied in the Preclassic, prior to the aboriginal discovery of the Jalapa outcrop.

IXTEPEQUE SOURCE AREA

To date, the best technological description of a Guatemalan obsidian quarry and workshop is that of Graham and Heizer (1968) for Papalhuapa/Ixtepeque. Papalhuapa is the name of the archaeological site, and Ixtepeque is the volcano and name of the obsidian source area. As with El Chayal, only a few comments will be made to amplify the Graham and Heizer report. What is currently needed is a sustained survey and testing program for the Ixtepeque area. It is not a single, discrete exposure of obsidian with a single workshop, but a sprawling complex of flows and beds of obsidian with associated quarries and workshops extending over some 30 km^2 from Agua Blanca to Volcan Ixtepeque. Williams et al. (1964:38) found it to be perhaps the largest exposure of obsidian anywhere in continental North America.

The road from Agua Blanca to Obrajuela and Papalhuapa has been improved since Graham and Heizer were there: it is now passable by 2-wheel drive vehicles with high clearance at any time of the year except after a heavy rain. Scattered nodules of obsidian cover fields from 1.5 km south of Agua Blanca to Papalhuapa and beyond. Nodule sizes vary considerably, many being over 0.5 m in diameter. A mahogany-colored red obsidian occurs in the Ixtepeque area in apparently larger amounts than at other Guatemalan sources.

Cortex in the Ixtepeque Source Area ranges from a faceted frosty appearance to an irregular frothy and perlitic surface. It is not known if any patterns exist in cortex variation within the source area.

Local informants at the town of Agua Blanca reported obsidian occurring at the 'Cueva del Diablo' 0.5 km to the east. The cueva is an overhang with a small cave, and at the top of the talus (the bottom of the cueva) is a massive band of obsidian about 1.5 m thick. Much of the talus is obsidian and some workshop debris intermixed with the natural obsidian. Agua Blanca obsidian (#12) is an opaque black color and of excellent flakeability. Two red hands, reported by local informants, were found painted on an overhanging ledge high on the cliff face above the cueva. These designs were achieved by painting around the hand while it was held against the cliff face. Neither chronologically diagnostic ceramics nor lithics were encountered to give a clue as to the time of aboriginal exploitation. The nearby spring with its milky colored water (hence the name Agua Blanca) would have supplied a water source to aboriginal exploiters in this somewhat arid area.

OBSIDIAN ARTIFACTS FROM THE SITE AND PERIPHERY OF QUIRIGUA—A PRELIMINARY ANALYSIS

The Maya lowland site of Quirigua is located in the Motagua River floodplain of eastern Guatemala at an elevation of 73 m. The strategic location of this site in the control of trade between Copan and the Southeast Maya Highlands to the south, as well as the Maya lowlands to the north, makes the understanding of Quirigua's obsidian artifact collections crucial.

The objectives of this preliminary study of Quirigua area obsidian artifacts are to derive a general impression of patterns and diversity in artifacts, to see if production and distribution information can be obtained from analysis of artifacts when combined with provenience-context data, and to try to determine the source(s) of Quirigua obsidian. The methods used to achieve the first two goals involved a readout of all obsidian lots collected by the project through the 1977 field season, followed by a more detailed analysis of certain artifacts or lots.

The categories into which the artifacts were classified for the lot readout analysis are becoming fairly standard in the Maya area (cf. Hester and Hammond 1976; Sheets 1978). Decortication flakes are flakes which carry some cortex (the natural outside surface of the original obsidian nodule) on their dorsal surfaces. No intent is implied by the term, that is, the claim is not made here that a decortication flake was removed for the sole purpose of eliminating cortex. Rather, in most cases there probably were a number of objectives, involving ridge straightening, thinning, trimming, sharpening, and/or cortex removal. A primary decortication flake has cortex on its entire dorsal surface, indicating it was the first flake removed from that area of the nodule. A secondary decortication flake carries one or more flake scars on its dorsal face, indicating that it was derived from a later stage in the manufacturing process.

Debitage refers to items which are wastage in the manufacturing process, or are portions of implements too small to be identified typologically. They are not industry-specific: they can derive from core-blade, core-flake, biface or uniface technologies, or from the resharpening of implements in any of these technologies.

Macroblades are large percussion blades, more than twice as long as they are wide, with relatively parallel sides. They usually come from core-blade technology just before the knapper shifted to pressure blade removal, but some are removed during pressure (prismatic) blade production to straighten a ridge or correct for hinge fracture. Unretouched macroblades, as the name implies, show no evidence of purposive percussion or pressure flake removal after their initial manufacture.

A scraper is a flake or blade which has been steeply retouched on its dorsal, or occasionally ventral, surface. It is unifacially retouched. The term 'scraper' is defined technologically, and an artifact so classified may or may not actually have been used for scraping. (It is extraordinary that only one scraper has been found by the Quirigua Project to date.)

A projectile point or knife is a bifacially-flaked implement. Detailed microscopic and replication studies are often needed to separate these two functions on a reliable basis in a research area. Such a detailed analysis was not performed in this study, so bifaces are identified here as projectile points or as knives only when clear evidence was available macroscopically or with 10x magnification. Bifacial thinning flakes are the distinctive flakes produced by the manufacturing or resharpening of these objects. Not only may a study of these flakes assist in functional categorization of the implements, it may also point out locations of biface manufacture or resharpening where they are encountered in primary midden deposits.

Polyhedral cores are the exhausted nuclei from the manufacture of prismatic blades. They, like biface thinning flakes for biface technology, are an index of prismatic blade manufacture; so are polyhedral platform spalls, the proximal segments of polyhedral cores detached after errors occurred in blade manufacture. These spalls were sectioned off the core to allow for continued blade removal.

The items classified as flake cores are the small nuclei for production of percussion flakes. Consistently, they were derived from small stream cobbles after a few flakes (generally less than 10) had been produced. The earliest flake or two would be primary decortication flakes, while most of the remainder would be secondary decortication flakes. A few of the flakes of this small cobble percussion industry may have no cortex, and would have been classified in this study as debitage.

Prismatic blades are the long, thin ribbons of obsidian found at all major Mesoamerican sites from the Preclassic through the Postclassic. They were removed from polyhedral cores by pressure, although the precise procedure or procedures used are not yet well understood.

RESULTS

The first step in synthesizing the lot-artifact type data was to tabulate frequencies and percentages into two contrastive groups: artifacts from the central area, i.e., the Quirigua Park, versus artifacts collected in the Peripheral Program. When these data are compared (cf. the first two columns of Table 2) some very strong differences are immediately apparent. Both primary and secondary decortication flakes are found in much higher percentages in the periphery. Only 6.3% of the artifacts in the park were secondary decortication flakes, while these accounted for 47.0% of the peripheral artifacts. Debitage frequencies in all columns are not sensitive indicators of technology and so these can be ignored for our purposes here.

These decortication flakes, along with flake cores (J in Table 2 and Fig. 2), are the remains of a percussion core-flake technology. The relative frequencies of flake

TABLE 2

OBSIDIAN ARTIFACTS BY TYPE AND LOCATION FOR THE QUIRIGUA REGION, GUATEMALA

Note: Nine loci, officially a part of the periphery program (L. 6, 26, 29, 35-7, 82, 92, and 116), were found to be typologically and technologically similar to the core area. The 3rd and 4th group of totals reflects the addition of these loci to the core totals.

Type/Location	Quirigua Park #	Quirigua Park %	Periphery Program #	Periphery Program %	Core-Revised #	Core-Revised %	Periphery Revised #	Periphery Revised %	TOTAL #	TOTAL %
A. Primary Decortication Flakes	13	0.8	137	4.1	17	0.7	133	4.9	150	3.1
B. Secondary Decortication Flakes	101	6.3	1566	47.0	135	5.9	1532	57.4	1667	34.1
C. Debitage	325	20.4	939	28.2	499	22.1	765	28.7	1264	25.8
D. Macroblades (Unretouched)	53	3.3	9	0.3	59	2.6	3	0.1	62	1.3
E. "Scrapers"	0	0	1	0.03	0	0	1	0.03	1	0.02
F. Bifaces (Proj. Pts./Knives)	9	0.5	4	0.2	10	0.4	3	0.1	13	0.3
G. Bifacial Thinning Flakes	12	0.8	11	0.3	14	0.6	21	0.8	23	0.5
H. Polyhedral Cores	14	0.8	16	0.4	28	1.2	2	0.06	30	0.6
I. Polyhedral Platform Spalls	0	0	6	0.2	6	0.3	0	0	6	0.1
J. Flake Cores	4	0.2	76	2.3	6	0.3	74	2.8	80	1.6
K. Prismatic Blades	1065	66.9	556	16.7	1488	65.8	133	4.9	1621	33.1
TOTALS:	1596		3331		2262		2667		4894	

cores also reflect this park-periphery dichotomy, with percentages of 0.2 and 2.3 respectively. Clearly, the manufacture and use of these percussion flakes from small obsidian stream cobbles were concentrated in the sites away from the Quirigua Park.

The prime indicators for Mesoamerican core-blade technology diverged markedly in patterning from the above core-flake artifacts. Macroblades, polyhedral cores and prismatic blades were found in much higher amounts in the park than in the periphery. The most significant of these, of course, is the prismatic blade (66.9% of park artifacts versus 16.7% of periphery artifacts). Apparently at variance with this is the fact that all six polyhedral platform spalls derived from the periphery, but, as will become clear below, all of these came from an outlier of the Quirigua site center.

Bifacial manufacture and use were more significant in the core than in the periphery, but the differences are not major.

In order to detect patterning within the general category of the Periphery Program loci individual lots and loci were inspected. This disclosed a total of nine loci which had relative artifact frequencies much more similar to those from the park than to other loci in the periphery; that is, in terms of indigenous lithic technology, they were culturally more a part of central than of peripheral activities. The park boundary itself is, of course, only a convenient demarcation between core and periphery (see *Quirigua Paper No. 6*, this volume). If we accept that a core-blade technology is characteristic of Mesoamerican civilization, as contrasted with a more rural (and likely antecedent in the Quirigua area) stream cobble percussion core-flake industry, then these nine loci should be considered a part of the center.

The nine loci are 006, 026, 029, 035-037, 082, 092 and 116 (Fig. 6.5), and it is significant that all but one are located adjacent to the park. In fact, seven of the nine are immediately north (NE to NW) of the park boundary, and one (Loc. 116) is only 1.5 km WNW of the park. These may be considered, again from the lithic point of view, to be culturally and geographically a part of the Classic Maya central place of Quirigua. Loc. 092, approximately 4 km southeast of the park, across the Motagua River and between the Jubuco and Morja Rivers, was culturally but not geographically a part of the Classic Maya phenomenon. Because it is located on the other side of the Motagua from Quirigua along the most likely trade route south to Copan, its apparent role as a Quirigua outlier is not surprising. The ballcourt nearby is ancillary evidence that this settlement was more than a small rural village.

The results of tabulating these lots with the central area artifacts instead of with those from peripheral loci may be seen in Table 2 and Fig. 2 as revised totals. Considering the core area first, very few of the artifacts from this zone are remnants of the stream cobble production industry. In fact, only 6.9% of the central area artifacts are decortication flakes or flake cores, indicating their slight importance to life at Quirigua and Loc. 092. That compares with 65.1% of the periphery artifacts being a part of the cobble percussion industry (a total obtained from adding percentages of decortication flakes to flake cores).

The indicators of pan-Mesoamerican core-blade technology, involving occupational specialization and long distance transport of obsidian in macrocore form, show a very different kind of distribution. Components of core-blade technology (macroblades, polyhedral cores and platform spalls, and prismatic blades) are strongly represented in the core area and weakly in the periphery. These core-blade artifacts represent 69.6% of the central area artifacts, while the same kind of artifacts account for only 5.1% in the periphery. Most of these core-blade artifacts are found at only seven peripheral loci: 011, 025, 051, 052, 086, 087 and 089.

The components of bifacial technology, specifically the bifaces and the thinning flakes deriving from their manufacture and maintenance, do not show a clear central-versus-peripheral pattern. Apparently, bifaces were more available to the people in the central area, but access was not severely restricted. The dispersed distribution of biface flakes indicates a pattern of widely scattered small workshops where bifacial manufacture and resharpening were carried out. A biface workshop was located south of the Motagua and west of Chapulco (Fig. 6.5) at Loc. 051, though the primary lithic activity at that village was the manufacture of percussion flakes from cobbles.

OBSERVATIONS ON SPECIFIC LOCI, LOTS AND OPERATIONS

Detailed information on microwear, technological variation within general categories, specific implement descriptions and the lot readouts are not presented in this preliminary summary. These data will be included, in modified form, in the final lithic report to be prepared by Andrea Gerstle. Comments are made in this section on collections of particular interest.

Locus 116. Loc. 116, a midden located 1.5 km WNW of Quirigua park, produced 11,000 sherds dating to the Terminal Late Classic. Some items, such as figurine molds and stamps, indicate a nearby ceramic workshop as well as the lithic workshop area (*Quirigua Paper No. 6*, this volume). Of the 91 obsidian artifacts recovered, 5 are secondary decortication flakes, 1 is an unretouched small macroblade, 4 are polyhedral cores and 81 are prismatic blades. The relatively high percentage of polyhedral cores (4.0% of this collection, compared with 0.1% in the total collection) argues for nearby prismatic blade production. The cores were deliberately smashed by harsh percussion blows after they had served their function. This action was apparently not involved with core rejuvenation as no reasons for rejuvenation were observable on any of the core fragments. All this suggests a small craft barrio, including at least ceramic and lithic workshops, for this central place residential zone.

Locus 039. Loc. 039 is a small plazuela site consisting of 11 structures on the south side of the Motagua River (Fig. 6.5). The sample of 138 obsidian specimens breaks down as follows: 8 primary and 38 secondary decortication flakes; 82 debitage; 1 unretouched macroblade; 1 small and irregular bipointed biface; 3 flake cores; and 5 prismatic blade fragments. There was an obsidian workshop at Loc. 039, one quite different from that at Loc. 116. Obsidian cobbles, generally smaller than 6 to 8 cm in diameter, were collected from the river alluvium, although the location of this deposit is not presently known. In a few hours of searching the Motagua alluvium in the Los Amates area I encountered only one obsidian cobble. Perhaps river deposits in the Jubuco-Morja area contain obsidian cobbles; at any rate, I suspect the source is within a few kilometers of Quirigua. Cobbles were reduced in an informal fashion by percussion removal of flakes. Cores were not unidirectional, and the cortex almost always served as the striking platform. The flakes probably were used as general utility cutting implements. Although this is a predominantly rural percussion flake industry, people in rural areas were able to obtain prismatic blades manufactured in the central places of Quirigua and Loc. 092 (see below). The stream cobbles themselves are too small for a core-blade technology.

Locus 013. Loc. 013 is a similar small site of six structures arranged into two plazuela groups on the first terrace north of the Motagua floodplain. It supported a cobble percussion workshop of considerable size, judging from the volume and nature of recovered artifacts. The 1463 obsidian artifacts subdivided as follows: 76 and 950 primary and secondary decortication flakes respectively; 39 flake cores; 1 large, roughly-shaped biface made from a macroblade blank which was used as a knife (judging from the parallel striae along the edge); 1 small polyhedral core fragment; 9 prismatic blades; and 387 pieces of debitage. This is the largest percussion flake workshop, probably representing a cottage industry, found by the project as of 1977. The polyhedral core fragment is enigmatic: its presence might indicate pressure blade manufacture, yet prismatic blades are rare at this location.

Locus 026. Loc. 026 is a residential area immediately northeast of the park. The lack of flake cores, polyhedral cores and biface flakes indicates a residential zone of consumption of lithic implements rather than of production. That prismatic blades represent 59.0% (31/52) of the sample indicated a central place residential area, not a rural residence.

Locus 082. Loc. 082, just north of the park boundary, is also a residential area, judging from the lithics recovered. However, the artifacts point toward a humble residential and craft area rather than the elite habitation of nearby Loc. 026. A total of 21 of the 145 obsidian artifacts recovered was from the stream cobble percussion industry, and two flake cores indicate local production in this zone. But the fact that 67.0% of the artifacts were core-blade, including a polyhedral core fragment, clearly indicates that craftsmen were manufacturing prismatic blades under the control of the Classic Maya elite. The cobble percussion flakes may have been for the craftsmen's own household use.

Locus 092. Loc. 092, a large site south of the Motagua and between the Morja and Jubuco Rivers, yielded 324 obsidian artifacts which subdivide as follows: 1 primary and 1 secondary decortication flake; 128 debitage; 4 unretouched macroblades; 6 polyhedral cores; 6 polyhedral platform spalls; and 178 prismatic blades. Although geographically peripheral to the dominant site of Quirigua, technologically it was an active participant in core-blade technology, almost to the complete exclusion of the rural core-flake percussion industry. The above frequencies of technological categories indicate that considerable core-blade manufacturing was performed here, involving frequent and apparently successful rejuvenation of polyhedral cores. The prismatic blades produced at this site were probably consumed locally or made available (in exchange for agricultural products?) to nearby rural villages on the south side of the Motagua.

One major difference between Loc. 092 and the center of Quirigua is the size of the prismatic blades produced. Quirigua prismatics are thicker and wider than Loc. 092 prismatics. The cutting edge per unit mass ratio (CE/M) for Loc. 092 is 304.1 cm/36.5 g = 8.3 cm/g. Knappers at 092 were much more miserly with their obsidian, deriving a maximum of cutting edge per unit weight, probably because they had more restricted access to it than did their contemporaries at Quirigua. CE/M ratios in the central area of Quirigua fall between 3 and 5 cm/g. Most probably, Quirigua controlled access to imported obsidian for core-blade technology, so Loc. 092 blade-makers would have had to obtain their macrocores from intermediaries at Quirigua, thus making them dependent on Quirigua in this respect.

It should not be surprising, then, that Loc. 092 has been described as the second most imposing site in the immediate Quirigua area after the site core itself (*Quirigua Paper No. 6*, this volume). Loc. 092 may have served as an intermediate station along the Morja River route connecting Copan with Quirigua (*Ibid.*).

Str. 1B-8 (South Group), Lot 7A/1. Redeposited debitage from a prismatic blade workshop was found at Str. 1B-8, the northernmost building of Morley's "South Group", within the Quirigua site core. Lot 7A/1 consisted of 133 prismatic blades, a polyhedral core and a bifacially flaked knife (5.4 x 3.2 x 0.8 cm). The knife has a pointed stem and an ovate blade (cf. Sheets 1978:Fig. 2b2), with moderate use abrasion at the shoulders, and was not manufactured at the prismatic blade workshop. The form is a common one for the Maya Late Classic and Postclassic.

The workshop was a specialized segment of core-blade technology, being devoted exclusively to pressure production of prismatic blades from polyhedral cores. The platforms of the cores were thoroughly ground, and only minimal overhang removal was effected before detaching each blade. In El Salvador this technology would date to the Postclassic. Platforms on prismatic blades are, as a result of minimal overhang removal, quite large. Most are between 0.7 and 1.0 cm in length and 0.2 and 0.4 cm in width. A CE/M ratio measured on 129 specimens yielded a 3.8 cm/g, which is about what one would expect with a powerful Maya site at an intermediate distance from core-blade source material (the straight-line distance to Ixtepeque is 115 km, to El Chayal 145 km).

The CE/M ratio of the small prismatic blade cache 6I/13, in the plaza of the Acropolis right in the center of Quirigua, is 4.75 cm/g, somewhat higher than the large 7A/1 workshop. The cache consists of 4 prismatic blades (Fig. 4), and 2 of these fit together, confirming their sequential removal from the same core. There is no evidence of use, and their technological identity and pristine condition indicate that they were produced by a single blade maker just before caching. The platforms are somewhat smaller than those of 7A/1, for scraping of the core edge to remove the overhang was more extensive, and are striated, not ground. These procedures, again judging from El Salvador, would date to sometime during the Late Preclassic or the Classic period.

6L/33—Special Deposit #10. It should be noted that one deposit of obsidian is not included in the totals of Fig. 2 or Table 1. A March 1977 discovery by Chris Jones, it is an extraordinary deposit of obsidian in the Acropolis of Quirigua west of Str. 1B-5 and north of Str. 1B-4. Found against the back wall of a room and above the floor, this deposit was deliberately sealed by a cobble fill after it was laid in place (see *Quirigua Paper No. 6*, this volume).

A total of 2145 artifacts was analyzed during this preliminary study, of which 1356 formed a random and hopefully representative sample of the deposit. The entire unit had not been fully excavated at the time of this study, so there was no way of judging sample representativeness or of determining the total number of obsidian artifacts which were placed there. A very rough estimate of the number of excavated artifacts may be made as follows: 2.5 lbs obsidian/9.5 lbs matrix sampled x 85.0 lbs (total excavated) x 1356 specimens in sample = 30,409. The final total may be between 50,000 and 100,000 obsidian artifacts.

The 1356 specimen sample, analyzed by type, breaks down as follows: 618 debitage (46.0%); 30 small pressure flakes (2.2%); 6 unretouched macroblades (0.4%); 72 small percussion flakes (5.3%); 7 polyhedral cores (0.5%); 1 flake core (0.1%); and 622 prismatic blades (46.0%). The small pressure and percussion flakes as well as the flake core are not a part of the stream cobble percussion industry. One extraordinary aspect of this deposit is that not a single primary or secondary decortication flake nor a flake core associated with the stream cobble percussion industry found its way into the sample, despite their ubiquity in areas surrounding Quirigua. The relative abundance of artifact types within the sample is more characteristic of the core than of the periphery of Quirigua, as indicated particularly by prismatic blades and polyhedral cores. If the sample is representative, I can only conclude that while this deposit was being assembled very great care was exercised that no implement or debitage from the rural stream cobble percussion industry be included. The peasant connotations of the rural obsidian industry and the elite attitude toward it may be reflected in the selective nature of this ritual deposit.

An alternative explanation, that this was a deposit of obsidian artifacts specially created for this layer by a few knappers, was rejected. The evidence for rejection lies in the high frequency of use wear among these artifacts, and the fact that extraneous sherds, worked bone and a few chert flakes were also in the deposit. This unit clearly was derived from midden areas, evidently from both obsidian workshops and household middens.

SUMMARY

In general, obsidian tool production in the Lower Motagua Valley during the Late Classic was organized into two quite different industries. One, a cottage industry, involved the collection of small obsidian nodules from stream alluvium. The location of this source is as yet unknown, but it is probably within a few kilometers of the study area. The reduction strategy was informal: percussion blows were directed at the cobble from many different directions, detaching flakes which could be used for manifold cutting, shaving and sawing tasks. Both production and use of these stream cobble percussion flakes are primarily in the smaller rural villages and hamlets which dotted the Precolumbian countryside. Occupational specialization, if any, was minimal.

On the other hand, the Classic Maya elite who established themselves at the site of Quirigua and at Loc. 092 brought with them the knowledge of core-blade technology, and the ability and power or wealth to obtain obsidian of a size and quality sufficient for blade production. Obsidian for the core-blade technology was imported from greater distances than the small stream cobbles were transported. In addition, the core-blade obsidian came into the site in preformed condition, while the cobbles were taken to percussion workshops in the villages in unmodified form. Core-blade obsidian arrived at Quirigua and Loc. 092 as macrocores. A few macroblades could be removed, as needed, by percussion, but most of the items derived from this long-distance obsidian were prismatic blades which were produced by a pressure technique. Considerable skill was required, and the Classic Maya elite maintained occupational specialists for the task. These specialists probably resided in assigned habitation areas. Most of the prismatic blades they produced were utilized within the major central places, but about 8.0% of their blades were used and discarded in rural zones.

AFTERWORD

I am grateful to a number of individuals and institutions for making this small research project possible. The Council on Research and Creative Work of the University of Colorado graciously provided funds for fieldwork and analysis. The Quirigua Project of the University Museum, University of Pennsylvania, directed by Drs. William Coe and Robert Sharer, provided housing and laboratory space for artifactual analyses. Wendy Ashmore patiently and promptly answered my many queries regarding provenience of surface and excavated samples.

Dr. Luis Lujan, at the time Director of the Instituto de Antropolgia e Historia of Guatemala, was particularly helpful during all stages of fieldwork. It was a pleasure to deal with him and his competent staff. Other Instituto staff members who contributed in various ways include Licda. Dora de Gonzalez, Enrique Monterroso and Guillermo Folgar. Sam Bonis of the Instituto Geografico was of assistance in source collecting. Peter Mueller and Kent Johnson, then SUNY Binghampton geology graduate students, were of assistance in laboratory analyses and in source collection.

Finally, it should be noted that this paper was written in 1977.

QUIRIGUA REPORTS

REFERENCES CITED

Ashmore, W.
    1977   Research at Quirigua, Guatemala: The Site-Periphery Program. Paper presented at the 42nd Annual Meeting of the Society for American Archaeology, New Orleans.

Cobean, R., M. Coe, E. Perry, Jr., K. Turekian and D. Kharkar
    1971   Obsidian Trade at San Lorenzo, Tenochtitlan, Mexico. *Science* 174: 666-671.

Coe, M. and K. Flannery
    1964   The Pre-columbian Obsidian Industry of El Chayal, Guatemala. *American Antiquity* 30: 43-49.

Feldman, L. H.
    1971   *A Tumpline Economy: Production and Distribution Systems of Early Central-East Guatemala*. Ph.D. Dissertation, Department of Anthropology, Pennsylvania State University.

Jones, C.
    1977   Research at Quirigua, Guatemala: The Site-Core Program. Paper Presented at the 42nd Annual Meeting of the Society for American Archaeology, New Orleans.

Graham, J. and R. Heizer
    1968   Notes on the Papalhuapa Site, Guatemala. in *Contributions of the University of California Archaeological Research Facility,* No. 5: 101-125. University of California, Department of Anthropology, Berkeley, California.

Heizer, R., H. Williams and J. Graham
    1965   Notes on Mesoamerican Obsidians and Their Significance in Archaeologic Studies. in *Contributions of the University of California Archaeological Research Facility,* No. 1: 94-103. University of California: Department of Anthropology, Berkeley, California.

Hester, T. and N. Hammond
    1978   *Maya Lithic Studies: Papers from the 1976 Belize Field Symposium*. Special Report 4, Center for Archaeological Research, University of Texas, San Antonio.

Sharer, R. J.
    1976   The Quirigua Project: 1976 Season. *Quirigua Report I* (Paper No. 5). Museum Monograph, 37. Philadelphia: University Museum.

Sharer, R., C. Jones, W. Ashmore and E. Schortman
    1979   The Quirigua Project: 1976 Season. *Quirigua Reports I,* (Paper No. 5). Museum Monograph, 37. Philadelphia: University Museum.

Sheets, P. D.
    1975   Behavioral Analysis and the Structure of a Prehistoric Industry. *Current Anthropology* 16(3): 369-391.
    1978   Artifacts. in *The Prehistory of Chalchuapa, El Salvador*. R. Sharer ed. Vol. 2, Pt. 1. Philadelphia: University of Pennsylvania Press.

Sidrys, R., J. Andersen and D. Marcucci
    1976   Obsidian Sources in the Maya Area. *Journal of New World Archaeology* 1: 1-13.

Williams, H.
    1960   Volcanic History of The Guatemalan Highlands. *U. C. Pubs. Geol. Sci.,* 38: 1-88.

Williams, H., A. McBirney and G. Dengo
    1964   Geological Reconnaissance of Southern Guatemala. *U. C. Pubs. Geol. Sci.,* 50: 1-54.

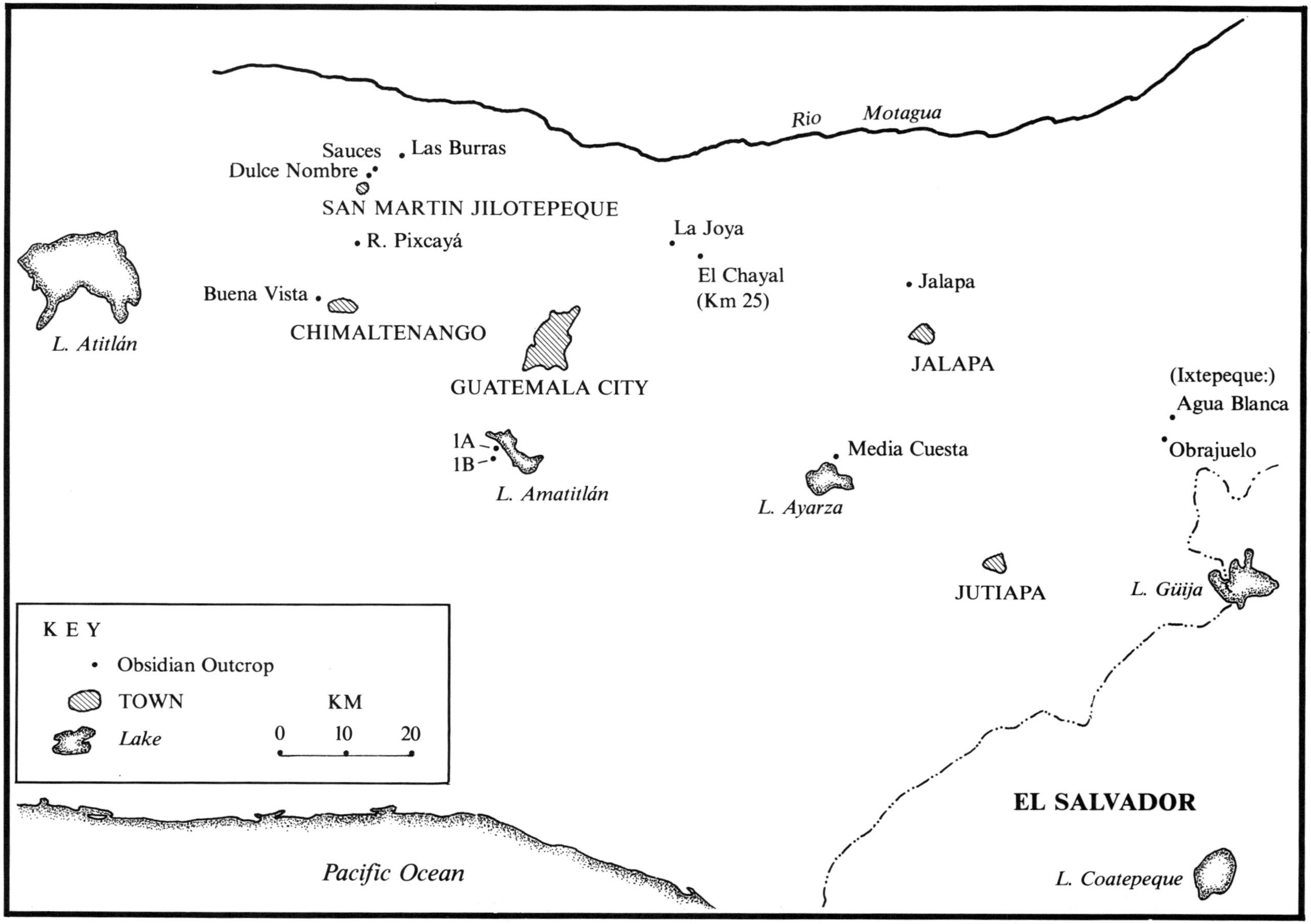

Figure 10.1. Location of Guatemalan obsidian outcrops collected for this study.

CORE (revised)

PERIPHERY (revised)

TOTAL AREA

KEY

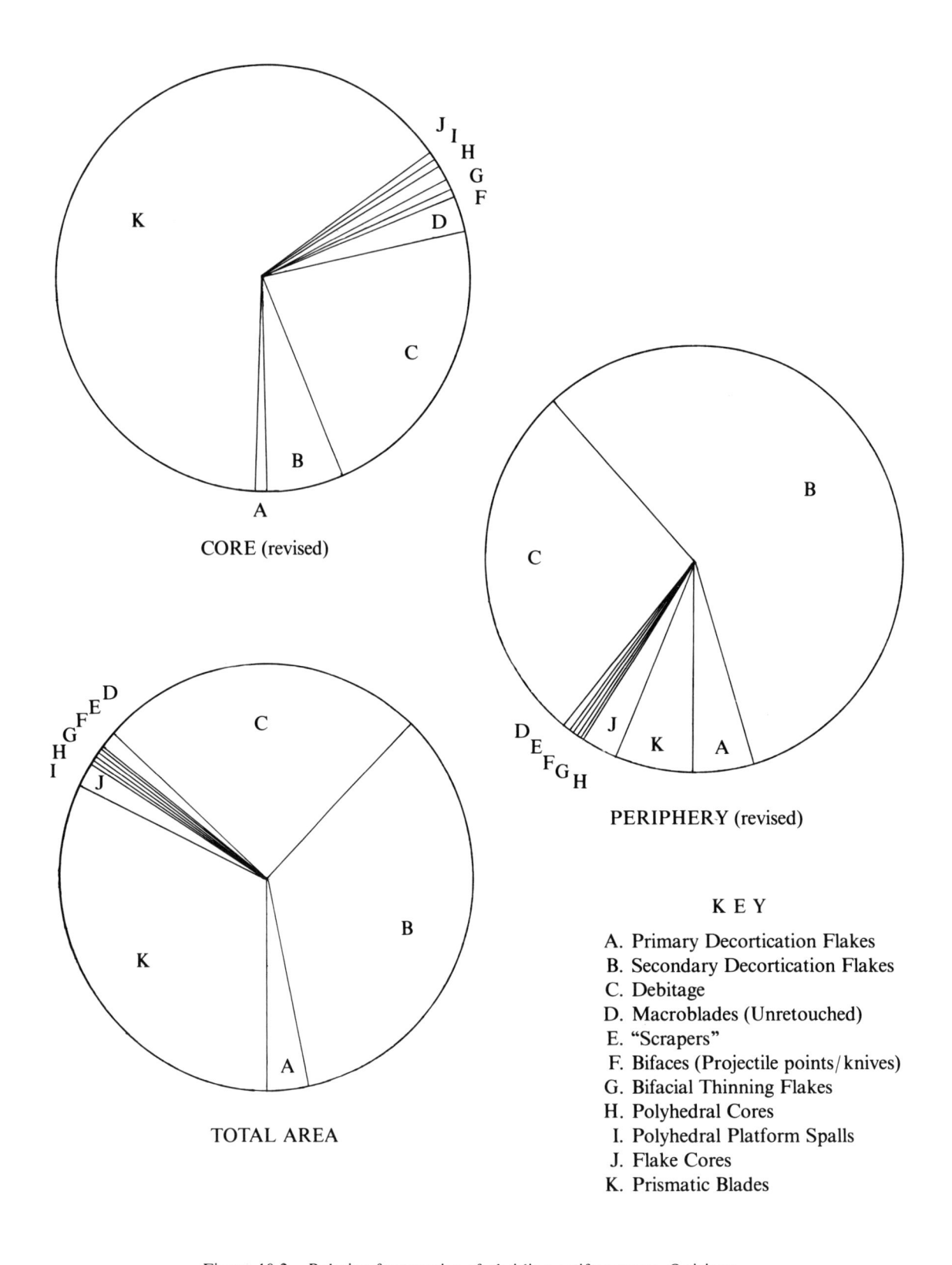

A. Primary Decortication Flakes
B. Secondary Decortication Flakes
C. Debitage
D. Macroblades (Unretouched)
E. "Scrapers"
F. Bifaces (Projectile points/knives)
G. Bifacial Thinning Flakes
H. Polyhedral Cores
I. Polyhedral Platform Spalls
J. Flake Cores
K. Prismatic Blades

Figure 10.2. Relative frequencies of obsidian artifact types, Quirigua.

Figure 10.3. Obsidian artifacts from Quirigua center and peripheral sites. All specimens except E oriented with platform at top.
    A-D. Primatic blades from 6I/13 Cache in Acropolis. A and B fit together, B was removed before A.
    E.   Bifacially flaked knife from 17BC/1, Quirigua Plaza.
    F.   Projectile point from 6L/27, Acropolis.
    G-O. Percussion flakes from obsidian stream cobbles, from various contexts. G-J are primary decortication flakes, and K-O are secondary decortication flakes.

PAPER NO. 11

CONTROL OF BIOLOGICAL GROWTHS OF THE MAYAN ARCHAEOLOGICAL RUINS OF QUIRIGUA, GUATEMALA

by
Mason E. Hale, Jr.

INTRODUCTION

Archaeological ruins are common in many tropical regions, with perhaps the greatest concentration in Guatemala and southern Mexico. While the existence of many of these sites had been known for centuries, it was not until the latter half of the nineteenth century that they were first visited by scientists. In the period 1895-1935 many ruins were rescued from dense jungle growth, at least partially reconstructed and opened up for visitations by tourists. The archaeological remains now constitute a significant cultural and economic asset for these countries.

The opening of the forest cover, however, has drastically altered the environment of the ruins. There is more light as trees are cut down, often increased soil moisture because of drainage problems, and greater exposure to extremes of wetting and drying without the protective canopy. As a consequence, lichens, mosses, algae and even epiphytic ferns and orchids have invaded and flourished. The growths, depending of course on local conditions, have totally covered many remains (stelae, walls, altars, buildings, etc.) obscuring features carved on the surfaces and most importantly contributing to weathering and breakdown of the stone surfaces (see Figure 1; Anonymous 1976). The ability of lichens in particular to penetrate and disintegrate stone by mechanical and chemical means is well documented. This phenomenon is most clearly seen in a comparison of a step from the Escalinata at Copan removed to Harvard University during the reconstruction in 1935 and a similar step exposed to biological fouling since then at the site (Fig. 2).

One of the earliest reported observations of biological fouling was made at Borobudur Temple in Indonesia (see Hyvert 1972) in the mid-1800's. Mechanical brushing was employed at that time to clean stone surfaces, but archaeologists soon discovered that this caused greater damage as stone crystals and fragments were also scoured off. More recently, various biocidal solutions have been sprayed on to kill existing growths without mechanical action and to ultimately control recolonization (Anonymous 1972). There are, however, very few published reports dealing specifically with this problem in tropical regions, although the British have done much to solve it in England (Richardson 1973).

This study, which was originally encouraged by Dr. William Coe of the University Museum, University of Pennsylvania, in 1973, attempts to attack the problem as it exists at the site of Quirigua, Guatemala, and to present recommendations for general treatments of other archaeological ruins in similar environmental settings.

This report represents that portion of a final report on the National Geographic Society Research Project "Control of Lichen Growths on Mayan Archaeological Ruins" (awarded 25 June 1975 with work completed in February 1978; funded for a three-year period) which relates to the site of Quirigua. The Principal Investigator has been Mason E. Hale, Jr., Curator, Department of Botany, Smithsonian Institution, Washington, D. C.; and photographs were taken by Julia Gould, Washington, D. C.

CONTROL OF BIOLOGICAL GROWTHS

INVENTORY OF THE MICROFLORA

A very large number of lichens, mosses, liverworts and several algae were collected at the site. These species are in fact common throughout the region, often occurring naturally in disturbed forest sites and on open rock outcrops, particularly in the humid lowlands which extend into the Peten and Yucatan. Samples of many species have been preserved as documentation in the herbarium, Department of Botany, Smithsonian Institution. Some specimens could not be sampled since collecting methods would have damaged the monuments.

Lichens

The dominant species in order of estimated coverage were *Phyllopsora corallina*, *Chiodecton antillarum* (see Fig. 1), *Leptotrema santense*, *Dirinaria picta* and an unidentified partly endolithic white crust. Other species with less coverage, often occurring on only one or two monuments, included crustose *Bacidia* sp., *Blastenia* sp. and *Leptotrema glaucescens*, and foliose *Coccocarpia cronia*, *Collema* sp., *Leptogium* sp., *Parmeliella pannosa*, *Parmotrema endosulphureum*, *P. praesorediosum*, *P. sulphuratum* and *Physcia sorediosa*.

Bryophytes

The coverage by mosses and hepatics (see Fig. 1) was often quite extensive, especially in moist areas under shade. Species encountered included *Bryum coronatum*, *Calymperes* sp., *Euosmolejeunea clausa*, *Frullania squarrosa*, *Groutetiella schlumbergeri*, *Mastigolejeunea auriculata*, *Octoblepharum albidum* and the common *Sematophylum caespitosum*.

Algae

The blue-green alga *Oscillatoria* sp. occurred on every monument but was best developed on the tops and flat surfaces (Fig. 3), often in full sunshine. *Trentepohlia*, less common, occurred mostly in shade. Later invaders are the blue-green *Phormidium* and green *Dermococcus*, coming in after the spraying treatments.

Others

Other plants encountered were orchids and the fern ally *Selaginella armata*.

TREATMENTS

SOLUTIONS USED IN TREATMENTS

The main purpose in employing biocidal solutions is to avoid the damage caused by mechanical brushing. The primary effect on the lichens is apparently to kill the green algae in the plant body, thereby depriving the plant of its food source. The bryophytes are bleached almost instantly as the chlorophyll is destroyed. In both cases the plant remains ultimately crumble and fall off naturally. If desired, one could brush away the detritus after a few months to hasten cleaning of the surface in preparation for scientific observation of hieroglyphs, sculpture and so forth.

I followed recommendations presented by Richardson (1973) who had tested a number of solutions. Two were selected on the basis of local availability, ease of application, effectiveness and safety: Clorox (diluted from commercial strength 1:5 parts water) and borax (5% aqueous solution). The solutions were applied with a standard hand-pressurized 8 liter capacity sprayer (Fig. 4). When treating heavily infested monuments, Clorox was consumed at the rate of about 300 cc/m^2 and borax, somewhat less easily absorbed, at 500 cc/m^2. As the lichen-moss cover dies away, much less solution is needed. Approximately 200 m^2 of monument surface can be treated in a day. The monuments were not washed down later to remove traces of the sprays since it was hoped to retain some residual effect, especially with borates and with Thaltox, a commercial organo-tin spray developed in England. A trial plot in Quirigua (Monument 11; Stela K) was washed down immediately following treatment without any obvious lessening of the biocidal effect. In any event, the solutions are reported to be harmless to most stone or other structural surfaces in the low concentrations recommended.

Samples from two monuments at Quirigua were analyzed at the end of the project in 1978 for the presence of sodium, boron, chlorine and tin ions in order to determine levels of residues. The very low values obtained indicate that the heavy rains during the wet season effectively wash out any ions that remain on the stones after spraying.

OUTLINE OF TREATMENTS

In 1975 a series of one meter square plots was laid out on Mon. 11 and Mon. 2 (Zoomorph B) at Quirigua to compare the effectiveness of various treatments. In general, all of the dominant species were killed off rapidly with either Clorox or borax, probably within hours. This was especially true of *Chiodecton antillarum*, *Phyllopsora corallina* and all the large lichen species, including *Physcias*. However, *Leptotrema santense*, a crust that is apparently not wetted easily, required several treatments to be killed and then only with borax. On the other hand, Clorox was most effective in eliminating the peprous white crust which was killed only very slowly with borax. One species of *Caloplaca* forming conspicuous orange colonies 2 to 5 cm broad and the crustose lichen *Blastenia* required repeated sprayings with borax and Clorox before any visible effect was evident. All bryophytes were killed off rapidly. It should be noted, however, that bryophytes can become re-established very quickly in a single growing season, even on monuments thoroughly sprayed. Cutting down adjacent trees to dry out the monuments usually prevented re-invasion.

The alga *Oscillatoria*, as one might expect, was resistant at first but responded after 2-3 treatments, especially with borax. Clorox alone was not very effective. Monuments 13 and 14 have developed greenish coloration after complete cleaning, caused by *Dermococcus* and *Phormidium*, soil algae, which can be controlled with Thaltox.

As a result of these experimental treatments, a program of spraying all the monuments at Quirigua (about 25) was begun in 1976. Clorox was applied one day and borax the next, the application being made at about six-month intervals: one in the dry season (December-May) and one in the wet season (June-November; Hale 1979).

The first treatment with Clorox and borax probably killed 90% of the microflora. The follow-up treatment six months later reached any colonies missed the first time as well as any resistant species. The third treatment approximately a year later effectively killed the resistant species. While some monuments received a fourth and even a fifth treatment, this was probably not needed and merely served to eliminate totally any residual plants.

Once the organisms had been sprayed, the only remaining problem was the length of time needed for them to crumble and fall away. I have summarized below the times for the major species at the site of Quirigua.

Chiodecton antillarum: after 5 months, dead; after 11 months, dead with some crumbling; after 23 months, 90-100% gone.

Phyllopsora corallina: after 5 months, bleached and dead; after 11 months, decaying and flaking off; after 12 months, 20-50% fallen off; after 21 months, 50-100% gone; after 23 months, essentially all fallen off with few remnants left.

Dirinaria picta: after 5 months, dead and just starting to flake; after 11-12 months, noticeably flaking away; after 21-23 months, more or less gone with few flaking remnants; after 31 months, completely gone.

Parmotrema endosuphureum: after 5 months, bleached and dead; after 11 months completely fallen away.

Leptotrema santense: after 5 months, no change; after 11-12 months, nearly unchanged; after 21-23 months, dead and crumbling with some falling away; after 31 months, all dead, 50-80% fallen away.

Oscillatoria: after 5 months, no change; after 11-12 months, about 50% gone or attenuated; after 21-23 months, much attenuated to about 90% disappeared; after 31 months, 60-95% gone.

A very large series of photographs in black and white and in color has been taken to document the mocroflora and changes in cover with each treatment. These are on file in the Department of Botany, Smithsonian Institution, along with interim reports.

FUTURE PROBLEMS

RECOLONIZATION

New wind-borne propagules (soredia, isidia, fragments, spores, etc.) will constantly re-invade treated sites and fall in stone surfaces, where they will resume growth under favorable conditions. The source of these propagules is nearby forest at least as far as 10-20 km, or even more distant. Studies on temperate lichens suggest a lag phase of about 2 years before the microscopic propagules attain visible size. In general, at Quirigua present evidence shows that about two years are needed for re-establishment and initial growth of the propagules and that after 2-3 years rapid growth occurs. Preliminary measurements of growth rates at Quirigua indicate that a monument could be completely colonized and covered in 10 years. Specific growth rates measured during this study are as follows: *Chiodecton antillarum* 4.5 mm/year; and *Dirinaria picta* 3-4 mm/year; both measured at Quirigua.

CONTROL OF BIOLOGICAL GROWTHS

Treatment of monuments must accordingly be done continuously, since it is impossible to eliminate natural sources of these mocroscopic, wind-borne propagules. Some degree of control can be achieved by spraying the monuments, all stone surfaces and tree trunks in a site, essentially sterilizing the area. In practical terms, a program of re-spraying with any one of the solutions (preferably Thaltox or Clorox) every 4 to 8 years would be more than adequate to kill off the tiny re-invading propagules, which are very susceptible to the sprays and quickly die off.

CONSOLIDATION OF STONE SURFACES

After the monuments are rendered free of fouling organisms, the equally serious problems of weathering, stone disintegration and exfoliation, often obscured by plant cover, become more urgent (Knopman 1975). This stage, which is beyond the scope of the biological program, involves improvement of drainage, isolation of the monuments from soil moisture and, in extreme cases, either application of silicone consolidators or protection of selected monuments with roofs or shelters.

SUMMARY

The microflora (lichens, bryophytes and algae) fouling archaeological ruins has a deleterious effect by chemically and mechanically breaking down the stone surfaces. These organisms can be killed off by spraying the monuments with dilute solutions of biocidal agents such as Clorox or borax, or special preparations such as Thaltox.

The remains of the lichen and bryophyte plant bodies crumble and fall away naturally 6 to 24 months after treatment, depending on site conditions and species involved. No brushing is necessary.

The recolonization of stone surfaces begins in 3-4 years, and without further treatment the monuments will be fouled again in about 10 years. Sprays must be re-applied to previously affected monuments at intervals of 4-8 years or more, depending on local conditions and on the results of follow-up observations. These treatments will have to be continued even after consolidation solutions are applied, but would not be needed if the monuments are protected from rain and moisture under shelters.

REFERENCES CITED

Anonymous
    1972   Control of Lichens, Moulds and Similar Growths. *Building Research Station Digest.* No. 139: 1-4

Anonoymous
    1976   Lichens on Stone, Beauty or Blight? *British Lichenological Society Bulletin.* No. 39: 1-2.

Hale, M. E., Jr.
    1975   Informe Sobre el Crecimiento de Liquenes en los Monumentos de Copan, Honduras. *Yaxkin*, Vol. 1: 6-9, 16.

    1979   Control of the Lichens on the Monuments of Quirigua. *Quirigua Reports I* (Paper No. 3). Museum Monographs, 37. Philadelphia: University Museum.

Hyvert, G.
    1972   The Conservation of the Borobudur Temple. *UNESCO* Serial No. 2646: 1-75.

Knopman, D. S.
    1975   Conservation of Stone Artworks: Barely a Role for Science. *Science*, Vol. 190: 1187-1188.

Richardson, B. A.
    1973   Control of Biological Growths. *Stone Industries*, Vol. 8, No. 2: 2-6.

Figure 11.1. Portion of Monument 11 (north side) before treatment (upper photograph) and after 23 months at Quirigua. The microflora includes mosses and *Chiodecton antillarum* with *Leptorema santense* and the white leprous crust in the lower right portion.

Figure 11.2. Comparison of a portion of the stairway preserved at Peabody Museum, Harvard (upper photograph) and a comparable stair in situ at Copan.

Figure 11.3. Comparison of black algal cover (Oscillaroria) on Monument 7 before (upper photograph) and after 3 treatments during 23 months at Quirigua.

Figure 11.4. Technique for spraying monuments (upper photograph) and an example of *Dirinaria picta* sprayed twice and peeling off in 12 months at Quirigua.

PAPER NO. 12

QUIRIGUA AND THE EARTHQUAKE OF FEBRUARY 4, 1976

by
Bruce Bevan and Robert J. Sharer

INTRODUCTION

Some 20 km southwest of the lowland Maya site of Quirigua, which is situated adjacent to the Motagua fault, was the epicenter of the 4 February, 1976, earthquake which devastated a wide area of Guatemala. This brief report summarizes what is known about this event (taken to include the primary shock and subsequent aftershocks) and is based principally on observations made by the authors at Quirigua during the days following 4 February. We offer a description of the physical damage to the site of Quirigua, a few hypotheses regarding earthquakes and the prehistory of Quirigua and some suggestions that may be of practical use to safeguarding the site in the future. A preliminary technical report of the 4 February earthquake is provided by Espinosa et. al. (1977; see also Plafker 1976).

TECTONIC BACKROUND

In the global synthesis of plate tectonics, the site of Quirigua is located on the northern side of the Caribbean plate (Molnar and Sykes 1969). The boundaries of this plate are shown by Plafker (1976:Fig. 6; see also Le Pichon, Francheteau and Bonnin 1973). The Caribbean plate is moving east relative to the Americas plate at a rate of about 3 cm/year.

Off the shore of Guatemala, in the Caribbean Sea, the northern side of the plate is marked by the Cayman (or Bartlett) trough. On land, the boundary motion is distributed between two parallel faults, the Polochic and the Motagua; both of these faults are named after the rivers which partly define their courses, and both are now left-lateral strike-slip faults (Kupfer and Godoy 1976). However, there is evidence that during the late Paleozoic northward motion of the Caribbean plate relative to the Americas plate resulted in the collision and suture of the two continental masses (Newcome 1973; Schwartz and Newcome 1973).

Historical records indicate a series of major earthquakes in Guatemala prior to 1973 (Espinosa 1977) including those of 1586, 1773, 1830, 1852, 1854, 1862, 1874, 1902, 1918, 1919 and 1942.

EVIDENCE OF TECTONIC ACTIVITY AT QUIRIGUA

The magnitude of the 4 February earthquake was 7.5 on the Richter scale (Plafker 1976:1201) and extensive displacement along the Motagua fault was recorded by aerial and ground observation (Espinosa et. al. 1977).

THE EARTHQUAKE

The authors observed a left-lateral displacement of about 0.75 m along the paved highway crossing the fault near Rio Hondo, Zacapa, approximately 60 km southwest of the site. The principal earth rupture at Quirigua was mapped in two locations (Fig. 1) near the northwest corner of the Park. A disrupted railroad bed near the town of Quirigua indicated horizontal displacement of only a few centimeters there; the direction of the fault was not measured. However, possible fault creep is indicated by cracking of masonry in the expedition houses in Los Amates beginning within two months of the earthquake; this would possibly mark the extension of the railroad bed rupture near the town of Quirigua. There were no ruptures found in the railroad bed between the two mapped areas of the site, and no investigation was done to the east of the Quirigua site-core. It is not expected, however, that the fault zone would be much wider than 1 km. A vertical shift observed in the road at the bridge entering the Park was probably due to slumping of the road fill.

The fault was traced for about 1 km near the site (see Fig. 1). It may be traceable for many kilometers on either side of this segment, but this was not attempted. The dashed line in Fig. 1 shows the extrapolation of the trend; however, it is expected that a true picture of surface faulting would show broken segments at varying angles within the fault zone. The earth rupture near the site shows the *en echelon* crack pattern which is common in alluvium. The left-lateral character of the fault is seen in the shift of the railroad rails and in the barbed-wire fence lines (a fence line crossing the fault at 260° is tensioned while one at 350° is slackened).

The measured fault offset near the site was 6 cm, much less than it was near Rio Hondo; this may imply a spreading of the faulting among parallel lines or a diminution of the total surface rupture. However, the stockyard fence on the north side of the park shows a left-lateral offset of 0.8 m at the site of recent earth rupture (see Fig 2a; this stockyard and fence overlie the foundations of banana farm buildings which were torn down between about 1935 and 1945). This discrepancy of 0.74 m must be due to either prior earthquake (such as the 1942 quake) or to fault creep. It is interesting that the railroad line shows no indication of correcting for this large displacement.

Seismomagnetic changes of between about 2 and 20 gammas (nanoteslas) have been measured as earthquake precursors and also during the faulting (Rikitake 1976); during the magnetic survey in March 1976 (*Quirigua Paper No. 9*, this volume) changes like this were not detected, but they probably would have been undetectable if they did occur.

EARTHQUAKE DAMAGE AT QUIRIGUA

Damage to the site of Quirigua caused by the 4 February earthquake was confined to two areas: masonry structures in the Acropolis and two of the monuments in the Great Plaza. In addition, several archaeological excavations suffered partial collapse, and the threat of aftershocks causing further damage restricted the investigations to shallow probes for at least a month after the quake.

The most conspicuous damage involved partial masonry collapse of both interior and exterior walls of Str. 1B-1, the southernmost building on the Acropolis (*Quirigua Paper No. 6*, Fig.1, this volume). As far as could be determined by inspection on 4 February, most of this collapse involved the walls re-set and mortared during the restoration undertaken in 1912 (Morley 1935:123). Most of the surviving original walls of this and other structures remained intact. Of course, the vaults and upper walls of these buildings had collapsed long ago (probably due, at least in part, to earlier earthquakes); as a result, the surviving masonry appears to have reached a fairly stable level.

The specific areas of damage noted for Str. 1B-1 include the near-complete collapse of the exterior wall on the west side of the building (Fig. 2b), partial collapse of the rear (south) exterior-outset wall and minor displacement of masonry blocks on the front (north) and west exterior walls. Interior walls collapsed in the east room (Room 1), including the complete failure of the east wall. In the central room (Rm 2) the south wall collapsed. In the west room (Rm 3) the upper portion of the south wall was severely damaged. The glyph blocks in all three rooms, however, escaped further injury (Fig. 2c).

No additional masonry collapse was observed for either Str. 1B-2 or 1B-3. Str. 1B-4 suffered damage to the unrestored masonry of three interior walls, but all had been weakened and out-of-plumb before the earthquake. The south wall of the south room (Rm 2) partially failed and both the east wall of the east room (Rm 3) and the north wall of the north room (Rm 4) completely fell in.

Damage to the original interior masonry was also noted in Str. 1B-5 where the upper portion of the north doorjamb leading to the southwest room (Rm 2) was destroyed. The roof of the west chamber of the rear central room (Rm 5) failed partially, although it had been on the verge of collapse prior to the quake.

In the Great Plaza Mons. 8 (Stela H) and 10 (J) suffered injury from this earthquake. Both of these monuments had broken at their bases and fallen antecedent to their discovery in the late nineteenth century (see Maudsley 1889-1902:Plate 45). Mon. 8, repaired with cement and reinforcing rods, had been re-set about forty years ago in a concrete slab placed just beneath ground level (Stromsvik 1941:81-83). Movement resulting from ground motion appears to have fractured the monument shaft at ground level, immediately above the concrete slab. Some cracking and spalling of the sandstone occurred above the fracture, especially on the east face, but damage to sculptured elements was minimal since the reinforcing rods did not burst from their setting (Fig. 3a).

Mon. 10, however, suffered more severely. Like Mon. 8, when re-set ca. 40 years ago its shaft was joined to its base using cement and medially embedded steel reinforcing rods. The movement of the shaft caused by the earthquake burst the reinforcing rods from their concrete mantle, cracking the stone and detaching spalls of both concrete and sandstone, resulting in damage to sculptured elements. Loss to the front (west) face was restricted to the plinth beneath the sculptured figure. The sculpted glyphs on the south face escaped serious injury. On the east face the lowest row of glyphs was almost completely destroyed and the row above was damaged. On the north face portions of the two lowest rows of glyphs were heavily damaged. The detached glyph fragments were taken to the Project laboratory for safe-keeping. As a precaution, both Mons. 8 and 10 were braced by wooden supports until permanent repairs could be undertaken by the Instituto de Antropologia e Historia (Sharer et. al. 1979).

ARCHAEOLOGICAL SIGNIFICANCE

The site of Quirigua appears to be immediately adjacent to the Motagua fault zone; it is also possible that lines of rupture do pass, or have passed, through the site since its occupation by the Maya. No clear evidence of ancient ruptures was revealed by excavation, although indications of past destruction and repair of masonry were noted on the east facade of Str. 1B-Sub3. It is possible that the corner buttressing present on most Acropolis buildings and the western terraces behind Str. 3 was a response to earthquakes occurring during the occupation of Quirigua (Fig 3b). Some cases of structural collapse revealed by excavation might be attributable to ancient quakes. Inferences supporting a case for ancient earthquake destruction may be drawn from the apparently sudden failure of an adobe building (Str. 1B-18) which collapsed and sealed its contents (see *Quirigua Paper No. 6*, this volume). The adobe-block building atop Str. 1A-10 may have been destroyed by a past quake, although other causes for its collapse cannot be ruled out.

If future investigations were to reveal the remains of masonry structures which contained evidence of actual ruptures resulting from movements along the Motagua fault, we would have firm geological information on the rate of movement along the fault during the last thousand years.

The present tipping of several of the monuments in the Great Plaza may be related to previous earthquakes at the site. It is interesting to note that Mons. 8 and 10, both of which fell anciently and were victims of damage during the most recent quake, have their short axes facing or roughly parallel to the line of the Motagua fault. During a strong aftershock on 6 February a Project member observed Mon. 8 rocking in an east-west motion. The two stelae that remain acutely out-of-plumb (Mons. 4 and 6) both lean to the east (Mon. 5 leaned severely to the northeast before finally falling in 1917; it was re-set by Stromsvik in 1934 and remains vertical). Recent geological studies have begun investigating earthquake ground motion near a fault, seeking in particular to define the forces and their directions during a quake. Some of these studies indicated that the initial strong motions are predominantly transverse to a fault (Hudson and Cloud 1967). Other work concludes that strong motions are parallel to a fault along its length, but transverse to the fault line in areas beyond both ends of the fault (Abe 1974). One might infer from the evidence regarding the Quirigua monuments that the strongest ground motion has been east-west (parallel to the fault) during earthquakes at the site.

THE EARTHQUAKE

SITE RESTORATION

Since earthquakes will occur in the future along the Motagua fault at Quirigua, consideration must be given to the protection of the architecture, monuments and visitors. It is very difficult to estimate the earthquake forces which are possible at the site. It is likely that the horizontal acceleration on structures could be as much as the vertical acceleration of gravity. Current research on the strong motion of earthquakes in other areas will help to specify more accurately the forces to be expected at Quirigua.

The damage to the stelae in the February 1976 earthquake indicates that they probably need to be safeguarded. The monuments and their fragile sculpture might be protected by either damping the earthquake forces or otherwise isolating the stelae from them. The fate of Mons. 8 and 10 shows that embedding stelae in concrete is not advisable. Instead, resting the bases in a pocket of sand might help dissipate an earthquake's forces. It is also possible that the stelae might be allowed to topple during a severe quake, but if protective barriers continue to be used around the monuments they should be designed so as not to damage falling sculpture.

The reconstruction of the architecture should also allow for the strong horizontal forces which can be expected in the future. There are a number of good sources available which discuss earthquake engineering(Weigle 1970; Newmark and Rosenblueth 1971; Okamoto 1973; and Solnes 1974). The information on restoration in this report is only preliminary and suggestive, but precautions taken now should mitigate the destructive effects of future tremors.

QUIRIGUA REPORTS

REFERENCES CITED

Abe, K.
    1974   Seismic Displacement and Ground Motion Near a Fault: The Saitama Earthquake of September 21, 1931. *Journal of Geophysical Research*, Vol. 79, No. 29: 4393-4399.

Espinosa, A. F. (ed.)
    1976   *The Guatemalan Earthquake of February 4, 1976, A Preliminary Report.* Geological Survey Professional Paper 1002, U. S. Geological Survey, Washington, D. C.

Hudson, D. E. and W. K. Cloud
    1967   An Analysis of Seismoscope Data from The Parkfield Earthquake of June 27, 1966. *Bulletin of the Seismological Society of America*. Vol. 57, No. 6: 1143-1159.

Kupfer, D. H. and J. Godoy.
    1967   Strike-Slip Faulting in Guatemala. *Trans. American Geophysical Union.* Vol. 48, No. 1: 215.

Le Pinchon, X., J. Francheteau and J. Bonnin.
    1973   *Plate Tectonics.* Elsevier.

Lomnitz, C.
    1974   *Global Tectonics and Earthquake Risk.* Elsevier.

Maudslay, A. P.
    1889-
    1902   *Archaeology. Biologia Centrali-Americana.* 5 vols. London: Porter

Molnar, P. and L. R. Sykes
    1969   Tectonics of the Caribbean and Middle America Regions from Focal Mechanisms and Seismicity. *Geological Society of America Bulletin.* Vol. 80, No. 9: 1639-1684.

Morley, S. G.
    1935   *Guide Book to the Ruins of Quirigua.* Carnegie Institution of Washington, Supplementary Publication 16, Washington, D. C.

Newcomb, W. E.
    1973   Late Paleozoic Tectonics of the Motagua Fault: A Subduction-Collision Scar? *EOS (Trans. American Geophysical Union).* Vol. 54, No. 4: 471.

Newmark, N. M. and E. Rosenblueth
    1971   *Fundamentals of Earthquake Engineering.* Prentice-Hall.

Okamoto, S.
    1973   *Introduction to Earthquake Engineering.* Wiley.

Plafker, George
    1976   Tectonic Aspects of the Guatemala Earthquake of 4 February 1976. *Science.* Vol. 143, No. 4259: 1201-1208.

Rikitake, T.
    1976   *Earthquake Prediction.* Elsevier.

Schwartz, D. P. and W. E. Newcomb
    1973   Motagua Fault Zone: A Crustal Suture. *EOS (Trans. American Geophysical Union).* Vol. 54, No. 4: 477.

Solnes, J. (ed)
    1974   *Engineering Seismology and Earthquake Engineering.* Leiden:Noordhoff.

Stromsvik, G.
    1941   *Substela Caches and Stela Foundations at Copan and Quirigua.* Carnegie Institution of Washington, Publication 528, Contributions to American Anthropology and History, No. 37, Washington, D. C.

Weigel, R. L. (ed.)
    1970   *Earthquake Engineering.* Prentice-Hall.

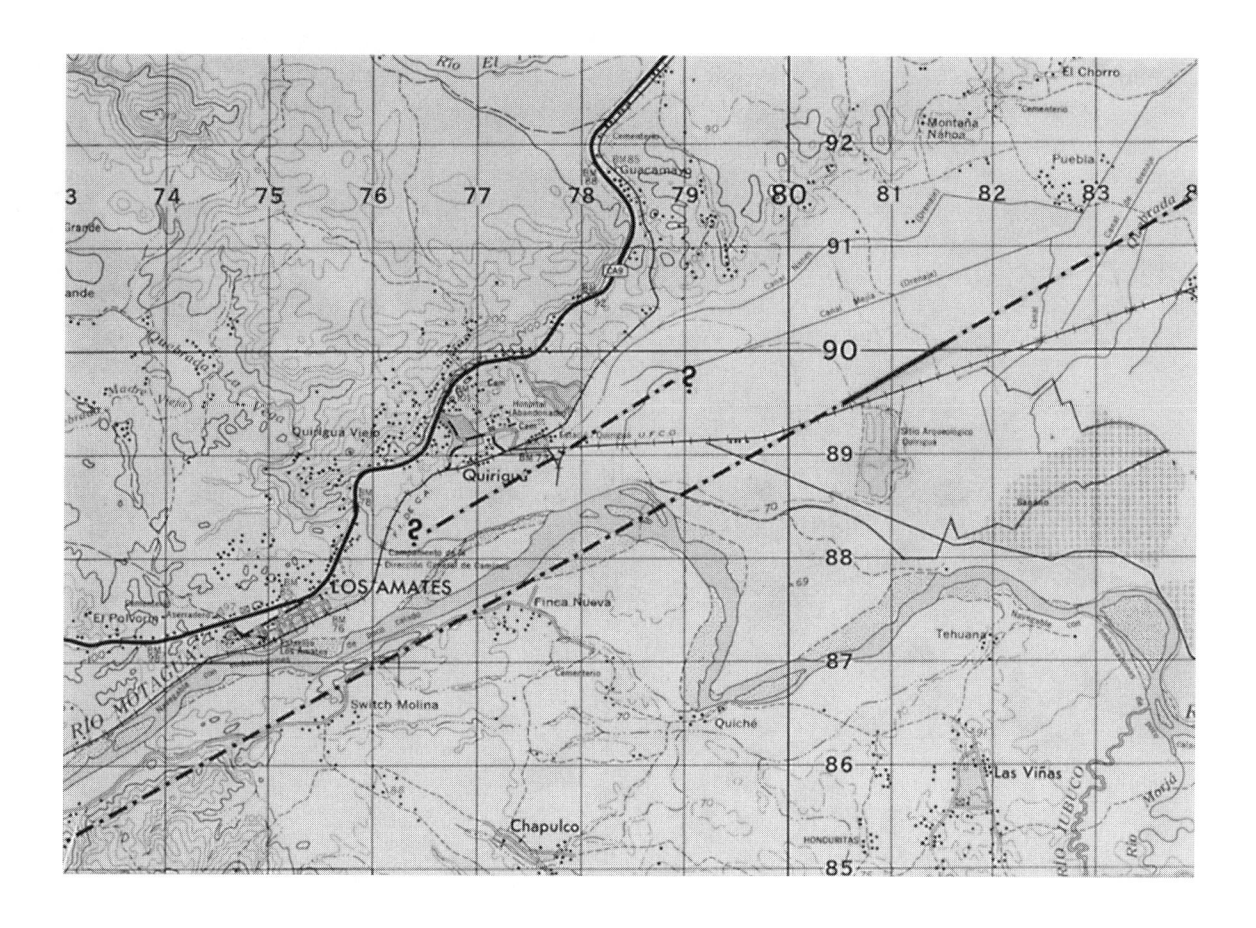

Figure 12.1. Map of the lower Motagua valley in the vicinity of Quirigua showing the approximate trace of earth ruptures resulting from the 1976 earthquake (solid line represents traced rupture; broken lines represent approximate alignments beyond traced extent).

Figure 12.2. a. Metal stockyard fence immediately north of the Quirigua main group showing the lateral off-set due to earth rupture.
b. 4 February, 1976 earthquake damage to reconstructed masonry, west side of Str. 1B-1.
c. 4 February, 1976 earthquake damage to the southern wall of the central room, Str. 1B-1; note glyph panel bench.

Figure 12.3. a. 4 February, 1976 earthquake damage to south base, Monument 8 (Stela H).
b. 4 February, 1976 earthquake damage to east base, Monument 10 (Stela J).
c. Large secondary masonry buttress against the west wall of the Acropolis Platform, typical of reinforcements probably added in response to ancient earthquake activity.

PAPER NO. 13

MONUMENT 26, QUIRIGUA, GUATEMALA

by
Christopher Jones

INTRODUCTION

In November of 1978, BANDEGUA fruit company drainage operations around the site of Quirigua in the Motagua valley of Guatemala uncovered two large fragments of a new stela less than a kilometer north of the site center. The discovery was reported jointly to Marcelino Gonzalez C. of the Instituto de Antropologia e Historia de Guatemala and to David Sedat of the Quirigua Project and the University Museum of the University of Pennsylvania. The fragments, representing the top and bottom sections of the stela, are presently in Guatemala City under the protection of IDAEH. The middle section of the stela has not been found. (See Figs. 1 and 2).

Recognizing the importance of establishing context for the monument, Wendy Ashmore, with the help of BANDEGUA and funds from the National Geographic Society, supervised in 1979 the clearing and excavation of a broad earthen platform (Platform 3C-1) and rectangular structure(Str. 3C-14) exposed by the dragline at the reported location of the monument fragments (*Quirigua Paper No. 8*, this volume). On the platform was found a plain, circular schist slab (Monument 27), and within the structure itself a cache (SD 21) of three paired vessels containing six intact worked jadeite pieces, bone fragments, bits of pyrite, cinnabar and liquid mercury. The platform rests on what seems to have been an Early Classic level of floodplain silting; the vessels are probably Early Classic; and comparison of the jadeite pieces with similar ones from Kaminaljuyu and Copan also indicate an Early Classic date (Ashmore 1980). The following epigraphic and stylistic study of the monument adds confirmations to these chronological assessments, and suggests that the monument formed a part of this assemblage of platform, structure and cache.

Our drawing of Mon. 26 (see Fig. 1) is by Carl Beetz. It is based on a series of controlled-lighting photographs by Ashmore, supplemented by photographs by Gonzalez and a recent series of artificially lighted shots taken for the Quirigua Project by Joya Hairs. Layout of the wrap-around design is derived from a rubbing by John Keshishian. A full-scale photograph of the rubbing was furnished by George Stuart of NGS and after reduction to quarter-scale, provided the guide for the inked drawing. On the drawing, solid lines represent information which can be confirmed on more than one photograph, dotted lines indicate questioned features, and broken lines are reserved for reconstruction. The original 1:4 drawing is here reduced to 1:10 scale.

Monument 26 was carved from a column of hard blue-gray schist, a material which was commonly utilized in Quirigua architecture for paving stones and lintels. This material tends to develop erosion and fracture lines along the length of the shaft. As can be seen from the photographs, breakage at the top of the lower fragment occurred mostly along a single transverse plane, with the exception of a small fragment missing from the rear. The break at the bottom of the upper fragment is more irregular, suggesting that the missing portions of the stone are probably fragmented. Several of the breakage planes continue along the shaft as cracks, with one extending through the face of the front figure and another up the center of the left-hand column of glyphs. The even break at the butt contrasts with the uneven one above, suggesting that the shaft broke off its butt while standing erect, as did the sandstone Mons. 8 and 10 (Stelae H and J) of later times.

Aside from the breakage, the stone suffered three recent gouges on the rear surfaces, two on the right edge and one on Block C5. These look as though they were caused by the dragline bucket. Some older, more weatherd battering can be seen on the nose, lips and right eye of the front figure and was, perhaps, deliberate. In spite of the crisp appearance of most of the carving, a close examination shows that the entire shaft was exposed to cosiderable erosion, perhaps on the front more than on the back. The top of the shaft appears weathered and broken as well, indicating a long upright exposure.

I have tentatively reconstructed the position of the upper fragment relative to the butt, assuming that the distance from the eyes to the top of the belt was around 37% of that from the eyes to the bottom of the feet. This ratio was seen as a relative constant in three similar early monuments: Tikal Stela 2 (36%), Tikal Stela 31 (38%) and Uaxactun Stela 20 (36%). Presumably, such consistency would be created by the proportions of the human body, rather than by costume.

Our reconstructed position for the lower fragment also allows for a fairly even row height on the rear glyph columns. Room for adjustment in restored glyph heights must be allowed, however, since glyph heights in Columns C and D are considerably smaller on the bottom fragment than on the top. We have taken the caution of labelling the glyph blocks of the lower fragment zA1, zB1,... to allow for the possibility of an error in the row count.

As restored, the stela stands 1.80 m from the base of carving to the slightly restored top. Total shaft length is 2.23 m. Maximum dimension from side to side is 0.33 m and from front to back is 0.24 m.

EPIGRAPHY

The back of Mon. 26 is carved with a hieroglyphic text. The inscription begins on the left half with a large-sized initial series introducing glyph and large-sized initial series period glyphs. Since the text divides into quarter-sized blocks on the lower monument fragment and continues in the smaller size in the right-hand columns, we have labelled the left half columns A and B and the right half columns C and D. This conforms to Morley's standard labelling schemes for other Quirigua monuments in which large initial series glyphs are similarly followed by smaller blocks (Morley 1937-38 IV:123 ff.). As mentioned above, the blocks of the lower fragment are provisionally labelled with a small letter "z" in anticipation of the recovery of the missing middle section of the stela.

A likely reconstruction of the missing segment of the initial series as we will see below, is for a large-sized sacred round glyph and subsequent divided columns to follow the *kins*. Uneven row spacing calls for more rows in Columns A and B than in Columns C and D. In our reconstruction, there would therefore be 19 rows in Columns A-B and 17 in Columns C-D, producing a total of 51 glyphs in 72 labelled blocks.

The first glyph of the inscription, the initial series introductory glyph (Table 1), displays as its patron of the current month a reptile head with curved teeth, snake-like scales and a fat hook-shaped element (perhaps a tail) projecting behind the head. This reads best as patron for the months *Zotz*, *Yax*, *Zac*, or *Cumku* (Thompson 1950: Figs. 22 and 23).

The next glyph must be read as 9 *Baktuns*, thus placing the date within the main 400-year period of Maya history from A.D. 435 to 830 (using the GMT correlation). The following coefficient at A5-B6 contains two large dots. This would read as 2 *Katuns* without question, except for the peculiarity that the dots are connected by a thin bar. Next follows a clear 18 *Tuns* and then the *uinal* glyph with an eroded but indisputable Zero coefficent.

A problem arises with this seemingly unequivocable initial series when we discover that none of the twenty days of the *uinal* from 9.2.18.0.0 to 9.2.18.0.19 occurs in the months *Zotz*, *Yax*, *Zac*, or *Cumku* but rather in *Pax* and *Kayab*.

A possible choice for resolution of this set of conflicting information is to assume that the carvers of the text substituted the frog head *Pax* month glyph itself for the diety which normally serves as the patron of the month *Pax*. If so, the date would most likely be the period-end 9.2.18.0.0 10 *Ahau* 8 *Pax*. No Eighteen *tun* period end notations are noted by Morley (1937-38, Vol. IV: Table 139, p.291) for Maya inscriptions, but four 17 *tun* endings are noted and therefore 18 should not be unexpected.

Peter Mathews (personal communication) points out that the toad head month patron for *Zac* would allow a date at 9.3.18.0.0 8 *Ahau* 8 *Zac*. In addition, the reptile head patron of the month *Zotz* would also fit what we see on the monument, and allow a date at 9.8.18.0.0 11 *Ahau* 13 *Zotz*. Both of these positions must assume that we have misread the strange *katun* coefficent.

This date need not be a *tun*-ending at all, of course, since we are missing the *kin* glyph, the Sacred Round, the Vague Year, Glyph G and any helpful lunar information. However, if we assume a month patron of *Zotz, Yax, Zac* or *Cumku*, the choices are still limited. The only possibilities with 18 *tuns* and 0 *uinals* within the first half of *Baktun* 9 are:

9.1.18.0.17 3 *Caban* 0 *Zotz* (also 18-19 *kins*)

9.7.18.0.7 7 *Manik* 0 *Yax* (also 8-19 *kins*)
9.9.18.0.2 11 *Ik* 0 *Cumku* (also 3-19 *kins*)

Once the *katun* or *tun* coeffiecents are doubted, actually the monument cannot be tied down to a specific *katun* by calendric manipulations. A mistake in the number of bars or dots in the *tun* coefficent would allow the stela to be placed at period ends within *Katuns* 0, 2, 4, 6, 7, 9, 11, and 13, assuming again a period-end *Baktun* nine. On the basis of the well-defined two dots of the *katun*, we prefer 18 *tuns* and 2 *katuns* (at 9.2.18.0.0 10 *Ahau* 8 *Pax*) and the reptile head in the introductory glyph as a variant of the *Pax* patron. The alternative *tun* ends in *katuns* 3 and 8, plus many possibilities for non-*tun* ends and scribal errors should nevertheless be kept in mind.

TABLE 1

QUIRIGUA MONUMENT 26: GLYPH CLASSIFICATION AND CHRONOLOGICAL DECIPHERMENT

	A1-B2	Initial Series Introductory Glyph (patron *Zotz, Yax, Zac* or *Cumku*, possibly *Pax*)
	A3-B4	9 *baktuns*
	A5-B6	2 *Katuns* (coefficient oddly joined)
	A7-B8	18 *Tuns*
	A9-B10	0 *Uinals*
	A11-B12	*Kins* (coefficient missing, portion of head glyph preserved)
Date A (9.2.18.0.0?)	A13-zA1	9 missing blocks? (possibly reconstructable as: large-sized Sacred Round; Glyph G; Glyph F; Vague Year; Glyph E; Glyph D)
	zB1-zA2	Glyph C? (zero); Glyph A (30)
	zB2-D9	21 non-calendric blocks (Emblem Glyph at D1?; 3 *hel* succession at D6; 4 *hel* at D8)
	D10-	10 missing blocks?
	zC1-xC2	3 non-calendric blocks
Date B (9.2.2.7.17?)	zD2-zC3	10 *Caban* (or *Cauac*); Seating of *Yax*?
	zD3	non-calendric block (Emblem Glyph?)

MONUMENT 26

A remnant of the opening calendric information appears to survive on the lower fragment. At the block which we have labeled zA2 can be seen the characteristic postfixed coefficient 10 of Glyph A, signifying that the current lunation was counted as thirty nights in length. The preceding block is a young head with a lunar postfix. This might well be Glyph C of the lunar series, which registers the number of the current lunation within a series of six. The lack of coefficient is proper for the first lunation, the young head and lunar postfix are as they should be, but the characteristic open hand under the head is missing. A precedent for the lack of the hand in Glyph C can be found on Tikal Stela 31 at block B10 (Coe 1965: Fig. on p. 33). Unfortunately, neither glyph helps to position the initial series in time. Presumably missing are the Sacred Round glyphs, Glyphs G, F, E, D and the Vague Year position. These can be fitted into either 3 to 5 blocks with ease, thus not in themselves determining an exact number of missing rows.

The inscription ends with a date near the bottom of Columns C and D. At block zD2 can be seen the full frame and pedestal of a day sign, surmounted by coefficient 10. The curved lines in the glyphic interior are characteristic of early *Cauac* day signs, as on Tikal Stela 31, but can also be seen on early *Caban* signs as well. In the next block a *Cauac* main sign and bow superfix suggest a vague year glyph; one of the *Cauac* months *Chen, Yax, Zac* or *Ceh*. The upper affix might be that for either *Chen* or *Yax*. The block lacks either a coefficient or a seating prefix to place the date within a particular day of the month. However, there is a local precedent for this in the Leyden Plate, wherein the 0 *Yaxkin* position is represented without a seating glyph (Morley and Morley 1935; and Coe's drawing in Shook 1960: 34). If we read 0 *Chen* or 0 *Yax*, the two positions for this date near 9.2.18.0.0 are:

9.2.2.7.17 10 *Caban* 0 *Yax*
9.3.2.11.17 10 *Caban* 0 *Chen*

The earlier of these two dates is to be preferred, since inscriptions tend to relate historical information preceeding or immediately following the dedicatory date.

Within the long non-calendric statement from zB2 to D9 are two glyphs which also suggest an Early Classic date. At blocks D6 and D8, the main signs are Thompson's *hel* glyph, meaning succession, or count (1950:161-162). Both glyphs carry a spiral prefix (T21) and identical subfixes. The first carries the coefficient 3 and the second the coefficient 4. In a recent paper, Riese (1979a) has postulated that these numbered *hel* notations, when they appear at Copan, Tikal, Quirigua and other sites, record the number of the ruler in a successive count of reigns. Riese demonstrates that the occurrences of the glyph generally fit his hypothesis throughout Maya epigraphy with only a few exceptions.

If a count of succession is indeed stated here, then Mon. 26 would most likely date to early within *Baktun* 9. Cauac Sky, inaugurated at 9.14.13.4.17 was counted as the 14th ruler and Jade Sky as the 16th (Sharer 1978:69). Assuming that Mon. 26 was dedicated at 9.2.18.0.0 to a fourth ruler, then ten reigns would have passed within the space of 235 *tun*-years. The resultant average of 23.5 *tun*-years per ruler seems high but not impossible. By comparison, Tikal reigns averaged 17.5 *tun*-years each in the 313 *tun*-years between the putative inauguration of Stormy Sky around 8.19.10.0.0 (Coggins 1975: Table 3) and that of Ruler B at 9.15.3.6.8 (Jones 1977). I suspect, however, that the 9 *hel* ruler mentioned on Stela 31 is not Stormy Sky but a predecessor. If so, then the Tikal average would be lengthened and more comparable to that of Quirigua.

STYLE

In the absence of an unequivocal epigraphic date for Mon. 26, it is necessary to compare the carving with that of other Maya monuments in order to define some limits in our choices of chronological possibilities. The closest stylistic analogy lies in a previously discovered Quirigua monument, Morley's Stela U, which we have renamed Mon. 21 (Morley 1937-38, IV:89-94; V:Pl. 169; Coe and Sharer 1979: 19, Table 2). In spite of an unmistakable two *katun* coefficient in the initial series of that stela, Morley provisionally dated it to 9.14.0.0.0. The primary reason for doing so was to bring the date more in line with a 9.13.0.0.0 date on Monument 20 (Stela T) from the same hill-top location (Group A) north of the site core (Morley 1937-38, IV: 91-92). The *katun* coefficient on Mon. 20 is clearly higher than 10, and so in spite of earlier suggestions to the contrary (*Quirigua Paper No. 6*, this volume), I think we are safer not to assume an early date for that stone.

Mons. 20, 21 and 26 are of similar, short and narrow dimensions as compared with the later Quirigua giant monuments. They are also all made of schist and feature a front figure with spread-open feet. Nevertheless,

Mon. 20 is of a brown schist and has plain sides whereas Mons. 21 and 26 are fashioned from a blue-gray schist and the front designs wrap-around onto the stela sides. In addition, they share a particular glyph (C2 on Mon. 26; B6 on Mon. 21). This might be a name of a ruler, since on Mon. 21 it is carved in a larger size than the surrounding glyphs and this trait is characteristic of nominal glyphs on later Quirigua monuments such as Mons. 23 and 24 (the Altars of Zoomorphs O and P).

Our recent photographs of Mon. 21 (Jones and Sharer 1980) reveal design elements similar to what we see on Mon. 26. The front figure on Mon. 21 is mostly flaked off, but the feet and the side carving are still well-preserved. The feet point out in both directions and extend onto the sides as they must also have done on the even narrower Mon. 26. Similar open-mouth serpent bar heads can be distinguished as well. Thus the stone type, the wrap-around composition, the pose with horizontal serpent bar, the two *katun* initial series dates and the non-calendric glyph combine to unite the two monuments chronologically and to suggest that they are both *Katun* 2 monuments.

Other fruitful comparisons can be made to Tikal Stelae 1, 2 and 28 and to Uaxactun Stela 20, all of Early Classic date (Maler 1911:Pl. 12-14; Coe 1965:drawing on p. 32; Morley 1937-38, V:Pl. 61). On the Tikal monuments the front figure carries over onto the stela sides. Apart from this basic design, Mon. 26 shares many specific features with Tikal Stela 2, style-dated at 9.3.10.0.0 ± 2 *katuns*. Although the face and feet of the Tikal monument are shown in profile, it has the full-front torso pose with symmetrically-placed cupped hands and arms cradling a rigid serpent bar. We also see (in profile) the same large squarish tied ear ornaments, the twisted cords on the side of the face and over the ear ornaments, the large-nosed, large-eyed diety headress with featherless wing attachments and superior glyphic medallion and trefoil, the delineation of a prominent upper lip, the small necklace head medallion with widely flaring beads, the bead fringe across the forehead, the in-curving split end of the serpent tongue, and the generally blunt-ended scroll-work. Many of these stylistic elements are those utilized by Proskouriakoff (1950) to distinguish early monuments from late. Most of them drop out of the Maya artistic repertoire by 9.6.0.0.0. Uaxactun Stela 2 (9.3.0.0.0) shows the same frontal pose as on Mon. 26, with a similar headdress.

The hieroglyphs of Mon. 26 also show some indications of an Early Classic date. The *tun* and *uinal* heads in particular feature a head-band with a three-pointed tassel projecting over the forehead. These are seen on the following monuments only:

Tikal Stela 29	8.12.14.8.15
Leyden Plate	8.14.3.1.2
Copan Stela 24	9.2.0.0.0
Tikal Stela 6	9.4.0.0.0
Yaxchilan Lintel 48	9.4.11.8.16

In summary, then, Mon. 26 is stylistically early, most likely from *Katun* 2, even though the patron of the month glyph does not appear to be appropriate to a 9.2.18.0.? date as written. The supporting arguments for this assertion are: the two-*katun* coeffect itself, the two-*katun* date on the similar Quirigua Mon. 21, the similarity to Tikal Stela 2 and Uaxactun Stela 20, the early-style period glyphs, scrolls, headdress, ear ornaments and other items of costume. Even though individual costume features might persist until later (c.f. the headdress of Copan Stela P at 9.9.10.0.0), such a constellation of features can probably only exist on a genuinely early monument.

CONCLUSIONS

If we assume, then, that Mon. 26 dates at or near 9.2.18.0.0, and Mon. 21 to around the same time, the monuments become important for an understanding of the history of Quirigua and of the Maya.

In the first place, we find, somewhat to our surprise, that monument carving is of considerable antiquity at Quirigua, establishing itself almost as early as the first dated monuments at Copan (Stela 20 at 9.1.10.0.0? and Stela 4 more securely at 9.2.10.0.0). Equally important, perhaps, is the fact that the two Quirigua Mons. 21 and 26 are the earliest epigraphically dated figural art of the Classic Maya tradition outside of the core Peten area. Copan and Altar de Sacrificios have earlier stelae, but these are all-glyphic. The newly-discovered Stela 30 of Copan (Riese 1979b), is also probably very early, but there are no surviving hieroglyphs and as Baudez (1980) indicates, the figural style might be judged to stem directly from the same Late Preclassic El Baul-Kaminaljuyu style from which the Peten sculptural traditions were drawn.

As discussed above, the figural arrangement, pose and costuming of Mon. 26 are linked to that of the Peten, particularly to that of Tikal and perhaps to Uaxactun. In turn, the full-front pose, symmetrically cupped hands and horizontally held serpent bar of this early Quirigua monument become the hallmarks of the later figural stelae of both Quirigua and Copan. Whereas Morley postulated that Quirigua was colonized by Copan, it now seems clear that the two sites were viable and somewhat independent entities since the Early Classic as Miller (1980) has also suggested.

One might postulate that the great sequence of Copan full-frontal stelae grew out of the traditions established by these early Quirigua monuments. The Copan stela tradition is characterized by a trend towards full-round statue-like representations. The combination of full-frontal pose and wrap-around composition on Mons. 26 and 21 can be thought of as a necessary first step toward this tradition. The step was never taken in Peten art, where the wrap-around stelae retain the profile face and feet, and the full-front figures are carved only on the front surfaces of the stelae. Thus it is curious that it is here in the Southeastern Maya area that this approach toward a statue is made so early. As Miller has pointed out (*Quirigua Paper No. 14*, this volume), the early monuments show none of the deep carving and open work of the later Copan masterpieces, but retain the flat planes and bas-relief of the Peten.

Within Quirigua itself the later stela-carving sequence also seems to owe much to these early pieces, which were almost surely still standing and visible in Late Classic times. Mon. 8 (Stela H) at 9.16.0.0.0 especially utilizes the wrap-around concept in its design and carries the text on the back. Mon. 10 (Stela J) at 9.16.5.0.0 continues this arrangement to some extent, although hieroglyphs occupy much of the sides. After these monuments, the stelae depict figures on front and back and the wrap-around concept is minimized.

Thus Mons. 8 and 10, the early monuments of Cauac Sky's long stela sequence appear to draw upon these early Quirigua monuments for basic design, although increasing greatly the scale and cutting far more deeply into the stone. It seems clear that we no longer need to view late Quirigua stelae as merely stemming from Copan stela traditions, but instead as emerging out of a local Quirigua format, perhaps as a conscious renaissance (Jones and Sharer 1980). Along these lines, as Sharer (1978:65) points out, the above-mentioned Peten connections of Mons. 26 and 21 might be paralleled by the fact that Cauac Sky's name glyph, a split-sky glyph surmounted by a celestial deity head and two upraised arms, is an exact replica of the name glyph of Tikal's Early Classic ruler, Stormy Sky, who probably died shortly before the carving of Mon. 26. Was the naming of Cauac Sky a direct recognition of Tikal royal ancestry? Was Early Classic Quirigua established as a direct colony from the Peten? These are, of course, difficult questions. Nevertheless, when a drain for a banana orchard produces a monument which can so alter our view of the historical connections of a whole region, we are reminded that what we know is infinitely less than what we do not.

QUIRIGUA REPORTS

REFERENCES CITED

Ashmore, W.
- 1980   The Classic Maya Settlement at Quirigua, Guatemala. Paper presented at the 45th Annual Meeting of the Society for American Archaeology, Philadelphia.

Baudez, C.
- 1980   Iconography and History at Copan. Paper presented at the 45th Annual Meeting of the Society for American Archaeology, Philadelphia.

Coe, W. R.
- 1965   Tikal: Ten Years of Study of a Maya Ruin in the Lowlands of Guatemala. *Expedition.* Vol 8 (1): 5-56.

Coe, W. R. and R. J. Sharer.
- 1979   The Quirigua Project: 1975 Season. *Quirigua Reports* I (No. 2). Philadelphia: University Museum.

Coggins, C.
- 1975   *Painting and Drawing Styles at Tikal..* PhD. Dissertation, Harvard University. University Microfillms, Ann Arbor, Michigan.

Jones, C.
- 1977   Inauguration Dates of Three Late Classic Rulers of Tikal, Guatemala. *American Antiquity.* Vol. 42 (1): 28-60.

Jones, C. and R. J. Sharer
- 1980   Archaeological Investigations in the Site-Core of Quirigua, Guatemala. Paper presented at the 45th Annual Meeting of the Society for American Archaeology, Philadelphia.

Maler, T.
- 1911   *Explorations in the Department of Peten, Guatemala: Tikal.* Harvard University, Peabody Museum, Memoirs, Vol. 5 (No. 1).

Miller, A.
- 1980   Stylistic Implications of Monument Carving at Quirigua and Copan. Paper presented at the 45th Annual Meeting of the Society for American Archaeology, Philadelphia.

Morley, S. G.
- 1937-38   *The Inscriptions of Peten.* Carnegie Institution of Washington, Publication 437, Washington, D. C.

Morley, F. R. and S. G. Morley
- 1938   *The Age and Provenance of the Leyden Plate.* Carnegie Institution of Washington, Publication 509, Contribution 24, Washington, D. C.

Proskouriakoff, T.
- 1950   *The Study of Classic Maya Sculpture.* Carnegie Institution of Washington, Publication 593, Washington, D. C.

Riese, B.
- 1978   Estructura 4 - Informe Sobre sus Esculturas Jeroglificas. Proyecto Arqueologico Copan, Honduras, Manuscript.
- n.d.   Die Hel Hieroglyphen. Paper presented at SUNY-Albany Hieroglyphic Conference.

Sharer, R. J.
- 1978   Archaeology and History at Quirigua, Guatemala. *Journal of Field Archaeology.* Vol. 5 (1): 51-70.

Shook, E.
- 1960   Tikal Stela 29. *Expedition.* Vol. 2: 28-35.

Thompson, J. E. S.
- 1950   *Maya Hieroglyphic Writing.* Carnegie Institution of Washington, Publication 589, Washington, D. C.

Figure 13.1. Quirigua Monument 26, front and sides (drawing by Carl P. Beetz). Scale 1:10.

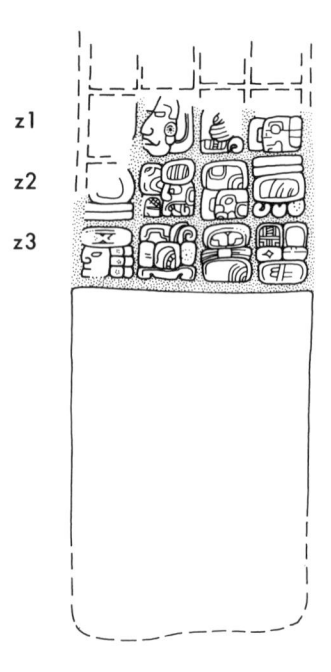

Figure 13.2. Quirigua Monument 26, back (drawing by Carl P. Beetz). Scale 1:10.

Figure 13.3. Quirigua Monument 26 (upper fragment), photographs of front (left), and front and right side showing wrap-around design (right). Not to scale.

Figure 13.4. Quirigua Monument 26 (upper fragment), photograph of back. Not to scale

PAPER NO. 14

STYLISTIC IMPLICATIONS OF MONUMENT CARVING AT QUIRIGUA AND COPAN

by
Arthur G. Miller

QUIRIGUA AND COPAN

Morley (1935) gives four principal reasons why Quirigua was "probably established as a colony from Copan": 1.) geographic proximity; 2.) Copan was very "monument-minded"; 3.) Copan was a "metropolitan center of culture and learning perhaps for the whole Maya area, and as such is...likely to have possessed the necessary elements, the intellectual, esthetic and physical equipment for the venture at hand (i.e. colonization)." 4.) "Indeed, inherent probability strongly indicates that Quirigua was organized and established under the leadership from Copan, which fact is strongly supported by the similarity between the sculpture, architecture and ceramic art of the two cities" (*Ibid.*:31).

Morley is not alone in suggesting that the art styles of both sites are similar. Spinden (1913:175) also suggests that Quirigua may have been founded by colonists from Copan, but Proskouriakoff (1950:131) doubts Spinden's suggestion of the relationship between Copan and Quirigua because "there are enough differences in style and in building practices between the two sites to make this a dubious conclusion." Kubler (1962:153-154) describes Quirigua and Copan sculptural style to be fundamentally different.

Pollock (1965:390-391) finds "extraordinary similiarity of the plan of Quirigua to that of Copan." But comparison of the plan of Copan and Quirigua reveals fundamental differences in the layout of structures. "Copan is an assembly of open volumes rather than a collection of buildings" (Kubler 1962:128). The building masses of Quirigua do not form close-knit "open volumes" as do the courts and courtyards of Copan. Quirigua lacks the tightness of spatial control relating masonry structures to open spaces as in the Copan Acropolis.

Significant differences between the two sites relate to the manner of monument erection: the nature of substela caches and foundations differ between the sites (Stromsvik 1941).

Although iconography is not a consideration of this paper it is important to mention that the manikin scepter appears at Quirigua but not at Copan.

The similarity of artistic style between Copan and Quirigua is, however, not totally indefensible. During the beginning of Quirigua's monumental series, we find strongly outlined and bolder, more architectonic feather design appearing at both sites.

Perhaps the most significant stylistic characteristic contrasting the monument carving is implicit in the manner of planning each site's sculptural design. Proskouriakoff (1950:129) implies that Late Classsic Copan monuments must have been made with the help of scale models. Because the design of late Copan stelae is so very intricate, it is simply inconceivable that a plan or design of some sort was not used in the process of its manufacture. The simple economics of quarrying and transporting a huge piece of stone must have alone induced the Copan sculptors to plan ahead and "get it right the first time".

Both Spinden (1913) and Proskouriakoff (1950) have

shown that Copan sculpture progresses towards the full-round; Proskouriakoff (1950) has therefore suggested that in order to form a scale plan for monumental high relief sculpture that is almost in the full round, a full round scale model was probably used. New England ship builders made perfect scale models for the great sailing vessels they produced. The builders would multiply each detail in the model by a standard factor to build their ships. The Copan Maya probably did much the same thing in making their monumental sculpture.

The method of planning Quirigua sculpture must have been quite different from that of the sculptures of Copan. Because the Quirigua design is largely restricted to flat planes, a drawing instead of a full round model was probably used as a scale plan; in Proskouriakoff's (1950:129) words, "A drawing on the front or the side of such a stela involves virtually no foreshortening. The artist could design the monument by sketching or blocking it out directly on the surface of the stone, establishing his principal planes and then rounding the forms."

MEDIA AND STYLES

Hardness or softness of a material may and often does restrict the kinds of forms a sculptor can produce. The low relief of almost all Mesoamerican jade is an example of an extremely hard stone dictating the style of carving. A Mesoamerican sculptor's tool kit of hard stones and abrasive sands made cutting a very hard stone such as jade a lengthy and tedious task. Adherence to low relief in hard stone carving seems to be a natural, or rather human, result of working the material.

Yet technique does not always dictate form. The history of art has demonstrated again and again that the restrictions imposed by technical limitations are not ultimate controlling factors in the shape of things. For example, a bronze head from Nineveh (c. 2300 B.C.) exhibits the same broad facial planes and low relief linear incisions for hair as can be seen in similar and contemporary representations in diorite. The facial features and hair patterns of the Nineveh bronze head were modeled in soft wax, a concomitant of the bronze sculpture technique.

The heads of common Teotihuacan Tlamimilopa figurines, found by the handfuls in the modern agricultural tracts of the massive site, are made of supple clay. Yet they share the same broad and generalizing geometric treatment of facial planes that characterizes the style of "classic" Teotihuacan masks made of jade and other extremely hard stones.

Why are soft materials treated like hard ones in the art of a culture? Perhaps the limitations imposed by materials were important in making a style at first. But it seems evident that something more than physical limitation is at work when soft materials come out looking like hard ones. It is, I suppose, possible to say that the hard materials first established the norms to be followed. Perhaps that is part of it. I think a better explanation lies in the notion that a habit of rendering kinds of form is established early in a culture, independent of technical restrictions, and that habit continues or evolves in a particular manner through time. We call this formed habit style.

If we chose to believe that materials may dictate forms more than I have suggested, we cannot account for the differences of monumental stone carving in the Copan and Quirigua monuments on the basis of very different hardnesses of stone. Only style makes for differences between the two. Compare these two descriptions of Copan and Quirigua stone made by two archaeologists of the Carnegie Institution who have excavated at both sites: Copan (Stromsvik 1947:14):

The ancient sculptors were fortunate in having close at hand a limitless supply of excellent material, a greenish volcanic rock which was relatively soft when freshly quarried from the ridge to the north of the ruins, but which hardened on exposure to air.

Quirigua (Morley 1935:28):

The Quirigua sandstone, for the most part, is close grained and of even texture. When first quarried it is somewhat soft but hardens with exposure to air. The close even grain of this stone made for uniform results under the chisels, since it provided an evenness of resistance upon which the ancient sculptor could rely, thereby permitting him to carve as and how he would; while its softness, when first quarried, made for ease in carving with his tools of flint, diorite and basalt.

STYLISTIC COMPARISON OF COPAN AND QUIRIGUA MONUMENTS

Copan Stela A (9.15.0.0.0)
Copan Stela N (9.16.10.0.0)

Quirigua Monument 6 (9.16.10.0.0)(Stela F)
Quirigua Monument 4 (9.16.15.0.0) (Stela D)

The style of carving at Copan during what Proskouriakoff (1950) calls "the Dynamic Phase of the Late Classic Period" is different from the style of Quirigua stone work during the same period. At Copan, the stelae bear figures almost completely sculptured in the round. A heavily ornamented figure, such as Copan

MONUMENT CARVING: STYLISTIC IMPLICATIONS

Stela A or Copan Stela N, is a high relief sculpture which breaks from the matrix of the stone mass. When one looks at Copan Stela A or N from the side, one is, in fact, looking at a full lateral view. Such nearly full round presentation of a figure is very different from the presentation of the figure on the Quirigua stelae. When one looks at a side view of a Quirigua stela which bears a frontal figure, one cannot see the figure's side view. One sees very little of that frontal representation (see Mon. 6, Stela F, east side). Instead, we are presented with a flat vertical rectangle whose design is independent of the figures on the front faces. We see a separate composition enclosed in a vertical rectangular frame. Most often this two dimensional composition on a single flat plane is an elaborated glyph panel. The top of the east side of Mon. 6 appears from the side as an abstract feather design, unrelated to the frontal figures.

Whereas the Copan "Dynamic Phase" stone carvers seemed to have, "boldly attempted to free the body from the stone block" (Kubler 1962:153), "Quirigua sculptors imprisoned the figural design inside "prismatic envelopes"(*Ibid.*:154) of stylistic conventions. The relatively soft sandstone of Quirigua did not induce the sculptors to cut deeply as did the equally soft material of Copan. Quirigua stelae makers were controlled by stylistic cannons which adhered to the decoration of flat two-dimensional surfaces. Copan design elements are curvilinear whereas those of Quirigua are rigidly rectilinear. "The governing idea of the sculptors of Quirigua was like that of a diamond cutter: to conserve the weight and bulk of the stone at the expense of other aims" (Kubler 1962:154). The analogy misses a bit. Unlike diamonds, Quirigua sandstone is soft and easy to carve.

I would characterize the Copan style of monumental carving in the "Dynamic Phase" as being one in which exaggerated curvilinear elements hang in precarious balance over, to the sides, behind and below a three dimensional figure. The deeply cut passages between curvilinear forms, as can be seen between the ear plugs of Stela N and lateral areas, constantly vacillate with the changing direction of the sun; the balance of forms varies with the changing light. The massive bulk of the figure's paraphenalia appears to change in varying light.

The relatively flat planes of the Quirigua stelae are not capable of such variegated illusionary movement. Where there is exaggeration of curvilinear forms at Copan reminiscent of the twisted, tortured forms of the "Southeastern Maya Frontier" (Longyear 1947), Quirigua style is restrained and hieratic, more reminiscent of the mainstream of Maya Classic art. Quirigua sculptors restrict the figure and his paraphenalia to a two dimensional plane. The Quirigua sculptural style is more rigid, formalized, more hieratic and less animated than the Copan monumental sculpture.

Another difference between Copan and Quirigua can be seen in the striking contrast of the monuments' size. Although the Copan monuments are larger than life size, they do not approach the colossal proportions of Quirigua monoliths. Mon. 5 (Stela E) at Quirigua is no less that 35 feet high, by far the largest monolith ever erected in the Maya area (Kubler 1962:153). The awesome effect of these monoliths recalls the huge heads of Olmec civilization.

COPAN AND QUIRIGUA EPIGRAPHIC EVIDENCE

Proskouriakoff (1950:131) suggests that Quirigua Mon. 8 (Stela H) 9.16.0.0.0 (Morley 1935:61), is the earliest monument of the known Quirigua series, which continues by *hotuns* for almost three *katuns*. Kelley (1962:334) thinks that this same Mon. 8 represents a prince of the Copanec dynasty. He interprets the prince's name glyph to be "Two Legged Sky" and calculates his age to be 27 when Mon. 8 was erected. Kelley (*Ibid.*) further suggests by means of epigraphic evidence that Quirigua Mons. 10, 6, 5, 1 and 3 (Stelae J, F, E A and C respectively) were erected to "Two-Legged Sky" during his lifetime and that during the erection of Mons. 1 and 3 (Stelae A and C) he was 52. Mons. 2 and 7 (Zoomorphs B and G) were erected when "Two-Legged Sky" was approaching 62 (9.17.15.0.0), and he may have died at this time (Kelley, *Ibid.*). At 9.18.5.0.0 Kelley (*Ibid.*) suggests that Quirigua Mon. 16 (Zoomorph P) "seems to show a ruler whose glyphs are of an entirely different family." Kelley (*Ibid.*) points to Mon. 9 (Stela I) five years later in the sequence as bearing the ascension motif which he sees to be similar to that of Piedras Negras: "Here, clearly, we have still another ruler, although the identification of his glyphs is by no means certain." Kelley (*Ibid.*) describes Mon. 11 (Stela K, 9.18.15.0.0) as bearing hieroglyphs of the last ruler of Quirigua who "may well have been a remaining grandson or great-grandson of "Two-Legged Sky" who survived dissension and disagreement to rule at least slightly longer than any of his three immediate predecessors."

Kelley's epigraphic evidence indicates that the history of Quirigua during the 75 year period from 9.16.0.0.0-9.18.15.0.0, punctuated by fifteen major monuments of the Quirigua monumental sequence, was one of political change. The rule of "Two-Legged Sky" seems to have initiated the monumental series. A 40 year period, at the beginning of the sequence, may have been controlled by a member of the Copan dynasty. The next 35 years produced four changes of government at Quirigua.

What are the implications of Kelley's work? Was Quirigua in fact established by a scion of the Copan dynasty? Are we really looking at monuments set up by hereditary rulers as Proskouriakoff and others argue? Or are we considering works which are manifestations of public ritual obligations of different cargo holders implicit in projecting back the ethnographic present from Zinacantan? If so, how do we account for the process of disjunction between form and meaning that may have been operative in the Maya past? These are all unanswerable questions at the moment, but which come to mind in considering the implications of Kelley's epigraphic study.

Ruling dynasties or rotating "cargos," the epigraphic evidence indicates changes in the history of Quirigua rulership. While the scale of Quirigua monumental sculpture after "Two-Legged Sky" becomes less spectacular, the actual style of carving stone does not correspondingly change. Specialized activities such as stone carving traditions seem to have resisted political change; the fluctuations in control of government do not filter down to the stone carving workshops. Indeed, the highly trained specialists whose skill is held in high esteem by the ruling power seems to be unaffected by political shifts. A specialist such as Werner von Braun is doing much the same work, with improvements in technique, under the tutelage of a patron who literally flattened the political and moral, or amoral, structure of his former employer. The monument carvers at Quirigua worked for different patrons, possibly representing different political systems, without changing their manner of carving, just as musicians play the same tune the same way no matter who is paying them.

EXTERNAL SOURCES OF THE SCULPTURAL TRADITIONS

Copan

Proskouriakoff's monograph on Classic Maya sculpture(1950) has charted Copan's sculptural evolution with comparisons to the general development of Classic Maya sculpture (Proskouriakoff 1950:109;115-117;129-131;143-145). Certainly Copan's geographical position on the southeastern frontier, at an extremity of Maya lowland civilization, was an important factor in its stylistic evolution. The curious "frontier flair" of Copan art style is a phenomenon which is not unique to Copan. It is not the purpose of this paper to investigate factors which contributed to Copan's unique artistic florescence. We are not interested here in characterizing Copan's unique artistic development. Spinden (1913) and, to some extent, Morley (1920), and, more significantly, Proskouriakoff (1950) have already made this fundamental contribution to our knowledge of Classic Maya civilization.

Significant here is that Copan receives some of its artistic forms from areas other than the Peten. Proskouriakoff (1950:129-130) implies that the Copan manner of carving in very high relief was inspired "by some peripheral style of carving in full round." Proskouriakoff points to Tonina as a possible direction for the source. I bid for a southerly direction. Small stone objects sculpted in full round are hallmarks of the Comayagua Valley tradition (cf. Stone 1957:Figs. 40,56,78,80,83,84) and may have been a factor in forming Copan's unique sculptural style.

Pollock (1965:421) makes the observation that the lack of heavy apron mouldings in Copan architecture is a factor that separates Copan from the Peten. He also notes that the architecture at Copan shares elements reminiscent of the Rio Bec and Chenes style (Pollock 1965:428). In light of this observation, the published letter from Licenciado Diego Garcia de Palacio to Phillip II takes on new meaning. Written from Guatemala, dated March 8, 1579, Palacio states:

I endeavored, with all possible care, to ascertain from the Indians, through the traditions derived from the ancients [of Copan], what people lived here, and what they knew or had heard from their ancestors concerning them. But they have no books relating to their antiquities, nor do I believe that in all this district there is more than one, which I possess. They say that in ancient times there came from Yucatan a great lord, who built these edifices, but at the end of some years returned to his native country, leaving them entirely deserted. And this is what appears most likely, for tradition says that the people of Yucatan anciently conquered the provinces of Ayajal, Lacandon, Verapaz, Chiquimula and Copan... (from Gordon 1898:48).

Pollock's suggestion of the architectural connections of Copan and Rio Bec-Chenes may find support in Palacio's reference, but whether or not there were movements of people from Yucatan to the southeast or *vice-versa*, and when, may have little to do with the transference of architectural style. Political geography may not, after all, reflect artistic, specifically architectural, style distributions.

MONUMENT CARVING: STYLISTIC IMPLICATIONS

There are significant differences between the two styles of architecture noted above. The Rio Bec-Chenes style exhibits a rigid geometricizing of forms, which cannot be seen in the serpentine doorway of Temple 22 at Copan. There are also no towers at Copan. The ready availability of lime mortar in the Rio Bec-Chenes *versus* its relative scarcity at Copan must have resulted in radically different means of consolidating construction fill and putting buildings together. That the architects of both areas restricted their architectural sculpture to upper facades and adapted the serpent mouth or serpentine doorway is too superficial a comparison to be significant. Nevertheless, the style of Copan architecture looks less like that of the Peten and more like that of the Rio Bec-Chenes.

While architectural ideas may have come from the north, the sculptural style of Copan relates to the art of the "southeastern Maya frontier" (Longyear 1947). These voluptuous curvilinear, intertwining serpentine forms are reminiscent of the non-monumental, yet *portable* ceramic designs and carved stone objects and metates of the neighboring southern area (cf. Stone 1957:Fig. 43). The frenetic configuration of curvilinear elements, so characteristic of Copan monumental sculpture after 9.8.0.0.0 is in keeping with the twisted and convoluted forms of the southern area which it borders.

The parrot head seems to be a distinctly southern iconographic motif that comes from the south (cf. Stone 1957:Figs. 56 and 84), and appears at Copan in the form of ball court markers (see Stromsvik 1947:29).

On the basis of high relief figural sculpture, Copan is related to the nearby site of Los Hijos. While the stela cult of Los Hijos most probably came via Copan, its sculptural style may have been inspired by the same southern ideas influencing Copan.

Quirigua

The Late Classic monumental series of extant stelae at Quirigua begins shortly before 9.16.0.0.0. A very distinctive style of stone carving appears at this time and continues virtually unchanged until the end of the series at 9.18.15.0.0. It is certain that the unique Quirigua style of carving did not come about by some sort of spontaneous generation. It had to come from somewhere, and if the sources of the style are not extant at Quirigua, a consideration of outside sources is in order.

Proskouriakoff (1950:144) suggests that "there is a particular quality of some of the Quirigua scroll designs which vaguely recalls the decoration of yokes found in the Totonac region, and the panels of the ball courts at Tajin...This type of design is characterized by abrupt changes of direction in the outline of forms, by the use of interlaced elements, and by features of internal decoration of scrolls not typical of pure Maya forms." Proskouriakoff (*Ibid.*) points to Mon. 15 (Zoomorph O) as possessing rounded, slightly notched forms containing an element shaped like a hook. Another example of the scroll interlace at Quirigua can be seen in the base of Mon. 5 (Stela E).

One does not have to look as far as Tajin to see sources for this particular decorative pattern which Proskouriakoff describes. Yaxchilan Lintel 25 in the British Museum displays characteristics of the Tajin-like scroll design. Interior decoration of scrolls in the shape of the serpent form, as well as the reversed hook shapes and slightly "notched-shaped forms containing elements like a hook", and even the "abrupt changes of direction in the outline of forms", can be seen in Lintel 25 from Yaxchilan. Restriction of the design to flat planes, so characteristic of Quirigua carving, is apparent at Yaxchilan. While the hard crystaline limestone of Yaxchilan may have imposed technical limitations upon its stone carvers, the soft stone of Quirigua imposed no such restrictions. Quirigua carvers seem to have chosen the Yaxchilan low relief style as a matter of choice. Another stylistic affinity between the two sites can be seen in the use of rectilinear design elements in contrast to the curvilinear ones employed at Copan.

Portable objects such as the modeled carved bowl said to have been found at San Agustin Acasaguastlan, about 50 miles from Quirigua (Kubler 1962:159), may be another source for the Quirigua Late Classic style. The San Agustin bowl is decorated with scrolls not unlike those found at Quirigua. Unfortunately, the archaeological associations of this piece are unknown. Because Thompson (1943:115,116) has questioned its authenticity, we must also question this putative stylistic relationship. It would be useful to know if design on portable objects found at Quirigua influences its stone carving traditions. At this point, those data are simply not available.

A more secure source for the Quirigua sculptural style comes from Salinas de los Nueve Cerros. Showing the frontal face, headdress and pectoral of a stela fragment, the sculpture was published by Seler (1908, Vol. 3, no. 3:pl. 1); the illustration reveals three sides of an undated fragment, which he describes as being made "...in rothem Sandstein"(Seler 1908:589-590), indicating that the stela may be composed of a material with physical properties like those of Quirigua sandstone. Proskouriakoff (1950:117) has suggested a Formative

Copan association for this piece, and she describes the Tonina style, to which she links the Salinas sculpture, as not being very different from the Quirigua style (*Ibid.*:129-130): "The figure alone was designed on a three-dimensional basis. All the ornaments and accouterments were conceived on subsidiary surfaces that followed the main mass." I would eliminate the Late Classic Copan link with Salinas. In any event, the Salinas carving style is close to that of Late Classic Quirigua: in the Seler illustration (1908, Vol. 3, no. 3:pl. 1), we see a human face projecting from the stone mass, while the rest of the design adheres to a flat rectilinear surface behind the face in the manner of Late Classic Quirigua monuments. The headdress band around the forehead is reminiscent of the similar form of Quirigua Mon. 4 (Stela D). The shape of the face is restricted between vertical design elements in a manner similar to Quirigua Mons. 4, 5 and 6 (Stelae D, E and F).

Although the Salinas fragment shows only the top part of what was once a vertical monolith, I would predict that the lower part of the design probably formed a vertical rectangle inside of which the lower body was flattened in the Quirigua manner.

I suggest that the Salinas de los Nueve Cerros fragment may be part of a common stylistic sphere that extends from Palenque along the foothills of the highlands to Quirigua. Proskouriakoff (1950:117) incorporates the Salinas example into an even larger sphere that extends along the northern border of the highlands, from Tonina in Chiapas to Copan:

It is not likely that this (the Salinas piece) is an isolated occurrence; there probably are other sites in this region which use round relief and full front presentation of the figure.

I doubt that Copan is on the receiving end of the foothill tradition on the basis of sculptural style, at least not after "Two Legged Sky" became the patron of Quirigua stone carvers. Minimal archaeology in this region might establish the basic time depths that would clarify these sculptural style relationships.

GLYPH BLOCK STYLES

Glyph arrangements on monumental sculpture and the manner of carving individual glyphs can be seen as a diagnostic characteristic that can indicate sources of stylistic influence. I suspect that the carvers of Classic Maya glyphs were a corps of specialists who were commissioned to carry out the translation into stone of a glyphic text supplied by another corps of specialists —probably court scholars of one sort or another. The style or manner of rendering hieroglyphic passages into stone of each glyph carving school would have been logically formed by glyph carving traditions, possibly related to their respective figure carving traditions.

The style of glyph carving on the back of Quirigua Mon. 8 (Stela H) is unusual. An arrangement of six diagonally tilted rhomboids are stacked upon each other; two similarly tilting rhombuses form the top and bottom member of the panel. These tilting units are contained by a steeply arched vertical frame which touches and confines the rhomboids and rhombuses at their two exterior corners. The rows of glyphs are enclosed in each tilting frame; the glyphs themselves are slightly rhomboidal in shape. An Initial Series introducing glyph fills the upper rhombus.

As far as I know, this particular arrangement of glyph panels is not found at Copan. The back of Copan Stela J is closest in arrangement to Quirigua Mon 8, although really quite different, showing a plait design—a translation into stone of a mat weave design with glyphs following the weave pattern.

Like Quirigua Mon. 8, Cancuen Stela 3 reveals a configuration of diagonally arranged rhomboidal glyphs enclosed in a larger rhomboidal frame, also tilted diagonally. Like Mon. 8, the two outside corners of each Cancuen rhomboid touches the outer edge of the stela. Also like Mon. 8, the position of the introducing glyph in a frame is situated at the upper right in Cancuen Stela 3. Despite the similar appearance of the glyph block arrangement, there are differences. The Cancuen fragment is limestone whereas Quirigua Mon. 8 is brownish red sandstone. The sizes of the individual glyphs are smaller at Cancuen than those at Quirigua. There seem to be at least five glyphs on the diagonal at Cancuen, whereas there are only four at Quirigua. Nevertheless, the similarity between the glyph block style of Quirigua Mon. 8 and Cancuen Stela 3 is striking. Located on the Usumacinta drainage in southern Peten, Cancuen glyph block carving tradition suggests a connection with Quirigua, providing another monument carving attribute linking Quirigua to the north.

Another stylistic characteristic related to glyph rendition connecting Quirigua with the Usumacinta drainage is evident in the use of stucco architectural decoration. At Quirigua, stucco was a far more common medium of decoration on architecture than at Copan (Proskouriakoff 1965:486). Stucco decoration relates to the Usumacinta drainage sites. During a 1967 reconnaissance at Cancuen, I found some stucco glyph fragments in a small plaza in what we have designated as "Group C."

MONUMENT CARVING: STYLISTIC IMPLICATIONS

RELIEF CARVING JUXTAPOSITION

A comparison of the back of Quirigua Mon. 9 (Stela I; 9.17.0.0.0 ±2 *katuns*; 9.18.10.0.0, Morley 1935) and the back of Copan Stela B (9.16.0.0.0±2 *katuns*) is suggestive of how Quirigua, in contrast to Copan, exhibits ties to the Usumacinta drainage monument carving traditions. Both carvings represent a seated figure in a niche over complex designs that are reminiscent of the elaborated ladder forms associated with the "ascension motif" at Piedras Negras (Proskouriakoff 1961; Kelley 1962:334). But style links Quirigua to the north. The depth of carving in Copan Stela B is similar in the lower curvilinear design areas and in the body and face of the small cross-legged figure of the niche above. In other words, the relief carving is consistently high throughout. On the other hand, there is no such consistency of carving in the rigidly geometric forms of Quirigua Mon. 9. Characteristic of all Quirigua stone carving, the relief is considerably greater in the face and in the tiny body than in the other parts of the composition. This difference in the depth of carving stone is not unlike the juxtaposition of high and low relief carving common at Piedras Negras.

CONCLUSIONS

Stylistic comparisons of Copan and Quirigua monuments have shown the two sites at odds in their sculptural traditions. What does this imply? What can we say about the sociopolitical relationship of Quirigua and Copan on the bases of comparing styles of stone carving and their sources? In a vacuum, we can only say that Quirigua did not have much intercourse with Copan *on the level of stone carving traditions*. I have suggested that Copan's Late Classic sculptural style is inspired from the south, spiced with the Peten influences charted by Proskouriakoff (1950). The Late Classic Quirigua stone carving tradition seems to draw from the foothills of the highlands, the Usumacinta sites, and the upper Rio Pasion.

Out of a stylistic vacuum, the epigraphic evidence suggests that Quirigua was connected with Copan. According to Kelley (1962) "Two-Legged Sky" was a Copan transplant at Quirigua. But how do the different sculptural traditions relate to the fact of "Two-Legged Sky"? The archaeology that has been done at the site certainly indicates that it is older than 9.16.0.0.0. But when "Two-Legged Sky" comes on the scene, monument carving takes on a remarkable vigor. Assuming the monuments were commissioned by "Two-Legged Sky" during his tenure as ruler of Quirigua, there are fascinating implications to be taken into consideration. The erection of gigantic monoliths seems to have been a variation of the stela cult, a kind of exaggeration that we could call mannerism. This interpretation sees the stela cult as a visual show, a way to awe the beholder, a sort of political billboard. Why was "Two-Legged Sky" so interested in impressing the stone testaments of his rule at Quirigua? What cultural factors account for such remarkable behavior? New-found wealth? Military success?

AFTERWORD

This paper was written in 1967 for a memorable seminar on the Maya conducted by E. Z. Vogt and G. R. Willey at Harvard University. Because the Peabody Museum has the somewhat unnerving practice of keeping on file its former students' indiscretions, it was inevitable, I suppose, that the Quirigua Project was to find that I had written on Quirigua *vis-a-vis* Copan at a time when still little was known about either site. When my friend and colleague, R. J. Sharer, asked me to submit what I had charitably described as a graduate student "earlier effort" for publication here, I felt sure it was his way of expressing what he thought about just having plowed through, at my insistence, a draft of my Tancah-Tulum monograph. But my immediate suspicions proved false. Despite the shortcomings in style and content, Sharer convinced me that there may be some actual use for this fossil unearthed from the Peabody cupboards because it relates to, although it could not incorporate, the Quirigua Project's new findings and interdisciplinary approach to understanding the Maya past.

Since the work of Tatiana Proskouriakoff most clearly points out that Maya stelae are, among other things, political documents, readers will not be surprised to learn that it was Tatiana Proskouriakoff who originally suggested the topic for this paper.

REFERENCES CITED

Gordon, G. B.
   1898   *Caverns of Copan, Honduras; Report of Explorations by the Museum, 1896-1897.* Peabody Museum, Harvard University, Memoirs Vol. 1 (No. 5).

Kelley, David H.
   1962   Glyphic Evidence for a Dynastic Sequence at Quirigua, Guatemala. *American Antiquity* Vol. 27 (3): 323-335.

Kubler, George A.
   1962   *The Art and Architecture of Ancient America; the Mexican Maya and Andean Peoples.* Baltimore: Penguin Books.

Longyear, J. M.
   1947   *Cultures and Peoples of the Southeastern Maya Frontier.* Cambridge.

Morley, S.G.
   1920   *The Inscriptions at Copan.* Carnegie Institution of Washington, Publication 219, Washington, D.C.
   1935   *Guide Book to the Ruins of Quirigua.* Carnegie Institution of Washington, Supplementary Publication 16, Washington, D. C.

Pollock, H. E. D.
   1965   Architecture of the Maya Lowlands. *Handbook of Middle American Indians,* Vol. 2, Part 1: 378-440.

Proskouriakoff, T.
   1950   *A Study of Classic Maya Sculpture.* Carnegie Institution of Washington, Publication 593, Washington, D. C.
   1965   Sculpture and Major Arts of the Maya Lowlands. *Handbook of Middle American Indians.* Vol. 2, Part 1: 469-497. Austin: University of Texas Press.

Seler, E.
   1908   *Gesammelte Abhandlungen Amerikanischen Sprach und Alterthumskunde.* Vol. III, Berlin.

Spinden, H. J.
   1913   A Study of Maya Art. Its Subject Matter and Historical Development. *Memoirs of the Peabody Museum.* Vol. Vi.: 285.

Stone, D.
   1957   *The Archaeology of Central and Southern Honduras.* Papers of the Peabody Museum, Vol. XLIX, No. 3

Stromsvik, G.
   1947   *Guide Book to the Ruins of Copan.* Carnegie Institution of Washington, Publication 577, Washington, D. C.

PAPER NO. 15

NEW DRAWINGS OF MONUMENTS 23 AND 24, QUIRIGUA, GUATEMALA

by
Christopher Jones

MONUMENTS 23 AND 24, QUIRIGUA, GUATEMALA

A major result of the 1975 field season was the cleaning and photographing of Monuments 23 and 24, the two large flat monoliths found in 1934 by Earl H. Morris and Gustav Stromsvik in front of Mons. 15 and 16 (Zoomorphs O and P). The stones have been known in the literature as the altars of Zoomorphs O and P, or simply as Altars O′ and P′. The present designations were assigned by the Quirigua Project as part of a less cumbersome and more easily expanded system of monument nomenclature for Quirigua (Coe and Sharer 1979:18-20).

The carvings on the two monuments have become well known through published photographs and descriptions by Morley (Anon. 1934:Frontispiece; Morley 1935:102-115; 1937-38, IV:185-196, 204-214, frontispiece to Vols. III and IV). Subsequently, Thompson (1945:189-199) published a radically revised chronological placement of the dates of Mon. 23, accompanied by an excellent set of photographs of the hieroglyphs. The latter were taken with the use of artificial light from Morris and Stromsvik's 1934 cast.

In light of the facts that no drawing of the carvings existed and the designs were still in fair condition, the stones afforded an excellent opportunity to begin an application of Tikal Project monument recording techniques to Quirigua. The altars were carefully scrubbed clean of their algae/fungus growths by Rebecca Sedat, Aura de Ortiz and Ann Coe. Plot plans of the carved elements were drawn on graph paper from exact measurements. In these drawings the carvings on the sides of the stones were included by means of a sort of Mercator Projection in which their elements were broadened in order to fit the two dimensions of the plans.

With the aid of a gasoline generator and flood-lights, Coe took four photographs of each portion of the surfaces under a variety of lighting conditions, intensities and angles. Several daylight shots were also taken. The drawings were composed and inked by Coe, using the plans for the basic outlines and filling in the figural and inscriptional details from the photographs. The positions of the hieroglyphs on Mon. 23 were further determined by the aid of a photograph of a rubbing on cloth. The glyphic portions of the drawings were subsequently reviewed by Jones, after which changes were made in details. This is especially true of Mon. 23, since important details which show up in the Thompson photographs have since eroded away and do not appear on any of ours.

Tables 1 and 2 are summaries of the decipherable chronological and non-chronological information in the two texts. Individual dates and distance numbers are identifiable in the tables by their positions in glyph blocks rather than by designations such as Date A or DN 1. The comments within parentheses are generally confined to questions and limits of possibilities without justification being given for what is clearly readable. In our block designations, we have eliminated the traditional yet clumsy use of u.h. and l.h. for upper half and lower half of a glyph block. Instead, we use the

QUIRIGUA REPORTS

TABLE 1

QUIRIGUA MONUMENT 23 ALTAR OF ZOOMORPH O)

A1-L4	9.17.14.16.18	ISIG (*Kankin* variable); 9 *Etznab;* Glyphs G9, F; Glyphs E-D (zero moon age); Glyph C (moon number 5); Glyph X, form 5; Glyph B. Glyph A (30-day month); 1 *Kankin* (18 *kins*, 18 *katuns* preferred; no coefficients on Glyphs E-D; thumb coefficient with *Kankin*).
M1		Hand/jog accession compound.
N1-O2		Name of Ruler II, *Batab*, blindfold glyph, Quirigua Emblem Glyph, *bacab*, bat.
R1a	1.2	DN (1-4 over moon-with-enclosed-dot).
R1b-Q2	9.17.15.0.0	5 *Ahau* 3 *Muan*, 5 *haab* lacking (*Ahau, Muan* not certain; PE 5 not indicated).
R2a		Scattering glyph (with PE's).
S1	-11.7?	DN (7 or 9 *kins*, any *uinal* possible).
	(9.17.14.6.13)?	12 *Ben* 16 *Zip* (not recorded).
T1	(9.17.14.6.5)?	4 *Chicchan* 8 *Zip* (*Muluc* preferred; 7 *VYr*).
S2b2		Capture glyph?
U1	8	DN (inverted *Ahau* variant; posterior date indicator).
V1	(9.17.14.6.13)?	12 *Ben* 16 *Zip* (*Ben* not certain).
V2		Name of Ruler II?, Quirigua Emblem Glyph?
X1	(9.17.15.0.0)?	5 *Ahau*, end *tun* (*Ahau* probable, with *ti* prefix; PE glyphs not certain).
Y1	-2.7.10.7?	DN (6 or 8 *uinals*; 7 or 9 *tuns*; 1-3 *katuns*).
X2	(9.15.6.14.6)?	6 *Cimi*?; 19 head glyph not *VYr*? (*Cimi* not certain, 11 preferred).
Z2-b '1a1		Name of Ruler I, *batab*, 5 *katuns*.
C '2a	(9.16.6.14.6)?	4 *Cimi*? (mainsign lost).
B '2	1.5.11.2?	DN (1-3 *kins*, 12 *uinals*, 15 *tuns*).
C '2a	(9.17.12.7.8)?	9 *Lamat* 1 *Zec*.
D '1b-E '1a1	4.17.1?	DN (1-3 *kins*; 16-18 *uinals*; 9 *tuns*).
E '1b1-a2	(9.17.7.8.7)?	9 *Manik* 5 *Yaxkin* (*Manik* not certain).
G '1b1	(9.17.8.2.9)?	4 *Muluc*.
G '1a2-b2	12.7	DN.
H 'b2	(9.17.8.14.16)?	4 *Cib*.
F '2b1	(9.17.8.15.4)?	12 *Kan*
H '2b1	(9.17.9.15.6)?	1 *Cimi*
H '2b2		Event postfix.
J '1-J '2		Name of Ruler II, *batab*, blindfold glyph.
I '3a1	14?	DN (written as 9).
I '4a1	(9.17.8.16.0)?	2 *Ahau*; 19 head glyph not *VYr*? (1-3 *Ahau*).
J '4a1-b1	1.0.4	(written 19.4); posterior date indicator.
J '4b2	(9.17.9.16.4)?	2 *Kan*.
I '6b2-J	(9.17.8.16.0)?	2 *Ahau*, posterior date indicator (1-2 *Ahau*).
I '6a1-a2	4.2.15	DN.
J '6b1	(9.17.13.0.15)?	2 *Men* (*Men* not certain).
M '1b2	(9.18.0.0.0)?	11 *Ahau* (*Ahau* not preferred).
P '1a1	9.18.0.2.16)?	2 *Cib* (*Cib* not certain).
Q '2a1		Name of Ruler II?

138

MONUMENTS 23 AND 24

numbers 1 and 2, as in block V2b2, designating the lower right quadrant of block V2.

Our table for Mon 23 follows that of Thompson for the most part. He recognized much that Morley did not and his Long Count positions for the dates in the text are supported strongly by the locations of the names of Rulers I and II (nick-named "Cauac Sky" and "Sky Xul" respectively). For Mon. 24, our table changes Morley's positioning of the dates to conform with Thompson. The two texts are obviously related in their organization and content. This relationship reflects the pairing of the two stones side-by-side in front of their respective zoomorphic sculptures, their similar size and shape, the airborne poses of the masked semi-human figures, and the *tau*-shaped glyph panels. Both texts emphasize the date 9 *Eznab* 1 *Kankin* (9.17.14.16.18) at the beginning and relate that date to a period ending and to the name glyph of Ruler II as identified by Kelley (1962:328-331). The date can now be positively identified as an inaugural by the hand/jog accession compound occurring between it and the name on block M 1 of Mon. 23 and on Mon. 7 (Zoomorph G). This compound was first recognized with Palenque inaugural dates by Mathews and Schele (1974:64).

TABLE 2

QUIRIGUA MONUMENT 24 (ALTAR OF ZOOMORPH P)

A1-H2	9.18. 5. 0. 0	ISIG (*Ceh* variable); 4 *Ahau*; Glyphs G9, F; Glyphs E. D (moon age 23); Glyph 23 (moon number 4); Glyph X, form 5; Glyph A (29-day month); 13 *Ceh*; end 5 *haab*.
J1b1-b2		Name of Ruler II, *batab*, blindfold glyph.
	- 10. 1. 2	DN (1 or 2 *kins*; 7 or 9 *uinals*).
J2a2-b2	(9.17.14.16.18)	9 *Etznab* 1 *Kankin* (*Kankin* preferred, but not certain).
K1b1	(9.18. 5. 0. 0)	4 *Ahau*.
K1b2-L1a2	9.18. 5. 0. 0	DN (*tun* 1 through 5; *baktun* 7-9, DN subfix).
K1b2-K2a2	(13. 0. 0. 0. 0)	4 *Ahau* 13 *Cumku*, end 13 baktuns (*Cumku* not indicated)
R1-Q2		8 preferred; 12 baktun possible). Name of Ruler II, *batab*, blindfold glyph
R2	(9.18. 5. 0. 0)	4 *Ahau* 13 *Ceh*, end 5 tuns (*ti* with *Ahau*; *Ceh* preferred).
P1a1-b1	- 10. 1. 2	DN (1 *kin* preferred).
P1a2-b2	(9.17.14.16.18)	9 *Etznab* 1 *Kankin* (*Kankin* not certain).
T2b2	6. 5 ?	DN? (4 *kins* possible, *uinal* sign and DN subfix probable; DN does not connect dates).
V1b2-U2a1	(9.17.14. 6.13)?	12 *Ben* 16 *Zip*? (11-13. any SR sign; *Zip*, *Zec* or *Ceh*).
V2a1-a2	- 1.10. 9.15	DN (all coefficients certain as written).
V2b2-W1a1		11 *Imix*? (*Imix* not certain); 19 head (cf. Mon. 23).
X1	2.10.12. 1 ?	DN (*uinals* nor certain; DN does not connect dates).
W2a1-b1	(9.17.12. 7. 8)?	9 *Lamat* 1 *Zec* (cf. Mon. 23 at 9.17.12.7.8?).
X2a1-b1	7.13. 2	DN (*uinals* 11-13 possible; DN does not connect dates).
X2a2-b2	(9.17. 7.18.17)?	9 *Manik* 5 *Yaxkin*? (or *Yax*; cf. Mon. 23).

After these opening phrases, both texts refer back in time. On Mon. 24, a lengthy distance number of 9.18.5.0.0 counts back 3965 years to the base date of the Maya calendar, 4 *Ahau* 8 *Cumku*. Mon. 23, on the other hand, seems to carry the chronology back by a 47-year distance number to the 6 *Cimi* date at 9.15.6.14.6 which Ruler I celebrated on many of his monuments and which has been suggested as the date of an important victory over the ruler of Copan (Proskouriakoff 1973:168). This reading of the date itself was first given by Thompson on the basis of the distance number, in spite of the apparent coefficient 11 rather than 6. It is

139

supported by the presence of Ruler I's name soon after.

Three additional dates are probably shared by the two monuments:

(9.17.14.6.13) ?   12 *Ben* 16 *Zip*
(9.17.12.7.8) ?   9 *Lamat* 1 *Zec*
(9.17.7.8.7) ?   9 *Manik* 5 *Yaxkin*

The Long Count position for these are as Thompson placed them in the Mon. 23 text instead of in the Early Classic as Morley had put them on the basis of a mistaken reading of *Katun* 6 at block Ua1. The first of the three is especially well fixed by two short distance numbers on Mon. 23. The other two dates are arrived at circuitously by means of lengthy distance numbers on both monuments, in which there appears to be an inordinate amount of Maya error in calculation. Nevertheless, the two dates are connected to each other on Mon. 23 by a distance number which would be correct with a relatively simple change from 9 to 4 *tuns*.

Mon. 24 ends with these dates, but the other text continues with a series of ten briefly written dates which are only ocassionally connected by distance numbers. All of these were positioned in Thompson close to each other in the seven years prior to the inaugural date. Our drawing does much to confirm Thompson's reading of the day signs and coefficients involved and of the two connecting distance numbers. The presence of Ruler II's name within this series also strengthens Thompson's Long Count positions. One might surmise that the passage relates several events within the pre-inaugural years of the new ruler, but the nature of the events is still unknown.

The second to last date of the series was read as 11 *Ahau* by Thompson, and suggested as the dedicatory date of the text, the same 11 *Ahau* 9.18.0.0.0 that can be read on the companion Mon. 15 (Zoomorph O). In our drawing the day-sign remains indistinct, however, and no tell-tale period ending signs are noticable.

In sum, even though we have not resolved the difficulties of the chronologies nor suggested a likely solution for the blatant contradictions between dates and distance numbers as written, Coe's drawing supports Thompson's reading for Mon. 23 and justifies its application to Mon. 24. Hopefully, they will advance a resolution of the difficulties of these texts and allow a fuller measure of historical information to be extracted from them.

REFERENCES CITED

Anonymous
    1934   *News Service Bulletin*. Carnegie Institution of Washington, Washington, D.C.

Coe, W. R. and R. J. Sharer
    1979   *The Quirigua Project: 1975 Season*. Quirigua Paper No. 2, University Museum Monograph 37, Philadelphia.

Kelley, D. H.
    1962   *Glyphic Evidence for a Dynastic Sequence at Quirigua, Guatemala. American Antiquity* 27:323-335.

Mathews, P. and L. Schele
    1974   Lords of Palenque—The Glyphic Evidence. In *Primera Mesa Redonda de Palenque, Part I*. M.G. Robertson, ed., pp. 41-76. Pebble Beach: The Robert Louis Stevenson School.

Morley, S. G.
    1935   *Guide Book to the Ruins of Quirigua, Guatemala*. Carnegie Institution of Washington Supplemental Publication 16. Washington, D. C.

    1937-38 *The Inscriptions of Peten*, 5 vols. Carnegie Institution of Washington, Publication 437. Washington, D. C.

Proskouriakoff, T.
    1973   The Hand-Grasping Fish and Associated Glyphs on Classic Maya Monuments. *Mesoamerican Writing Systems*. E.P. Benson, ed., pp. 165-178. Washington: Dumbarton Oaks.

Thompson, J. E. S.
    1945   *The Inscriptions on the Altar of Zoomorph O, Quirigua*. Notes on Middle American Archaeology and Ethnology. Carnegie Institution of Washington, Washington, D. C.